The Eternal Table

Big City Food Biographies Series

Series Editor

Ken Albala, University of the Pacific, kalbala@pacific.edu

Food helps define the cultural identity of cities in much the same way as the distinctive architecture and famous personalities. Great cities have one-of-a-kind food cultures, offering the essence of the multitudes who have immigrated there and shaped foodways through time. The **Big City Food Biographies** series focuses on those metropolises celebrated as culinary destinations, with their iconic dishes, ethnic neighborhoods, markets, restaurants, and chefs. Guidebooks to cities abound, but these are real biographies that will satisfy readers' desire to know the full food culture of a city. Each narrative volume, devoted to a different city, explains the history, the natural resources, and the people that make that city's food culture unique. Each biography also looks at the markets, historic restaurants, signature dishes, and great cookbooks that are part of the city's gastronomic makeup.

Books in the Series

The Eternal Table

A Cultural History of Food in Rome

Karima Moyer-Nocchi

with Giancarlo Rolandi

ROWMAN & LITTLEFIELD
Lanham • Boulder • New York • London

Published by Rowman & Littlefield
An imprint of The Rowman & Littlefield Publishing Group, Inc.
4501 Forbes Boulevard, Suite 200, Lanham, Maryland 20706
www.rowman.com

6 Tinworth Street, London SE11 5AL, United Kingdom

British Library Cataloguing in Publication Information Available

Library of Congress Cataloging-in-Publication Data
Names: Moyer-Nocchi, Karima, author. | Rolandi, Giancarlo, author.
Title: The eternal table : a cultural history of food in Rome / Karima Moyer-Nocchi
    with Giancarlo Rolandi.
Description: Lanham, Maryland : Rowman & Littlefield, 2018. | Series: Big city food
    biographies series | Includes bibliographical references and index.
Identifiers: LCCN 2018031037 (print) | LCCN 2018052953 (ebook) | ISBN
    9781442269750 (Electronic) | ISBN 9781442269743 (cloth : alk. paper)
Subjects: LCSH: Food habits—Italy—Rome—History. | Food—Italy—Rome—History.
    | Rome (Italy) —Social life and customs. | Rome (Italy) —Civilization.
Classification: LCC GT2853.I8 (ebook) | LCC GT2853.I8 M69 2018 (print) | DDC
    394.1/20945632—dc23
LC record available at https://lccn.loc.gov/2018031037

∞™ The paper used in this publication meets the minimum requirements of
American National Standard for Information Sciences—Permanence of Paper
for Printed Library Materials, ANSI/NISO Z39.48-1992.

Printed in the United States of America

To my beloved,
Tua

Contents

Acknowledgments

My sincerest thanks go out to Adrian Bregazzi and Andrew McGowan for their generous assistance as readers, consultants, and editors. Thanks also go to Simone and Venanzio Nocchi for research assistance, Yhara Formisano and Francesca Fabri for their "on-call" support, Sheena Vick my test reader, and Elizabeth Yorke, who helped compile the index.

I thank Mina Novelli, Alberto Manodori Segredo, Walter Levy, and Salumificio Porchetta Leopardi Srl for their kindness in allowing me to use images from their personal collections, and Katie Parla for her recipe contributions. Thanks to Gabriele Gatti and Elisabetta di Benedetto, whose kind hospitality in their San Lorenzo flat gave me one less worry.

Karima Moyer-Nocchi
July 2018

Ostium

I shall, at all events, derive no small satisfaction from the reflection that
my best endeavors have been exerted in transmitting to posterity the
achievements of the greatest people in the world.

—Titus Livius, *The History of Rome*

Writing about Rome is nothing less than a privilege. There is arguably no
other city whose history and culture have been so thoroughly researched and
written about in such minute detail as Rome. And yet, as its byname promises, the Eternal City is a source of seemingly endless curiosities waiting to
be explored and interpreted. I was therefore fortunate to have found a niche
that has afforded me the honor of writing the first concise cultural history of
the food of the Eternal City from pre-Roman to modern times.

While there are commendable cookery books with well-written overviews
of Roman food history, and studies that go into depth about particular periods, the aim here is to examine the role that food played in and alongside
the development of a city and its people, how it was utilized culturally and
politically, and how that led to the individuation of a gastronomy with a
uniquely Roman stamp. Such a project involved the daunting task of as-
sembling a succinct narrative outline that captured the underlying momen-
tum, both in terms of continuities and departures. The process of creating
a cohesive, illustrative framework spanning such a long and complex time
period necessitated bypassing some key points and reducing others to a bare

synthesis or risking oversimplification. Often histories of food become elaborate historical grocery lists, overlooking the social contours. Food history is
not, however, a list of plants, animals, or dishes, but a narrative—the story
of production, distribution, accessibility, demand, and control. It is about the
human partnership with what is raised, picked, fished, caught, slaughtered,
and cooked. It is about the meaning, expression, and manifestation of eating
and feeding as it is experienced and perceived along the continuum between
excess and dearth.

The cultural history of food in Rome is, like the city itself, made up
of multiple layers running both vertically and horizontally. It is therefore
treated here both thematically and chronologically, often necessitating a
two-steps-forward-one-step-back approach, underscoring connections as
they evolve through time and topic.

Numerous scholars, and many others, have made the study of Rome their
life's work. Both my own ideas in this book, and those of other authors whose
work I have relied upon, may thus run counter to positions put forth by others. As aptly put in Horden and Purcell's *The Corrupting Sea*, "To borrow an
evocative term from mathematics, the Mediterranean is a 'fuzzy set.'"[1] Rome,
as a focal point in the Mediterranean, as well as the subject of so many books,
films, television series, and vacation packages, makes it prey to sentiment
and idealization, from idyllic pastoralism to imperialistic grandeur. Such
emotional investments may stir resistance from those enamored of the patina
that shrouds the reality. We live in a time favoring journalism that gushes
about the Mediterranean, a *parti-pris*, that is not employed in this culinary
retrospect.

At the same time, affective, anecdotal literature—including works intended as serious histories—is an inseparable part of the texture and color
that create Rome's culinary portrait, regardless of its grounding in fact.
Often, these are the only extant historical sources available and as such are
invaluable. Such works describe through more emotionally charged language
how the culture, material and otherwise, was experienced, and, as such, they
add to rather than distract from the total picture.

There is also an extraordinarily large body of poetry inspired by and
dedicated to the pleasure (or not) of Roman food, drink, and conviviality.
Some of this has been quoted where it brings color, clarity, or poignancy to
the topic in a way that only poetry can. Most were originally written in the
plucky Roman dialect, whose earthy musicality is inevitably lost in translation. But, in those cases where the content and tone remain intact and are
accessible outside their sphere, they add a valuable layer to understanding
the history.

The foodways that characterize the gastronomy of Lazio often overlap those of other regions of Italy, but insofar as these foods and practices are recognized by the practitioners themselves as pertaining to the culinary grammar of Rome, they will be accepted and respected as such. The picture will not, however, be one with clean edges; there will be inconsistencies, as in life. Indeed, mutability and mobility are the themes that run throughout the book. Human agency and movement, the unprecedented ebb and flow of peoples of all descriptions in and out of Rome are, and have always been, the principal forces that forged the city's history and influenced its gastronomy. And, I too, as a long-established immigrant, am part of that great and ongoing wave of humanity, honored to have a position alongside the many who have had the privilege of writing about Rome.

QUI HIC MINXERIT AUT CACARIT HABEAT DEOS SUPEROS ET INTEROS IRATOS
(From a tombstone on the Appian Way)

Translation note: Unless otherwise indicated, all translations from Italian and Roman dialect into English are mine, including the text of Giancarlo Rolandi's contributions, featured in chapters 5 and 7.

A note on gender-inclusive language: When dealing with a patriarchal society in which women were in the shadows, having little or no say, and about whose lives, thoughts, and activities much less was recorded, the use of the masculine references for generalities is often the appropriate choice, because often the discussion is about men per se, and not people. There were very few occasions in which "s/he" or "his/her" would have been accurate, though each case was considered carefully.

Roman and *Romanesco*: Due to Rome's extensive history, I have when necessary made an artificial distinction between *Roman* food/cuisine and the *cucina romanesca*, the former spanning more or less from the Ancients to the eighteenth century.

CHAPTER ONE

The Roman Terrarium

The early Latins had little more than a subsistence economy based on the primitive cereals that had proliferated throughout the Mediterranean basin following the Neolithic or Agricultural Revolution,[1] principally emmer wheat and spelt, followed by barley and basic legumes. Abundant forests, the natural herding ground for pigs, and the grassy pastures and scrubland of Latium, well suited to raising sheep and goats, fed the livestock, whose meat and dairy products rounded out the diet. Fish occasionally came into play, but only as a supplemental food. For the overwhelming majority, these foods formed the common denominator, the basic leitmotif of ingredients that would sustain the life of sedentary communities.

Societies whose culinary traditions stretch back so far as to seem rooted in time immemorial often equate continuity with immutability. But how much of the description above would continue to define the food of the Roman people after two thousand five hundred years? Who exactly were the Romans? And in this handful of wheat and beans, in this scattering of pigs and goats—where lies the history of Roman food?

It was not so much environmental determinism as human enterprise, the tendency toward exploitive design, the irrepressible, insatiable, and indefatigable inventiveness of the Romans, that drove them to capitalize ever more on nature's pantry in the forests, swamps, plains, hills, lakes, rivers and coastal areas of Latium, transforming raw materials into social centerpieces that would distinguish, delineate, and bind the society ideologically—therein lies the story of Roman food, Roman gastronomy, and Roman cuisine. Be she clement or cruel, yielding or withholding, people found a way to force the hand of nature's limitations and transform her offerings into something that was worth eating—and selling.

No society aims at mere subsistence. Thus, with the springboard provided them by nature and their ability to select, master, and improve upon the best of foreign cultural influences, in combination with their legendary voracious ambition, Romans engaged in the development of a culinary history around these simple foundational foods that would nurture them along their long and perilous trajectory. Although parsimony and tradition were stalwart Roman virtues, their infamous hedonism would at times overshadow repeated claims of humble reserve. This tension between restraint and intemperance against a backdrop of stark social realities would exert a significant influence on the development of Roman cuisine. The road to power opened an irrepressible flow of importation and diversification that alarmed conservatives as much as it thrilled the inquisitive. Inevitably, albeit cautiously, novelties were accommodated into the ever-evolving culinary grammar that defined the Roman identity.

The fear of dearth, the wherewithal to profit from surfeit, and the yearning for the delectable and the exquisite were the stage upon which farming, consuming, cooking, storing, and selling played out the sociocultural history of food and eating in Rome. It is a history that is deeply scarred with inequality, want, and exploitation, but also rife with intrigue, and it cries out with hunger in every sense of the word.

The Land and Territory

The spatial delimitations of an area dubbed with the weighty appellative The Eternal City are best treated with indulgence. For most of its history, the word *frontiers* would be a more fitting term than *borders*, heaving as they were with manifest destiny, only to buckle later under the weight of excessive ambition. Rome was the felicitous offspring born of the interrelationship of natural resources laid out in the terrestrial cradle once called Latium, the unique combination of Empedocles's four elements that make up all matter: earth, wind, fire, and water. The geomorphic features of this triangular swath yielded the foundational groundwork upon which humankind would erect one of the most formidable civilizations in history. Cuisine, art, architecture, artifacts and items of material culture were the instruments that expressed the collective mythos, the innate human need to discover, create, and explain the story of ourselves. The unique underlying physical reality of the area that would be called Rome and the evolution of its peripheral landscape are an integral part of this vast cultural and culinary patrimony.[2]

The story begins with the lay of the land and the raw materials that would set the table and make the bed of the future inhabitants. The softly undulating landscape was formed following a stretch of intensely violent volcanic activity in the Pleistocene period, blanketing the surface with pyroclastic material that would be smoothed during the Würm glaciation.[3] These early layers of time, the volcanic stratigraphic by-products of tufa and travertine, would be exhumed as the building blocks of Rome and fashioned into the objects of civilization. The basaltic lava would pave the Roman roads; the metal ores would be forged into plough blades, weapons, and cooking vessels, and the underlying alluvial clay would make amphorae, bricks, and pottery. The hard leucitic basalts quarried from Bolsena provided durable stone for milling cereals.

The city of Rome, its outlying fields, and expansive countryside were respectively distinguished as *Urbs Romae*, the *Ager Romanus*, and *Latium Vetus*, later the *Campagna Romana*.[4] At any point 100 miles[5] from the city center, exile could officially begin. The Urbs was the nucleus, founded upon the Palatine Hill, one of the seven contiguous mounds where the city emerged, the others being Capitoline, Aventine, Celian, Esquiline, Viminal, and Quirinal. The Ager, or literally, "fields," a wide tract girdling the girth of the city, was delineated by a network of sacred locations where religious rites and celebrations were held.[6] The sprawling campagna that was Latium Vetus[7] was bordered on north by the Tiber River, which divided the Latin territory from that of the Etruscans—a piece of that greener pasture to the north of the Tiber would later be usurped, and called *Latium Novum*.

The land met the shore at the Tyrrhenian seaboard between Civitavecchia and Terracina on the west, and a string of pre-Apennine volcanic mountains enclosed the region to the east and south down to the promontory Mount Circeo. The Alban Hills, bordering the south, are older secondary volcanoes built up from their own wreckage, spewed over a deep layer of alluvial clay. The microclimate, south/southwest exposure, and potassium-rich soil mantle covering the broad craters lent the area to viticulture, which would develop early.[8] Long after the great age of tempestuous volcanic activity had simmered down, sporadic subterranean gurgling in the south would continue, the most notorious event being the sudden and tragic explosion of Vesuvius in 79 CE, which left posterity with a slice-of-life preserved in stone, revealing volumes about culture and daily life in Roman society. Even today, the occasional gaseous belch of carbon dioxide from the bowels of the earth, worsened by the frequency of earthquakes, threatens the health of the residents and animals in the Alban Hills. But *non tutti mali vengono per nuocere*—not all evil comes to cause harm. The dormant craters of the cooled calderas formed chalices that would cup the essential life-sustaining element: fresh drinking water. Lake Bolsena and Lake Bracciano are respectively Italy's second- and fourth-largest lakes, and to the south lie Lakes Albano and Nemi.[9] These inland resources of abundant fresh water were indispensable to the prosperity of the inhabitants, who tapped into them to irrigate surrounding farms and provide drinking water for themselves and their livestock.

The foothills of the mountains were once adorned with lush forests and diverse plant life, as was Latium's northern border with Etruria. In the name of human progress, these thick, almost impassable woodlands would undergo rampant deforestation as Rome grew, for which many geomorphologists consider the Roman era as the onset of the Anthropocene epoch. These forests supplied fuel wood and charcoal for smelting, cooking, heating, and brickworks. An exorbitant amount of wood was also required for funeral pyres: cremation had entered into the culture during the early Iron Age, and remained the standard until the end of the first century CE. The generous amounts of timber needed to construct the indomitable trade ships that kept Rome stocked with wheat, and later its fearsome war fleet, would further tax woodlands. Finally, by the time thermal baths were in their heyday, forests had been depleted to the point that the wood supply had to be regulated.

The chestnut tree, fundamental for its highly caloric, starchy nut and its durable hardwood, was a foreign import to the area that had been safeguarded in Latium during the last Ice Age. Along with the walnut tree, it supplanted much of the autochthonous forests and proliferated during the Neolithic Era, later being honored as the symbol of the Campagna Romana.[10]

The countryside was also thick with aromatic shrubbery native to the area, like rosemary, juniper, myrtle, and thyme. These flavorful herbs not only enhanced the quality of food, they also contain volatile substances that encourage the spread of fire. Fire, in this case part of a holistic ecology, enhances nutrient recycling and seed germination, thus encouraging fertility and constant renewal. Shrubs like these tend to occur in fire-prone areas, like Latium, with dry climates. Gentler aromatics like mint, fennel, chamomile, sage, and oregano were also indigenous.[11] From the hills and fields sprung a variety of edible wild plants,[12] some of which would be domesticated in time. Whether foraged or cultivated, most of those attested in ancient sources would remain part of the Roman culinary tradition until the twentieth century. The better known among the forageable leafy greens are wild chicory, arugula, chard, borage, dandelion, and nettles. Lesser known among these native comestibles are black mustard, wild asparagus, shepherd's purse, old man's beard, common mallow, poppy, hawkweed, purslane, milk thistle, sow thistle, and goats beard.[13] Most of these plants were quite bitter, for which it was (and is) believed that they were charged with medicinal and even magical properties. Among the naturally occurring species, *cynara cardunculus*, the cardoon, deserves separate and honorable mention as the native plant that would later be domesticated into the artichoke, or more specifically the globe-shaped cultivar *carciofo romanesco del Lazio*, one of the signature foods of Roman gastronomy. The flowers of the cardoon also contain a vegetable rennet used since ancient times to make sheep's milk cheese, now produced as *caciofiore della campagna romana*.

Much of the hinterland was cloaked in stretches of soft grassy hills with easy passes and fertile valleys that tapered off, surrendering their undulation into flatlands. Together with the wholesome sea air and temperate climate, Latium held great promise for settlement. The inland area is traversed by the mighty and mythic Tiber River, which departs from its source in Romagna on Mount Fumiaolo, then meanders down for two hundred fifty miles through Latium. Before reaching Rome, the Tiber is fed by many smaller rivers and streams, the most important of which is the Aniene, whose westward course compliments the Tiber's southerly flow, allowing for both north-south and east-west transport, fundamental veins for importing mountain resources and facilitating commercial trade. The lesser-known river was another key source of water for the ancient urban population, as the waters of the Tiber were suspect early on. The ancient physicians, including the revered Galen, warned that the waters of the Tiber weakened the liver, stomach, and kidneys, as well as increasing phlegm and leg infirmities.[14] Therefore, despite the presence of a freshwater source flowing directly through the city, it was aqueducts, the result of extraordinary human ingenuity, that brought the growing population of Republican and Imperial Rome an abundance of potable water imported from pristine sources. The city's main aqueducts tapped into the Aniene and the minor ones into local lakes. With no chemical analysis available, human trials were the proving ground for the salubriousness of aqueduct water for which the engineer Vitruvius advised, "Study the general health of the local consumers with special reference to complexion, strength of bone, and cloudy eyes." Aqueducts not only dispensed water for practical uses for farms and private homes, they also served aesthetic purposes, notably the public fountains, and fulfilled social functions by supplying a constant flow of clean water to the Roman baths.

That is not to say that the Tiber had been reduced to a mere murky waterway. It was teeming with a variety of fish and other comestible creatures, which would take on a significant role in the Roman culinary tradition. While the waters of the Tiber may have been disdained, the mouth of the river was an unimpeded gateway connecting the city to the sea. As a maritime power, Rome loomed large on the watery continuum of trade and communication, another essential element that would propel Roman society forward.

In spite of the long stretch of seaboard flanking the western Italic peninsula, there were not many areas along the coastline that lent themselves as natural salt beds.[15] After fresh water and fertile soil, the possession of salterns, the meeting point of land and sea, was an inestimable boon for any nascent settlement. As a preservative, salt was a form of life insurance. Therefore, possessing the mouth of the Tiber on both sides, where the Tyrrhenian salt water pooled and dried, was of dire importance for the prosperity of the community as well as the ambitions of its leaders. The salt supply at the base of the river was robust enough to set in motion, and for a time sustain, the exponential population growth of Rome that would know no rival until Victorian London.

From an economic standpoint, salt curing created long-storing products that allowed for stockpiling and surplus, as well as redistribution and resale for profit at a distance from its original location, giving rise to road networks reinforcing Rome's preeminence. The oldest and most renowned of the salt roads was the Via Salaria, a route already in use during the Bronze Age. The very act of salting pushed beyond the bounds of mere usefulness. Curing foodstuffs rendered products that were uniquely desirable in both taste and texture, so much so that this would eventually take precedence over the original purpose of salting to prolong shelf life. As Pliny the Elder affirms, "Without salt, one cannot live. It is necessary because it makes life pleasurable; it is the joy of life, it is rest after the fatigue of life."[16] Salt-cured products rendered commodities suitable for long-distance export, an enticing new concept whose promise of wealth accumulation piqued the enterprising mind. Salt was a necessary preservative, but when combined with its irresistible sensual appeal, the simple white crystals represented an indomitable source of power.

Despite its rosy potential, the Campagna Romana fell somewhat short of Eden. The flatlands receded into extended depressed areas that filled with stagnant water from the streams and rivulets that lacked the force to carve out a neat course through the dunes to empty out into the sea. The Pontine Marshes, now the Pontine Fields, cover nearly 310 square miles and were a perpetual haven for malaria, so named as it was first thought to be an airborne sickness. According to popular mythology, the marshes had been cre-

ated by Juno to punish the nymph Feronia, who stole away there to consort
with Jupiter, Juno's husband. Geologists have proposed the more staid and
scientific theory that the ancient riverbed of the Tiber had been blocked
with materials extruded by volcanic eruptions.[17] It would take thousands
of years to carve out a new course to the sea, and in the meantime, waters
pooled in the southwest, creating alluvial plains. The prospect of taking up
residency there may have seemed a precarious if not senseless venture, particularly given the quantity of arable land elsewhere. However, portions of the
marshes were above sea level and sparsely wooded, with abundant game and
wild life.[18] Therefore, while human habitation may have been sparse due to
the obvious drawbacks, wetlands harbored a richly varied ecosystem, whose
bounty attracted populations such as the Volscians. Nestled among reeds and
grasses were an abundant variety of aquatic creatures and fish, like mullet,
carp, and eel in quantities incomparable to what could be procured through
shoaling in the nutritionally paltry environment of the Tyrrhenian Sea.[19]
With the heat of summer, the stagnant brine in some areas reduced to a hard-
ened crust in the natural saltpans. Although the riddle of malaria bedeviling
the area would not be solved until the twentieth century—concomitant with
the transformation of marshland into arable land—swamps were not the ma-
leficent wastelands they are often depicted as being; they contributed to the
livelihood of the inhabitants, not only because of the fish and salterns, but
also as a habitat for water fowl and a feeding ground for livestock, as saline
vegetation improves the quality of meat. Later, and perhaps most notably for
Roman cuisine, they would be an ideal environment for water buffalo.

The marshes were also a source for reeds and fibrous plants to make baskets and sacks—durable, breathable, lightweight containers for transporting
goods, drying, draining, and sifting. This made a virtue of necessity, underscoring humankind's ability to assess and exploit whatever could be eked out
of the resources at hand. Reclaiming the land, in the end, simply redefined
the word "arable"; the marketplace, politics, and the pressure to supply high-
volume storable products to the swelling city destined "arable" to be defined
as "grain-producing." By harnessing the power of water, such as draining
marshes, the construction of aqueducts, fountains, ponds, canals and bridges,
or the Cloaca Maxima—the ingenious sewage system that flushed Rome of
its waste, eventually dumping its load into the Tiber—men hoisted themselves up on par with the gods.

The choice to establish permanent settlements here does not imply that
pre-Roman tribes were environmental soothsayers or carried out geological
survey assessments. Had they been shopping for prime real estate, the better
investment would have been the territory just north and south of Latium, re-

Figure 1.1. Water buffalo, imported into Rome in the sixth century, would adapt well to the watery habitat of the Pontine Marshes. Photo by G. Primoli, reproduced with permission from the Fondazione Primoli, Roma

spectively Etruria and Campania, which had richer, more fertile soil. Whatever might have influenced their choice, settle they did on this central-southwesterly plot. As for the upmarket land they had bypassed, no worries. In due time, that and more would be enveloped into the ever-expanding concept of Rome and the best of its bounty surrendered. But first, Rome had to be founded.

Who Were the Romans?

A Neanderthal cranium was discovered in the Guattari Grotto at Mount Circeo, Latium's southernmost point, just off the Tyrrhenian coast, dating back c. 50,000 years, to the middle period of the Würm glaciation. There is a curious hole in the back of it, first theorized as a part of a cannibalistic rite involving the removal and consumption of the brain. The skull was purportedly found in the center of a circle of stones, adding credence to the macabre claim. Later scientific observations deduced, however, that the victim's head had been brought into the grotto by a hyena who had made her den there—the hole bore signs of animal teeth, thus dashing the cannibal story. The Neanderthals would die out, while *Homo sapiens*, who had evolved alongside them, flourished. The earliest trace of humans in Europe was discovered in the heel of the boot of the Italian peninsula and dates back about forty-five thousand years ago. In the area of the Campagna Romana, the earliest verifiable evidence of human settlement dates to the Bronze Age, 1800–1200 BCE. These were few, transitory encampments, nothing more than the shelters of sojourners whose socioeconomic organization appears to have been based on transhumant pastoralism, the cyclical relocation of sheep and goats from upland pastures in the summer months to lowlands in the winter.[20] In the Late Bronze Age, permanent settlements appear that counted inhabitants in the hundreds, whereas a settlement in the early Iron Age often numbered a bustling one thousand or more.[21] Metalworking allowed for significant advances in agriculture, indicated by the variety of precision metal artifacts that have been unearthed in the vicinity of Rome. Alongside the refinement of artisan production, the population grew and cultural traits of the various peoples who had put roots down in Latium—among them the Sabines, Volscians, and the Falisci—began to differentiate, deviate, and express discrete features, where previously they were more culturally indistinct. The Italic tribe called

Figure 1.2. Vilanovan cinerary hut urn, c. ninth century BCE. Reproduced with permission from the Ministero dei Beni e delle Attivit. . . . Culturali e del Tourismo di Bologna e le provincie di Modena, Reggio Emilia e Ferrara, copyright.

the Latins was among first to so distinguish itself. Their burial rite included household items such as containers for food and drink, cups, bowls, plates, and a variety of pots, enough for a celebratory meal, as well as a human figurine with outstretched hands. The ashes of the deceased were placed in the center of a hut-shaped cinerary urn, a replica of their actual dwellings, as if they were cinders in the family hearth. The urn and funerary accessories emphasize the comfort of house and home and within that, the central role that domesticity and commensality played in easing travails. As in life, so after death. And so begins the story of the Romans.

The First Settlers

The Latins were not natives sprung up in situ by spontaneous generation, but a migrant people who had crossed over onto the Italic peninsula from Eastern Europe through the Alpine passes. Here they began their descent into the plains area under the Po Valley, eventually settling into Latium, between Etruria and Campania and bordered on the east and west respectively by the Tyrrhenian Sea and the Apennine Mountains. These newcomers may have been escaping turmoil or inhospitable conditions in their place of origin, finding in Latium a place that might offer solace. The survival of the society in the newfound land depended upon the successful interplay between the diverse geomorphic features on offer in Latium Vetus and the fears, beliefs, ambitions, tastes, and physiological needs of the new residents. If the human element successfully synchronized with local topography, climate, and biota into a choreography of mutual cooperation and imposition, it would yoke the people together, and to the land, as a systemic whole.

The Latins brought with them an evolved Indo-European social organization, a history of shared cultural and religious practices, and an economy based on pastoralism and cereal cultivation. The early Latins had been migrant stockbreeders and shepherd-warriors, which can be traced back to the Yamna culture of hunter-gatherers.[22] Both pastoralism and agriculture are offshoots of the hunter-gatherer. They developed largely in interdependent symbiosis, although domestication of plants was the forerunner. Hilly landscapes like Latium Vetus, whose vegetation varied with altitude, also fostered the greatest variations in tamable animal species, the evolutionary sequence of stockbreeding here and elsewhere in the Mediterranean being goats, sheep, pigs, then cattle,[23] some more predisposed to being herded than others.[24] There are comparatively few fossil remnants of horses in Italy. Their use as a war vehicle and status symbol translated into an aversion to equine meat, a cultural perception originating from the Middle East during the original Agricultural Revolution thousands of years earlier. The few extant protohistoric remains show no signs of butchering or cooking and are not found in the vicinity of other petrified faunistic meal fragments.[25]

Domestic animals intended for consumption are a form of stored food, on-the-hoof insurance against the lack of vegetable food. These herded animals transformed otherwise indigestible biomass into food that humans could not only ingest and assimilate, but relish. Through animals, humans were able to profit from the areas considered "marginal" landscapes, like forests, slopes, and marshes, making them an integrally productive contribution to the whole picture.[26] Ovicaprids (sheep and goats) grazing in scraggly scrublands and lush wetlands, or pigs foraging in forests and oak groves for foods, did not compete with the resources that humans themselves consumed, and thus they complimented the ecosystem. Feeding animals food that humans could digest themselves would have been illogical. Likewise, the consumption of animals that provided renewable resources, beyond what was nutritionally or ritually necessary, would have endangered potential emergency provisions.

"Transhumance" breaks down into the concept of travel between two ecological realities: vertical relocation between the summer highlands and the winter lowlands, or horizontal movement between biomass types in an effort to make the best use of available resources and climates. Centuries of transhumance carved out the famous *tratturi*, pathways joining these realities. However, environmental determinism was only part of what dictated these routes. Taxes, the proximity of markets, settlements, and property rights came to override environmental determinism as factors that that dictated where herds would graze and how they would be brought to their destination, ultimately affecting the quality of meat and dairy as well.

Herders themselves have long been subjected to a reputation as a primitive subset of cultivators—backward, violent, and slow-witted. Historian Ammianus Marcellinus, although writing in reference to his own age in the 390s CE, captures this well-worn stereotype calling them "savage beyond belief: they are beastlike in their ugliness, eat raw flesh, have no houses, living only on horseback and in wagons, never change their clothing have no government, no morality, no laws."[27] The marked distain for herders and the desire to relegate them to a subhuman rung was ironic in that agriculturalists had themselves first domesticated animals for human use. Indeed, in spite of the distinction, the roles were interdependent—pastoralists relied on agricultural products, such as the ground-dried wheat needed to make their daily gruel, a durable, portable foodstuff that could sustain the itinerant shepherd on his journeys; whereas the manure, heavy field work, wool, dairy, meat, skin, and bones of livestock variously complimented agriculture.

Domesticated animals also allowed men to appease the gods through sacrificial rites, live tokens offered up in exchange for a favorable glance. Sacrificial meat allowed humankind to commune with the gods, re-invoking a long lost golden age when men and gods dined together in harmony. Sheep- and goat-milk cheeses, the making of which was a laborious enterprise requiring the skill of experienced pastoralists, were also used as votive gifts. In the urban context, cheeses were placed at the base of statues of the gods, and their pungent smell became a pervasive reminder of the divine.[28] Yet, in spite of the importance of herding historically, politically, economically, and socially, the cultural dietary model in Rome disdained meat, at least philosophically.[29]

Whatever sparse extant communities from the preexisting Apennine culture the Latins might have encountered upon their arrival were absorbed or extinguished.[30] *Latinus*, the newly assumed identity, meant "man from the flat land." A sense of nationhood for the Latin League, as the consortium of small communities came to be called, was created by "the common language; the common annual sacrifices to the ancestral gods, the common myth of origin of the female boar who, by divine guidance, lured the ancestor of the tribe to follow her to Alba Longa, to his future seat as King of the Latins; the exclusive community of legal marriage, and the business arrangements between all the Latins."[31] The flexibility of unwritten religious myths allowed for the constant restructuring of alliances. As leading clans overtook others, their lineage would become incorporated into the creation myth, endowing them with a larger-than-life status that instilled confidence and adulation in their followers.

The confederation of Latin colonies convened yearly en masse to celebrate and reinforce their ethnic bond at the Latin Festival (*Feriae Latinae*). Amid feasting and sacred rites, disputes were settled, tokens of goodwill exchanged, matches made, goods marketed, and the myth of their origin reenacted. The gathering place was the Holy Mountain at Alba Longa. A ritual sprinkling of milk on the mount to encourage fertility set the festivities in motion, and a great banquet ensued featuring lamb, sheep's milk, and cheese. The crowning ceremony was the sacrifice of a white bull on a high altar to propitiate the gods. Its meat was then duly distributed among the tribal representatives. If any error was made in the ritual or the distribution, the whole affair had to be repeated.[32] Distribution was not "share and share alike." Sacrificial meat was carefully selected and apportioned so as to distinguish the dignitaries with the prime parts, and so on down the line. The open declaration of tribal pecking order held the potential for flaring tensions, but the act of consuming the same animal was intended as a sign of communal amity, in which every member was expected to gracefully acquiesce for the greater good.

In time, both rural and urban sedentism began to lay down indelibly deep roots. Shifting perspectives about belonging to the land and familiarity with local food sources gave way to the comforting predictability of seasonal scheduling and resource management.[33] Under the influence of the Greeks and Etruscans, structured stationary nuclei gradually became the defining sociopolitical feature of Latium. As colonies increased in number and size, group identities grew more pronounced, with contrasts often leading to conflict. Distinctions were made between "originals" and "newcomers," the embryonic Rome being among the latter. As the settlement clusters coalesced, and ethnogenesis progressed in concomitance with advances in food and travel technology, a network of trade routes also developed. Already by the eighth century BCE, Rome had become the central trading hub; the expression "all roads lead to Rome" came much later, but the idea was well established.

Ab urbe condita—The Mythological Founding of Rome

In lieu of flags, anthems, and other symbolic paraphernalia of nationalism, Rome would elaborate its own civic creation myth, glorifying its manifest destiny as divine will brought to fruition by human force. The first part of the myth is based upon a gastronomic prophecy. In Virgil's *Aeneid*, the survivors of the fallen city of Troy arrive on the coast of Latium. Exhausted and hungry after a long period at sea, they

> stretch out on the grass below the boughs of a tall tree,
> then set about their meal, spreading a feast on wheaten cakes—
>   Jove himself impelled them—heaping the plates with Ceres' gifts,
> her country fruits. And once they'd devoured all in sight,
> still not sated, their hunger drove them on to attack
> the fateful plates themselves, their hands and teeth
> defiling, ripping into the thin dry crusts, never
> sparing a crumb of the flat-bread scored in quarters.[34]

The bread plates mentioned in this excerpt were only meant as a base to hold the food. Eating them would have been gluttonous, akin to licking your plate. But the band of men was driven by hunger, and so, after consuming the food, they ate their trenchers. It is this very act that had been prophesied, and when they realize what had just happened, the Trojan prince Aeneas cried out:

Hail to the country owed to me by Fate!
Hail to you, you faithful household gods of Troy!
Here is our home, here is our native land!
For my own Father—now I remember—Anchises
left to me these secret signs of Fate:
"When, my son, borne to an unknown shore,
reduced to iron rations, hunger drives you
to eat your own platters, then's the moment,
exhausted as you are, to hope for home."[35]

The Trojans would integrate with the Latins, eventually establishing a lineage that would lead up to the founding of Rome. In the legend of Romulus and Remus, the four classic elements—earth, air, water and fire—are

Figure 1.3.   *The Trojan's First Meal in Latium.* Etching by Vaclav Hollar, reproduced with permission by Walter Levy

interwoven into the myth, as are Empedocles's two fundamental forces of life: Love and Strife. It proceeds thus:

Procas, King of Alba Longa[36] left two sons at his death, Numitor, the heir apparent, and his ambitious younger brother, Amulius. In short order, Numitor was dethroned, his sons killed and his daughter forced to become a virgin priestess of Vesta, goddess of the home fires. Their oath of chastity, the breaking of which was punishable by death, would, as Livy says, "deprive her of all hope of issue."[37] Thus, Amulius extinguished any future threat to his illegitimate claim to the throne. The name of the ill-fated priestess, Rhea Sylvia, is rife with symbolic meaning. Her divine namesake, the original Rhea, was the fruit of the coupling of Gaia, the earth goddess, and Uranus, the sky god, while Sylvia originates from the Latin word for woods. With the addition of her imposed vocation as a priestess of the hearth, she embodied three of the classical elements in herself.

"But," Livy recounts, "the fates, I suppose, demanded the founding of this great city, and the first establishment of an empire, which is now, in power, next to the immortal gods."[38] Rhea Silvia, the vessel of destiny, was lulled into slumber by the god of sleep Somnus,[39] so that the god Mars might more easily have his way with her. Then, when Rhea Silvia found she was with child, neither Mars nor any other deity intervened on her behalf. The usurper, King Amulius, was predictably indifferent to her claim of innocence (some ancient authors went so far as to suspected that this was a cover-up for an all-too-human affair). He ordered that her twin neonates be taken to the Tiber, the water artery that coursed through Latium, and dispatched posthaste. Whether from pity or indolence, the henchmen were haphazard in carrying out their mission; instead of drowning them in the river, they abandoned the infants in a shallow pool, which soon dried with the receding tide.

A she-wolf, or *lupa*, heard the cries of the babes and rushed to give them succor by nursing them from the bounteous dangling dugs so copiously depicted in Italian paintings and statues. It is fitting that generosity to foundlings should mark the beginnings of Rome, a city whose open doors have been compared to Dodge City[40] and present-day Dubai.[41] Not long thereafter, a kindly shepherd named Faustulus happened upon the twins and took them home, where he and his wife Laurentia would raise them. Some versions of the origin myth suggest that Laurentia was a prostitute, and therefore also referred to as a lupa, which may lay to rest some practical questions, but would sap the entertainment value out of the story.

The rambunctious boys ran with a motley crew of ruffians who plundered the lands of Numitor. In an ambush set up by rivals, Remus ended up as the fall guy and was presented before the deposed king. Spurred on by wishful thinking, Numitor put two and two together; meanwhile, Faustulus revealed to Romulus the truth about his august ancestry. The boys joined forces to restore Numitor to the throne, after which they struck out on their own to found a city. All might have gone peacefully had it not been for a flaw in their DNA, a twisted taint that would not allow them to rule together as equals.

Knowing now that they were of aristocratic birth, the brothers were allowed to use augury, the reading of the flight of birds sent by the gods, to determine who should rightfully rule and where. The twins staked their claim among what would become the Seven Hills of Rome, Romulus choosing the Palatine and Remus the Aventine. Remus was the first to be honored with the omen of six vultures. But before his victory had been confirmed, twelve birds appeared to Romulus. Both felt the throne was rightfully theirs, one through primacy of arrival and the other through primacy of number. In accordance with a sacred Etruscan tradition, Romulus wasted no time in plowing the line demarcating the city limits, materially carving his destiny into the surface of the Earth as a completion to the airborne portents. This raised a ridge, symbolizing the city's fortification wall, called the *pomerium*. Remus signaled his irritation at the presumptuous gesture by jumping over the sacrosanct marker, resulting in a bloody fight. "Romulus, enraged thereat, slew him, uttering at the same time this imprecation, 'So perish everyone that shall hereafter leap over my wall.'"[42]

Thus, according to legend, Rome was founded on April 21, 753 BCE.

In the Romulus saga, his followers were a ragtag band from different ethnic backgrounds of the area. The image projected by this legend was of an unpretentious people who welcomed diversity in an open cosmopolitan society. Strength came in numbers, and even freed slaves were not shunned.[43] The more the merrier. More sober forms of history provide some confirmation to this early diversity. The two main proto-urban settlements, of Latins and Sabines, were perched, respectively, on the Palatine and Quirinal Hills. Between them, in the location where the Roman Forum would be constructed, was the altar of Vesta, the Eternal Fire that symbolized hearth and home. Vesta ranked among the oldest and most sacred of divinities and at this juncture had not yet been anthropomorphized, maintaining her abstract spirit form. The vestal virgins priestesses were handpicked from ruling-class families and charged with stoking the hallowed fire lest it should go out and leave Rome unprotected. Once again, the comfort of home, and specifically the home fire that would provide cooked food and warmth, is given venerable status. In addition to maintaining the State Hearth, these elite priestesses prepared the sacred mola salsa, a mixture of toasted coarse-ground emmer wheat and salt for sacrificial and ceremonial purposes, a practice said to date back to the time of Romulus's successor, the Sabine Numa Popilius.

The use of toasted emmer meal in the preparation of the mystical concoction resonated in many ways. Toasting the grains proved an effective means of deterring parasites and increasing shelf life, a technique handed down from the Greeks and Etruscans. When coarsely ground into a dish called puls, this toasted wheat was the primary foodstuff around which the most basic and traditional repast was constructed, a pattern that recurred throughout most of the Mediterranean.[44] The Romans peered over at the table of the older, more established cultures for cues on what to eat, believing that comestibles had contributed to their seniors' success.[45] But they didn't merely ape their betters. By associating it with sacred rituals that were distinctly Roman and attributing it directly to King Numa, they reinvented the lumpy pap and enshrined it as a quintessentially Roman tradition—a humble food for a grounded stock of humble people. And it was this food, and the subsequent variations of it, that the hoards would come to identify as their basic righteous entitlement through to the present day. Any lack thereof had the power to make and break kings and empires.

Diversification, preservation, storage, surplus, and redistribution of foods loom large among the greatest contributors to human survival, firstly, and then to the civilization process. The development of ancient Rome was, thereby, Italy's cultural equivalent to the Cambrian explosion. Strategies such as salting, smoking, pickling and fermenting would develop as sophisticated methods of preserving food, but drying was the simplest and earliest form of prolonging shelf life. The reliable results of drying promoted cereals and legumes as the foods of choice that would fill the bellies of the multitude. Setting aside the romantic stories of priestesses, nascent royalty, and honest farmers, the predominance that wheat achieved in the Mediterranean diet, including at Rome, is directly related to the ease with which it could be managed as a commodity, "whatever is said about the taste and cultural fashion, and even nutritional return."[46]

Whether from envy or disgust, later ancient historians reviled the Etruscans, who preceded the Romans in central Italian dominance, as hedonists whose love of luxury had reputedly blunted their prowess. Indeed, Etruscan art celebrates their lavish banquets, depicting diners around tables in the semi-reclining position of the Greeks—the difference being the former's inclusion of women, who enjoyed a significantly higher status among them. This splendor at the table did not square with the portrait that Romans had painted of themselves as rough and ready, salt-of-the earth people. Regardless of the sumptuous imagery however, the basis of the Etruscan meal had been none other than those same cereal gruels made with ground emmer or barley and legumes, the selfsame inheritance of the Neolithic revolution revered by the Romans. The repast was supplemented with fruit, vegetables, dairy, and meat, principally sheep or goat, and rarely game. As a nonagricultural product, game would be recast as barbaric and hunting relegated to an elite sport, whose secondary purpose was the procurement of food.[47]

In spite of the austere ideals upon which their traditions were based, the early Romans were by no means impervious to the pull of luxury or the cultural advantages to be had from associating with an advanced society like the Etruscans. Quite the contrary. The fifth and sixth kings of the seven who, according to tradition, reigned before the Republican Era were Etruscan, reflecting a fruitful period of cultural exchange. The new order occupied the Capitoline Hill; thus, together with the occupied Palatine and Quirinal Hills, they created a triad with Vesta's fire at the center. Stone buildings with tiled roofs replaced the wattle and daub huts, signaling Rome's transformation during this monarchic period into a formidable urban society that now boasted a population of over thirty-five thousand. As nucleated settlements continued to grow and consolidate, the quality of funerary accouterments increased—the crude plate and cup was superseded by whole banquet services of fine imported ceramics and amphorae of wine. Material well-being reflects improvements in agricultural production; indeed, it is here, during the reign of Lucius Tarquinius Priscus, that vine and olive cultivation is thought to have developed.[48]

Well-being was not, however, evenly disbursed. Social stratification and the rise of a full-fledged aristocracy splintered the community into haves and have-nots—those who produced for those who consumed and traded. When combined with human greed and ambition, even the beneficent intention behind a simple concept like storage was subject to corruption. The dark side of storage is the inherent temptation to hoard and artificially create shortage, even in the presence of glut, and to manipulate prices in accordance with levels of public desperation. Wheat prevailed over dried legumes in versatility, firstly as gruel, then later and more importantly as flour for bread, the antecedents of pasta. Whereas leavened bread was best baked daily, pasta transformed flour into a product that could be stored for years and would prove even more impervious to external agents than dried cereals. Deliciousness was the felicitous counterpart to necessity, but pasta was not a "neutral ecology pursuing its natural course."[49] As a storable, versatile, transportable, resilient product, wheat was particularly attractive to urban dwellers, and its vulnerability as an exploitable commodity made it all the more alluring to shrewd merchants. The multifarious social delineations that arose as a consequence of advances in agronomics strongly influenced the close of the Era of Kings in 509 BCE, ushering in the establishment of the Roman Republic, during which time Rome would pursue its hegemony over the Mediterranean, exporting its own foodways and in turn opening the garden gates, larder cupboards, and kitchen doors encountered along the way.

CHAPTER TWO

◧◩◨

Quid tum—Then What?

Roman Kingdom (753–509 BCE)
Roman Republic (509–27 BCE)
Roman Empire (27 BCE–476 CE)

Caput mundi

Rome had embarked on a systematic trajectory of continual expansion. By consuming the sacred Latin heartlands like Alba Longa and thereby presiding over the Feriae Latinae, the annual convention, the focus of sacrality was shifted strategically to Rome itself. More than kinship or race, common ritual joined disparate clusters of people together. With Jupiter as their official god, a federation of peoples built up in Latium.[1] "Strangers in blood were brothers if they worshipped at the same house-altar; brothers by blood became strangers when one was banished from it."[2] A single political authority emerged, and a council of "fathers" (*patres*) who had no trace of slavery in their lineage was selected. Their descendants would become the patrician class. In the earliest times, these administered the common land, regulated private land ownership, and oversaw urban markets. The plebeians were the remaining free Roman citizens, who ranged from near nobility to poor working classes. The bottom rung was, of course, slaves.

The last battle of the Latin War in 338 BCE left the Roman Republic the undisputed ruler of the region. The victorious Romans dissolved the Latin League and allowed only Romans the privileges of citizenship, such as political assembly, commercial activities, and lawful marriage.[3] The combined area would later become the modern-day region of Lazio.

Over time, an intricate system of patronage and homage bound the society together socially. Patronage allowed persons of lower standing a channel through which they could interact within "better" society, to obtain justice, possessions, sponsorship, or even just a regular meal. The common client courted patronage through flattery, wit, talent, and/or declarations of unflagging loyalty. "A large clientage was the glory of a patrician family, and the number of adherents in some degree the measure of its eminence."[4] The balance of power and the preservation of social cohesion in Rome were centered on this arrangement of favor and obeisance. While its strictures and structures would evolve over time, the patron/client relationship formed the conceptual basis of Roman socioeconomic history, and thus the justification for who ate what, where, with whom, and why.

Living and the Land

In the civilized agricultural portrait the Romans painted of themselves, land was measured in units called *iugera*. The *iugerum* was the amount of land that one man with a plow and a beast of burden could reasonably till in a single workday—hence, one iugerum was about a quarter of a hectare—a human geographical feature that echoed the communion between land and laborer.

The land of Latium was fickle. Whereas in one place, the alluvial and volcanic soils might have given a good return, in another, the claylike earth was so thick as to be plow resistant. In yet another spot, the wispy topsoil proved too thin to produce a healthy crop. The gods were, of course, ultimately responsible for the bounty, for which sacrificial due was paid both Saturn, god of agriculture, and his fearsome consort, Lua Mater,[5] who would destroy the year's crop in the wink of an eye or shield it from harm, depending on her disposition.[6] A multitude of rituals, incantations, and homages were integrated into the Roman agricultural calendar to beg benevolence and assure a plenteous harvest.

Under the sixth and penultimate king of Rome, Servius Tullius, the first coins are said to have been minted, bearing the image of a sheep and a bull, a reminder that the ultimate source of power and wealth was still herding and agriculture.[7] Tullius was also said to have instituted a census requiring all citizens to register their rank, property, household, and income, and to have dubbed the outlying area of the city the "ager Romanus" to mark it as Roman territory, the garden that would supply the private homes and public markets of the Urbs with perishable goods.

As Rome's boundaries expanded through Italy and beyond during the Republican period, the government assumed ownership of all lands acquired through conquest, and would distribute this new *ager publicus* opportunely to compensate services rendered, or to maintain power relations. A notional

Figure 2.1. **Peasant farmers in the campagna romana. Ancient methods of farming continued throughout the nineteenth century. Photo by G. Primoli, reproduced with permission from the Fondazione Primoli, Roma**

limit of 500 iugera was placed on individual holdings, but in practice, wealthier citizens could and did ignore this, acquiring tracts far beyond prescribed limits, or treating rented lands as private property. This was the beginning of the *latifundia*, huge holdings that would burden Italy's economy through to the twentieth century. Conceptually, these vast estates, worked by slaves or, more often, left fallow, pitted the reality of empire and privilege against the Roman ideal of the industrious citizen farmer growing simple food for a family.

In 133 BCE, Tiberius Gracchus, one of two politically radical brothers from a distinguished family, set out to redress the imbalance of land ownership, and thus the availability of food, by enforcing the old laws, and making plots available to returned solders and to the urban poor. For his efforts, Gracchus was murdered by elite opponents. His law was later implemented, but despite having been conceived to assist the small landholder, to some extent it proved ill conceived.

In theory, the ager Romanus and the more distant public lands were meant to be a busy patchwork of small farms manned by veterans who had come back steely from combat, men who, as Pliny the Elder (23–79 CE) says, "tended the seed with the same care that they had displayed in the conduct of wars, . . . the same diligent attention in the management of their fields as they had done in the arrangement of the camp. . . . Under the hands of honest men everything prospers."[8] In reality, however, these land awards were often more trouble than they were worth, either due to poor land quality or to inadequate size. Family farms were no match for the latifundia, profitable large estates resulting from those same wars of expansion, first in Italy itself and then around the Mediterranean. Not only did slaves work them, but in high season, the owners could afford to also take on extra day laborers to bring in the crops.[9]

This reality sat awkwardly with the persistent ideal of a stalwart farmer race for Romans.[10] Ancient Greek and Roman writers on agriculture had always venerated the outdoor life. Pliny the Elder considered the centenarian Antonius Castor, a pioneering botanist and a freedman exemplary in that regard, proof of Juvenal's expression *mens sana in corpore sano*, "a healthy mind in a healthy body," owing to the fact that Castor spent every day tooling away in his garden.[11] The sermon "'getting your hands dirty is a sign of clean living,'" was, however, addressed to the literate and leisured, and did not necessarily imply any real exertion on their part.

As land holdings increased, local cultivation near Rome, particularly of the main staple, wheat, was considered an almost futile enterprise, and most of the land in large estates in Latium itself was left fallow. At the turn of (what is for us) the new millennium, many landholders and agriculturalists asserted that the soil would not produce as it once had, because it was suffering from old age. Agronomist Tremellius Scrofa compared the spent land to a menopausal woman who had simply become unproductive over the years.[12] The technical knowledge of how to restore the land to its fecund state was known to them, yet not put into practice, given the new tracts that had opened up farther afield, and perhaps because speculation on the expanded grain market had become more profitable, and less risky. Even Pliny the Elder, who sang the praises of Italian wheat, did so in reference to imports from Verona, Pisa, and Campagna, but not crops closer to Rome.

Columella (4–c. 70 CE), took a firmer stance, castigating his contemporaries who used the excuse that the land was unproductive: "I do not believe that such misfortunes come upon us as a result of the fury of the elements, but rather we ourselves are at fault; for the matter of husbandry, which all the best of our ancestors has treated with the best of care, we have delivered over to the worst of our slaves, as if to a hangman for punishment."[13] He implored town-loving, absentee landowners to devote more time to their farms: "Whenever he has an opportunity, let him stay in the country, and not pass the time he stays there in idleness and ease, and lolling in the shade, or keeping within-doors."[14] He, too, waxed poetic about the olden days, lamenting the misguided youth of his day and the lost Roman values of "parsimony, temperance, moderation and industry." Women, who were once dedicated wholly to their domestic burden, had become "so delicate, and such lovers of the town, that they could not endure to pass a few weeks in the country, and thought it greatly below themselves to cast their eyes upon the instruments of husbandry." Whereas the men, "by turning night into day, and day into night . . . were almost dead while alive . . . so that they soon became useless both to themselves, and to their country."[15]

Thus, the lackadaisical gentleman farmer had his part in forcing Rome's continuous expansion in order to sustain itself. Most estates could have produced the necessities for self-sufficiency and cash crops for export. Yet, from the time of the earliest Roman agricultural writer, Cato the Censor (d. 149 BCE) onward, wheat cultivation had been either disregarded or downplayed in favor of viticulture and oleiculture. Grapes (*vitas vinifera*) were native to the area, whereas olive cultivation in Rome was said to date back to the era of Kings.[16] According to Greek mythology, on the other hand, the olive tree was created by Athena (whose Roman counterpart was Minerva), and it was she who introduced the olive tree to the Italian mainland. Both were profitable ventures and considered in keeping with the decorum of the gentleman farmer.

The estate owners, the eating classes, were starvation brokers. These same often had a hand in masterminding food shortages—though blamed on the weather—greed was the driving force. Generally speaking, slaves were given an allowance of grain, salt, windfall olives, some pickled vegetables, and oil. Under Cato's directives, not only did they not have meat or cheese, they were not even given beans, though stringency and generosity varied from estate to estate, and some slaves might have enjoyed the occasional morsel of meat.[17] In the winter, dried fruit, especially figs, were added to the field workers' ration.[18] The standard peasant diet consisted of little more than what was allowed to farm slaves. The dietary practices of smallholders held little interest for ancient writers, and as these farmers lacked both the wherewithal and resources to write their musings about food, particularly when their reality was not characterized by variety, menus, or intricate preparation, little is known about their foodways. Among the few to shed light on the diet of the laboring wretched was the Greek physician Galen. Although he rubbed elbows with the *Roma bene* after his arrival in 161 CE, he nevertheless treated people of all backgrounds. In his observations on the state of tenant farmers, he does not don the same rose-colored glasses as his peers:

> When summer was over, those who lived in the cities, in accordance with their universal practice . . . took from the fields all the wheat, barley, beans and lentils, and left to the rustics only those annual products which are called pulses and leguminous fruits. . . . So the people in the countryside, after consuming during the winter what had been left, were compelled to use unhealthy forms of nourishment. I myself saw some of them at the end of the spring, and almost all of them at the beginning of the summer, afflicted with numerous ulcers covering their skin, not all the same kind in every case, for some suffered from erysipelas, others from inflamed tumors, others from spreading boils, others had an eruption resembling lichen and scabs and leprosy.[19]

Latifundia perdidere Italiam ("the large landholdings are destroying Italy").[20] Even though Pliny was himself a wealthy landholder, he recognized the *latifundia* of his era as a real-estate expression of moral decrepitude. As the ager Romanus emptied, and expansion continued elsewhere in the Mediterranean, the newly conquered lands did not, as logic might want it, simply add more revenue to the pot. On the contrary, the Urbs swelled with more mouths to feed. Among the circumstances leading up to the decline of Rome, the negligence of landowners ranks high,[21] in conjunction with a "progressive exhaustion of the soil . . . sufficient to doom Rome, as lack of oxygen in the air would doom the strongest living being."[22]

Urbs Romae, civitas aeterna— Rome, the Eternal City

Rome in her greatness! Stranger, look your fill!

—*Propertius*

But his besetting sins were luxury and cruelty. He divided his feasts into three, sometimes into four a day, breakfast, luncheon, dinner, and a drinking bout;

and he was readily able to do justice to all of them through his habit of taking emetics. Moreover, he had himself invited to each of these meals by different men on the same day, and the materials for any one of them never cost less than four hundred thousand sesterces. Most notorious of all was the dinner given by his brother to celebrate the emperor's arrival in Rome, at which two thousand of the choicest fishes and seven thousand birds are said to have been served. He himself eclipsed even this at the dedication of a platter, which on account of its enormous size he called the "Shield of Minerva, Defender of the City." In this he mingled the livers of pike, the brains of pheasants and peacocks, the tongues of flamingoes and the milt of lampreys, brought by his captains and triremes from the whole empire, from Parthia to the Spanish strait. Being besides a man of an appetite that was not only boundless, but also regardless of time or decency, he could never refrain, even when he was sacrificing or making a journey, from snatching bits of meat and cakes amid the altars, almost from the very fire, and devouring them on the spot; and in the cookshops along the road, viands smoking hot or even those left over from the day before and partly consumed.[23]

The dining habits of late first-century Emperor Vitellius, as described above by the historian Suetonius, were fodder for the Hollywood imagination, whose portrayals of the unbridled gluttony of the Roman upper crust titillated the appetites of audiences. The protagonist of Petronius's debauched *Cena Trimalchionis*, written around the same time as Vitellius was eating his way into history, holds a prominent place in the pantheon of excess. The fictional Trimalchio is a caricature of the uncouth ways of the nouveau-riche freedman, a lampoon of the clod whose cultural bearing cannot keep pace with his purse, a very real and unpleasant phenomenon lightened through satire. Trimalchio embodies a range of actual personages, in particular Vitellius's predecessor the notorious Emperor Nero, and the banquet he holds unfolds like an ancient "mockumentary."

Feasts of grotesque dimension and elaboration were certainly not unknown, and as the empire progressed, authors made it a point to pen them down for posterity or satirize them for public amusement. Criticism of infamous incidences of imperial gluttony, such as use of obscure bits of animals, or the tongues or brains of exotic birds, was almost a literary genre in and of itself. In the third century, critics railed against excess such as those of Maximinus Thrax, whose personal consumption of meat purportedly ranged between forty to sixty pounds daily, or Firmus, who single-handedly put away an entire ostrich in a day; they were also self-appointed watchdogs for uncouth practices, like those of Commodus, who ate in the baths.

Figure 2.2. *Les Romains de la d'cadence*, by Thomas Couture, is emblematic of the fascination with Roman debauchery. Thomas Couture, 1847

Yet these gastronomic departures were noteworthy precisely because they were extraordinary, and entertaining as they might be, should not be taken as a reflection of general custom or values. So enamored are we of the image of the overstuffed Roman that even some scholars perpetuated the idea of the *vomitorium* as an architectural structure wherein the full-to-bursting Roman would void the contents of his stomach so that he might recommence gorging *da capo*. Much to our modern dismay, the term simply refers to the entrance and exit tunnels leading into and out of amphitheaters, like the Colosseum,[24] where any vomiting was likely driven by the violent combats and executions. There were also numerous staid emperors of exemplary frugality through this same period, such as Pertinax, Severus Alexander, and Tacitus, and others who may have put on lavish public meals but were conservative in private.

Roman generals and emperors on military campaigns made it a point of supping on soldier's fare, and did so in full view.[25] The soldier's larder was by and large adequately stocked, although Rome found it behooved them to establish limits on food, drink, and sexual license, in order to uphold discipline and decorum. Lest the situation become too comfortably domestic, the spit was recommended as the most suitable means of cooking for soldiers, being the most basic and therefore an ancestral throwback reminiscent of a time of purity and righteousness. However, Roman soldiers also traveled equipped with vessels to boil and stew meats, a departure from the standard military kit.[26] Not everyone had forgotten the frugality and industry for which Cato and Pliny had yearned centuries before, and neither the infamous acorn-and-chestnut fattened, honey-dipped dormice adorned with a sprinkling of poppy seeds nor the curious fig-peckers splayed voluptuously over spiced egg yolk in Trimalchio's banquet were common features of the Roman table.

Civilized peoples, according to the Mediterranean mind-set, were those whose societies were stationary; thus cereals and pulses, the stolid and storable products of agriculture, embodied the triumph of civilized moderation over both catch-as-catch-can savagery and gastronomic frippery. It was through the repast structured around the Greek ideal of a starch staple, *sitos*, and accompaniments, *opsa*, that they expressed their civility and distinguished themselves from the meat-gorging, milk-drinking, beer-guzzling barbarians. Paradoxically, Rome had long been reliant on massive imports of grain from Sicily, Sardinia, and Egypt in order to meet the needs of the metropolis for their mainstay, wheat. Roman writers looked enviously upon the productivity of Egypt, attributing the fecundity of their women, who they believed commonly had multiple births, to the Nile, whose regular floods also nurtured the wheat fields.[27] The traditional Roman staple was *puls* or *alica*,[28] a gruel made most often of *far*, emmer wheat, and accompanied by or prepared with various additional foods and condiments, collectively called *pulmentarium*, consisting of vegetables, meats, cheeses, and the ubiquitous fermented fish sauce garum.

To make puls, wheat was hulled and winnowed by a *pistor*, generally a slave, given the arduousness of the task. The grain was then soaked, dried, and crushed into a coarse meal to be boiled into gruel as needed. The more finely ground grains might be used to make an unleavened flat bread called *libum*, an intermediate phase between puls and bread. The moralistic or nostalgic ancients would boast that they supped more on puls than bread.

In speaking of the goddess Carna's disdain for modern ways, Ovid evokes the image of this culinary ideal:

> You ask why fat bacon is eaten on these Calends, and why beans are mixed with hot emmer. She is a goddess of the old times, and subsists upon the foods to which she was accustomed before; no wanton is she to run after foreign foods. Fish still swam unharmed by the people of that age, and oysters were safe in their shells. Latium was unaware of the fowl that rich Ionia supplies, nor the bird that delights in pygmy blood; and nothing in the peacock but the feathers pleased; nor had the earth before sent captured beasts. The pig was prized, people feasted on slaughtered swine: and the ground yielded only beans and hard emmer.[29]

This protest alludes particularly to the Greeks, who through their colonies in southern Italy had introduced a variety of tempting new foodstuffs. The infiltration of such novel items led to fears that the invasion would corrupt tradition.[30] They were to blame for the Roman indulgence in fish, the high demand for which warranted private farmed fisheries and live imports, the most sought after being the moray eel from Sicily. Mollusks of all kinds were another delicacy the elite clamored for. Pliny abhorred the fashion for fish and was particularly wary of seafood: "Moral corruption and luxury spring from no other source in greater abundance than from the genus shell-fish. It is true that of the whole of nature the sea is most detrimental to the stomach in a multitude of ways, with its multitude of dishes and of appetizing kinds of fish to which the profits made by those who catch them spell danger."[31] He could not fathom why one would risk one's life fishing, searching for wild-fowl, and hunting for prey, when the less privileged guiltlessly obtain their food from the vegetable garden.[32]

Pliny doggedly extols the humble foods of the earth, in particular turnips, radishes, carrots, as well as cabbage and cucumbers as foods that embodied republican probity. Columella mentions fifteen varieties of cruciferous vegetables, from the common cabbage to brussels sprouts, from which Pliny imparts eighty-seven different remedies in accordance with the Hippocratic adage, "Let food be your medicine and medicine your food." Cato too ranks cabbage above all other vegetables and leaving this handy tip to posterity: "If during a dinner you should want to drink and eat abundantly, before dinner you should eat as much [cabbage] as you want dressed with vinegar. Then after the meal eat another five leaves; it will make you feel as if you hadn't eaten anything and then you can carry on drinking as much as you please."[33]

But these were the writings of men of means. For the urban poor, choice and variety were luxuries that were not part of their lot. Only occasionally could they afford vegetables, and then from the cheaper bins—cabbage, onions, garlic; most others were out of their range. Even those who grew vegetables for the urban market did not eat the cash crops from their own garden, nor did they spend their earnings on "upscale" foods as captured in this excerpt from a poem attributed to Virgil:

> But this was not the owner's crop (for who
> Than he more straightened is?). The people's 'twas
> And on the stated days a bundle did
> He on his shoulder into th' city bear,
> When home he used to come with shoulder light
> But pocket heavy, scarcely ever did

He with him bring the city markets' meat.
The ruddy onion, and a bed of leek
—For cutting, hunger doth for him subdue—,
And cress which screws one's face with acrid bite,
And endive, and the colewort."[34]

The unskilled or occasional worker in Rome supplemented the grain staple with low-quality fish (procured from polluted areas of the Tiber) and fish sauce, dry legumes, and olive oil, washed back with local wine, but again, all of the basest sort. Half a liter of wine, for example, cost half the daily wage of a menial laborer. At festivals one could count on eating more and various foods, but overall this made little impact nutritionally. The lot of those who were not eligible for the grain dole, the *cura annonae* was undoubtedly less varied, and particularly grim for pregnant and lactating women, nubile girls, and widows, for whom there was no direct provision.[35]

Cura annonae—The Welfare System

The fact that grain was the staple, in both reality and in noble yearnings for the past, did not itself put bread on the table. The urban poor, including numerous displaced farmers and former soldiers, were generally at a loss to feed themselves adequately. Rome, however, was not a city with a historical grounding in charity or philanthropy. Even the client/patron relationship was at best about mutual back scratching. Against this backdrop, the institutionalization of a grain subsidy for citizens might have been politically correct, but when made in the later days of the Republic the proposal was met with hostility on the Senate floor. Gaius Gracchus, younger brother of Tiberius, shared the family bent for reform but shifted the focus from land to food itself. In 123 BCE, Gracchus promulgated a *lex frumentaria* that provided for a distribution of subsidized grain to free inhabitants of the city. The conservative opposition in the Senate feared it would weaken the patron/client bond, placing the state above the plutocrats, the traditional dispensers of patronage.[36] Like his brother, Gaius was murdered, but the grain dole lived on.

With the *lex Clodio frumentaria* of 58 BCE, the lower classes were provided for gratis. In 22 BCE, Augustus personally assumed responsibility for the grain supply, in response to the protests of an angry mob during a particularly alarming food shortage. Altruism may have been part of his objective, but taking control of wheat distribution was part of the process by which he defined himself in the emerging office of *princeps*, the Roman emperor. Ensuring the food supply, including the grain dole, was foundational to holding power. The early *principes* took advantage of food crises in symbol as well as in substance, creating the goddess Annona Augusti, the deification of the grain supply to Rome, which helped affirm the emperor's emerging deity as well. She was inaugurated into the pantheon of gods by associating her with the better-established Ceres, goddess of agriculture, wheat, and motherliness, as well as Abundantia, who more generally represented prosperity.

When Augustus assumed personal guardianship of the dole, a large number of slaves were set free, especially those who were past their prime, but the emperor "announced that those to whom he had promised nothing were entitled to nothing."[37] Slaves and noncitizens, destitute or otherwise, were not eligible for the dole; had they been, mayhem would have been unleashed. This dole was not an indiscriminate charity but a privilege bestowed upon citizens, and even after the Edict of Caracalla (212 BCE), which awarded citizenship to all free men in the Roman Empire, certain restrictions were maintained.[38]

The new law did much to reinforce the position of the emperor, but it meant that a fifth of Rome's income from taxes was spent on filling the urban stomach.[39] At some points in the first century CE, no fewer than three hundred twenty thousand residents of Rome, out of a total population of about one million, were receiving thirty-four kilograms of wheat per month.[40] The dole was distributed to eligible males regardless of the number of dependent

Figure 2.3. A sarcophagus depicting the gods involved in the grain trade. Far left: Port, the lighthouse, flanked by Fortuna Annonaria, with the wheat dole register and an oar; second from the right is Abundance with her cornucopia, also used to symbolize the goddess Annona. Far right: the personification of Africa, Rome's primary wheat source, with a fistful of grain and an elephant headdress. Sarcofago dell'Annona, from the Museo nazionale romano, c. 280

mouths waiting at home to be fed. Therefore, while some were able to hoard and resell, others with families found that the thirty-five hundred or so daily calories it provided still had to be supplemented out of pocket. Furthermore, the daily dole had its problems:

> The grain had travelled far: if of Egyptian origin, it was at best the grain of the year before. More likely it was older than this by the time it reached the consumer, having been stored in warehouses for some time. Not all of it would have been fit for human consumption. It would have deteriorated further after distribution, while stored in some dark corner, waiting to be processed and eaten. Wheat easily deteriorates if not stored in optimum conditions (such as were not available in the crowded tenements of Rome), and it is prone to attack by sundry pests and diseases.[41]

Furthermore, the grain was distributed unprocessed, apparently leaving the recipient to pay for milling, or to simply crush it at home and eat it as *puls* or a crude flatbread.

The fear that all of this free food and public games were a breeding ground for indolence was written forever into history when Juvenal penned his stinging metonymic phrase *panem et circenses*—bread and circuses—denigrating both the government for its lack of integrity and the populace for its fickle mores.

The annona was an institutionalized form of the *patronus-cliens* concept, but in this case provided for those of lower socioeconomic standing, and made the state or the emperor the patron. The choice of wheat as the central handout was multifaceted: it was wholesome, traditional, and reinforced values, and as such, was nutritionally, affectively, culturally, and politically sound. Yet satisfying the grain needs of the city required anywhere between two thousand to three thousand voyages per year across the Mediterranean, each taking several weeks. Shipments changed hands many times before reaching their final destination, with costs rising each time. If a ship had sunk or been captured by pirates, it could take weeks before the merchants found out.[42] The goods were subject to spoilage and parasites, and would sometimes be worthless upon arrival, or would go bad under storage. It was a complex enterprise rife with risk—and prone to racketeering.

The senators, though initially disgruntled by the wheat dole, more than made up for their losses—because *they* were among the private merchants who ran it. Each senator was allowed only one ship with a capacity of no more than three hundred amphorae, but this obstacle was easily bypassed by simply registering ships in someone else's name. Other working merchants were either from the lower orders of the aristocracy (knights) or were enterprising freedmen. While punishments, rewards, oaths, and competitive pay were drummed up to promote honesty and fair conduct, double-dealing, and skimming off the top remained a concern every time the grain changed hands. As a result, guild systems were set up whose members were meticulously vetted. The social benefits derived from being attached to a guild also made them attractive, and the sense of belonging and camaraderie may have fostered honest dealing. Since Roman religion, unlike the more familiar monotheistic religions, did not connect a code of ethics directly to its ritual practices, trustworthiness had to be inculcated and celebrated by other means and in other contexts. Fair dealing in trade, probity in public matters, and morality in the home were equally matters of, in our terms, secular and sacred significance.

Ars pistorum—The Baking Arts

By 500 BCE, seed selection of free-threshing, or naked, wheat, whose grains more readily released the chaff, had developed to commercial levels in Sicily and North Africa. As the Romans developed a taste for wheat bread, it became an identity marker of culinary superiority. The traditional Greek barley bread was disdained as being suitable only for slaves and soldiers, although an older preference for the hulled form of emmer wheat known as far (today's *farro*) was remembered and sometimes formed part of Roman culinary nostalgia.[43] Dyed-in-the-wool traditionalists like Cato never warmed to the idea of bread, seeing it as a sign of decadence. For such purists, only gruel and the flatcake *libum* were deemed uncorrupted by foreign influence or frivolous modern whims.

Bread making had traditionally been women's domestic work, and development of a new profession dedicated to the process has often been attributed to vanity: "She who had a long been the wife of the peasant and the warrior and had been proud of her household work learned . . . that it was good for a woman to spare herself during the hot hours of the day. Mirror and rouge preserved youth; leavening and baking brought on age."[44] The expansion of Rome's empire added to prosperity, and to both the availability of food and the skilled artisans to prepare it. Numerous bakers are said to have arrived in Rome from Greece after its conquest in the mid-second century BCE.

The quality of bread varied not just from the grain used but in accordance with sifting, which produced varying grades of flour from coarse to fine. At the bottom of the barrel was bread for dogs (*panis furfureus* or *sordidus*) made with bran, closely followed by *panis militaris* and *panis nauticus* for soldiers and sailors. For these, flour was hand ground and the loaves baked under ashes resulting in a sort of hardtack (*bucellatum*), impervious to both molding and teeth. At the other end of the continuum was bread made with high-quality, soft wheat *siligo* flour (*panis siligineus*),[45] a circular loaf slashed to create eight equal servings.[46] The whiter and more refined the bread, the higher one's social status. Juvenal tells us that refined white bread was so rare that a poorer free man might have tried it once in a lifetime, at a dinner held by his patron.[47] In any case, the bran was only ever partially removed and no mention is ever made of picking out extraneous debris or washing the grains before grinding.[48]

Common folk partook in the rougher *panis cibarius*, an elongated loaf made with barley and emmer flour, while their inferiors ate the whole-grain *panis secundarius*, *plebeius*, or *rusticus*, whose very names comment on their quality.[49] Top-of-the-line breads could include costly ingredients such as honey, exotic spices, and candied fruit, whereas the poorest rural loaves were stretched with non-cereal flours derived from legumes, chestnuts, and other less likely fillers. Although Pliny discusses various leavenings, the impression given is that breads were essentially dense. He seemed quite impressed by a recent method from northeastern Iran, "It is not so very long since we have bread introduced from Parthia, known as water-bread (*panis parthicus* or *aquaticus*) from a method of kneading it, of drawing out dough by aid of water, a process which renders it remarkably light and full of holes, like a sponge."[50] The addition of the brewer's yeast on which modern baking depends was an exotic practice, known to the inhabitants of Gaul and Spain but only reported as a curiosity by Pliny.

Bread baking like other mercantile and culinary pursuits became a way for freed slaves to move up in the world, some becoming quite prosperous. The example *per eccellenza* was the freedman Eurysaces, whose outstanding wealth is manifest in the funerary monument known as "Tomb of the Baker" (c. 50–20 BCE) which still stands in Rome. The inscription on it reads, "This is the sepulcher of Marcus Virgilius Eurysaces, baker, contractor, and official," the latter term perhaps indicating that his position of baker was as a subordinate to a Roman magistrate. High-relief friezes depict the slaves in tunics carrying out the various phases of bread making, overseen by a toga-clad Eurysaces. His wife's urn is in the shape of a *panarium*, a bread chest.

The Emperor Severus Alexander (222–235 CE) decreed that the wheat dole be changed over to bread.[51] In the city, therefore, the government tightened control over bread production: bakers became civil servants and bakeries state institutions. As state-structured workers, they had a hierarchy that went in descending order: minister, vice minister, baker, kneader, assistant, delivery boy, and simply "the boy."

Figure 2.4. Detail of the tomb of the baker Eurysaces, a frieze depicting the bread-making process. Photo by Jeremy Cherfas, c. 2017

Legumes: Poor Cousins

Legumes, despite their subordinate rank to cereals, were their natural companion as staple. In their dried, stored state, pulses proved less vulnerable to insects, rodents, fungus, and damp, for which they played a fundamental role in feeding the rural poor and promoting urban stability; indeed, they were referred to as "the meat of the poor." Yet beans were not hailed and revered culturally, as were their cereal companions. There was no god of beans in the pagan pantheon of gods, nor would pulses assume a sacred dimension in Christian liturgy. Their indecorous gassy side effect and potential toxicity may have precluded this.

As a protein compliment, beans were fundamental in a society whose meat consumption occurred mainly on festival days. In addition to being a staple for humans, the straw and pods of legumes provided fodder for livestock. Given their ability to fix nitrogen in a usable form, they revitalized the soil, and were therefore a must for fruitful olive groves and vineyards. Although the scientific explanation would not come to light until the nineteenth century, ancient agronomists had noted this phenomenon in their own empirical observations. In times of drought and heat, legumes resisted longer than cereals, particularly chickpeas, lentils, and grass peas (or chickling vetch), called *cicerchia* in Italian. This gravelly, misshapen, beige bean is extraordinarily hardy and offered salvation as a buffer crop when most others failed. In recognition of its historic contribution to food security in Lazio, the chickling vetch has been conferred the coveted PDO status "Protected Designation of Origin" by the European Union, establishing Campodimele in southern Lazio as the epicenter of production. But there is a diabolical downside to the heroic face of this humble pea: lathyrism, a debilitating and sometimes fatal neurological disease. During severe dry spells, the chickling vetch thrived to the exclusion of most other plant foods, but overreliance on it and the concomitant lack of water to properly soak and thoroughly boil it accentuated its toxicity, adding insult to injury. Rural revivalism has brought it once again to the fore, exchanging the former stigma of poverty with a badge of honor. Indeed, Campodimele, historically an area of desperate poverty, marred with a reputation for brigandism, now touts itself as "The town of Longevity,"[52] owing to the high percentage of nonagenarians who reside there.

Lentils are mentioned more frequently in Roman literature than any other legume. Pliny warns that lentils can affect the eyesight, indicating that excessive dependence on them, like on the grass pea, might also produce a neurotoxic effect.[53] Perhaps for this reason Columella recommended rubbing the grains with the enigmatic North African spice silphium. According to *Herbal of Dioscorides the Greek*, this exotic root seems to have been a cure-all, as well as a flavoring for numerous dishes. In addition to its miraculous powers as an antitoxin, digestive aid, and contraceptive, it was reputed to restore "quickness of sight and, when smeared on with honey, disperses the dripping of fluids in the eyes."[54] By the first century CE, however, silphium had been foraged to extinction. The last root of it had reportedly been sent to Emperor Nero as a curiosity. Claims of silphium sightings persist, though none have been substantiated.

Evidence of the fava bean has been found in the earliest settlements, and it enjoyed a higher status than other legumes. Not only did it count among the ingredients used to add bulk to bread dough, in the form of gruel it was considered suitable as a sacrificial food. A bean brought home from the harvest was akin to a lucky charm. However, like the chickling vetch, fava beans were a double-edged sword. A genetic metabolic deficiency, called favism,[55] which strikes Mediterraneans in particular, leads to hemolysis, the rupturing of red blood cells. On the positive side, favism seems to be paired with resistance to malaria, which, given the vastness of the swamp-ridden lowlands of Rome, was a remarkably adaptive response.

The Irresistible Draw of Foreign Goods

Though singing the praises of beans, I'm really a gourmet at heart.

—Juvenal

As Rome grew and trade flourished, foreign luxuries inevitably poured in from the Middle East, Asia, North Africa, and elsewhere on the Italic peninsula. Among the earliest imports were pine nuts, sesame, quince, walnuts, hazelnuts, pomegranates, various plums, apricots, melons, some varieties of figs, sugarcane,[56] grape varietals, olives, capers, cabbage, fennel, garlic, onions, oregano, and basil.[57] Animal imports included chickens, horses, donkeys, sheep, pigs, dogs, alpine bovine, peacocks, ducks, doves, pheasants, and rabbits,[58] and war spoils like the chestnut, cherry, peach, and citron.[59] Imported foods were not only tasty in and of themselves, they held a fascination of the foreign that increased the salivation factor.

As tolerance gave way to curiosity and curiosity to desire, a resounding market demand grew for esoteric, exotic, and prime craft food items, whose prices were marked up in accordance with elite consumer enthusiasm. Knowing where the best of the best came from became a badge of cultural acuity. Horace speaks of the shellfish of Lucrine Lake being better than that from Baia, and Umbrian wild boar outranking that of Laurento. He also praises the superiority of oysters from Circello and the sea urchins from Miseno. Commercially minded agriculturalists close to home cast a sidelong glance to the lusty cultivars and varietals in gardens across the way—with a squinted eye on returns. Agricultural products, too, were "high-status disposable goods, an addition to the portfolio of good things for redistribution,"[60] "forms of wealth: . . . first devised for that reason."[61] Diversification and hybridization potentiated both quality and novelty, which upped profit margins in a luxury market geared ever more toward the conspicuous consumer,[62] or as Varro proposes, "If you get a revenue from flocks, what does it matter whether they are flocks of sheep or of birds? . . . And do you get more from the butcher for boars born on your place there than Seius does from the market-man for the wild boars from his place?"[63] To this end, villa husbandry aimed at replicating nature in a domesticated milieu with aviaries, fishponds, and hare warrens or hunting reserves for both profit and pleasure.

But in a city glutted with immigrant fortune seekers and menial laborers, the low-income buyer was the main consumer at the marketplace. By providing for this end of the alimentary continuum, a profit could be turned from the sale of quantity, if not quality, products. In catering to the most common purse, relatively mundane items like game and domestic meats were moved to the rack with the boutique selections, because while meat was not scarce, it was priced beyond the means of the masses. Reliance on vegetable food sources grew as the population swelled, prompting Pliny to call the vegetable garden, or *hortus*, the butcher shop of the plebs.[64] But as the need grew for vegetables to supplement aristocratic banquets, those too were subjected to the price laws of supply and demand.

Commensality

Daily life for the more fortunate was punctuated by three meals. *Ientaculum*, or breakfast, consisted of a bit of bread sprinkled with wine and perhaps a few leftovers from dinner; children were given sheep or goat milk and pastries.[65] *Prandium*, lunch, was a quick on-the-go affair, either leftovers again or, if one was out and about, a simple hunger stopper could be procured from one of the many hawkers or from a corner *thermopolion* or *popina*. Dinner was the main meal, which over time changed from being an afternoon event to an evening one. Families dined at home, but the *cena* and *convivium* were important social vehicles—and consequently important gastronomical occasions as well.

Contrary to the free-for-all image of Bacchic orgies, Roman conviviality was usually highly regimented. Like all manners codes, theirs was used by the collective to judge one another and to assert cultural superiority over nonadherent groups—praising the sheep and denigrating the goats. The glorified ideal of Romans as *pares* was, therefore, not always respected at the dinner table. It was the expectation, indeed the duty, of all patrons to entertain their clients. The private formal meal, or convivium, was the theater wherein the host not only reasserted his own status and reminded his guests of theirs, but also one in which he forged important alliances and sniffed out dissenters. The unlikelihood of upstaging rivals and garnering political favor with a patriotic crock of puls and a side order of vegetables, while your adversary might be serving stuffed roast peacock, threatened to set the elite on a spiraling course of extravagance. Superlative banquets had long been part and parcel to the aristocratic lay of the land, as evidenced by the infamous feasts of General Licinius Lucullus (c. 117–57 BCE), whose name is synonymous with lavishness.[66] As wealth flowed into Rome, pressure to impress or outdo reached such a fevered pitch that sumptuary laws were enacted.[67] These worked to level the political playing field of the convivium by curbing the ostentatious display of table luxury (*luxus mensae*) that might unduly influence or sway.

The *Lex Orchia* (182 BCE) limited the number of guests one could invite to a cena; the *Lex Fannia* (161 BCE) required senators to swear an oath promising to stay within the prescribed limit of expenditure on *obsonium*, sumptuous or exotic market foodstuffs, in particular fattened fowl and dormice; exotic birds; kid; imported shellfish and mullet; and much-sought-after swine delicacies like paunches, vulva, sweetbreads, and the unctuously soft udders—the latter being optimal when taken from a young sow who has just whelped but not yet suckled her litter.[68] Such was their delectability that clear depictions have immortalized them on no less than thirteen extant artifacts.[69] Predictably, restrictions did not include leafy greens (according to Plautus's cook: "weeds that cattle wouldn't touch"),[70] *far*, or domestic wine. The free reign given to foods that they themselves *could* produce resonated with Roman nostalgia for "self-reliant farmers, whose hard work strengthened their body and spirit, and whose simple life insulated them from the snares of sophistication, including the sophistication of monetary exchange,"[71] –that dirty money.

At any given organized meal, each dish was carefully selected and served according to type, quantity, and quality in descending order of rank. Individuation allowed for passive-aggressive slights by denying select foodstuffs in order to rebuff and marginalize diners or, likewise, indulging elect guests in delicacies that outclassed their status. Yet a competing ideal of dining as egalitarian continued to rear its head. The perpetually disgruntled client Martial (40–103 CE) makes this clear in his complaint about dining with his patron:

> Since I am asked to dinner . . . why is not the same dinner served to me as to you? You take oysters fattened in the Lucrine lake, I suck a mussel through a hole in the shell: you get mushrooms, I take bog funguses; you take turbot, but I brill. Golden with fat, a turtledove gorges you with its bloated rump; there is set before me a magpie that has died in its cage.[72]

In the late Roman period, artistic depictions of dining feature two or three large platters from which everyone partakes, suggesting a move away from "status dining" to "convivial dining."[73] Community building among the growing sub-elite, such as guild members, as well as the early egalitarianism of the Christian sect, may have favored the more equal model.[74]

The Theater of Fine Dining

The types of food served and the number of courses at a formal meal were elaborated in accordance with the invitees and the politics of the host. From the first century onward, the full-blown banquet lasting from dusk to dawn was divided into three phases. In the first phase, the guests were likely to have arrived genuinely hungry and food, rather than drink, was the main focus.

Promulsis—opening nibbles
Gustatio—antipasto

These are the lighter dishes, such as cured foods like olives, fish, and marinated vegetables. The dishes might also be meat morsels like dormice, sausage, small birds, or egg dishes, all of which was accompanied by bread and aperitifs: mead (fermented honey cordials), *mulsum* (high alcohol wine and honey), or something akin to vermouth. Guests imbibed from a communal bowl to evoke the spirit of conviviality.

Mensa prima—first main course
Mensa prima (cena altera)—second main course

The word mensa means both "course" and "table," so conceived because a new table was originally brought out for each course. The first main course would have been the moment for traditionalists to present *puls* with legumes or vegetables, or more refined dishes that would satisfy expectations but not exceed the second main course. This concluded the first phase of the *cena*. The table of mains arrived to begin part two of the dinner, the more substantial dishes. It is here that the cook might pull out the stops with dishes that ranged from the exotic to the purely bizarre. Petronius's *Satyricon* offers such a scene:

A tray was brought in after them with a wild boar of the largest size upon it, wearing a cap of freedom, with two little baskets woven of palm-twigs hanging from his tusks, one full of dry dates and the other of fresh. Round it lay suckling-pigs made of simnel cake with their mouths to the teats, thereby showing that we had a sow before us. These suckling-pigs were for the guests to take away. The carver, who had mangled the fowls, did not come to divide the boar, but a big bearded man with bands wound round his legs, and a spangled hunting-coat of damasked silk, who drew a hunting-knife and plunged it hard into the boar's side. A number of thrushes flew out at the blow. As they fluttered round the dining room there were fowlers ready with limed twigs, who caught them in a moment. Trimalchio ordered everybody to be given his own portion, and added: "Now you see what fine acorns the woodland boar has been eating." Then boys came and took the baskets which hung from her jaws and distributed fresh and dry dates to the guests.[75]

Mensa secunda—dessert and wine

Dessert was not necessarily sweet, as sweetness was an important feature of many dishes throughout the meal. It signified the closure of the dinner, and therefore, just as the meal often opened with an egg dish, the symbol of beginnings, so it closed with seasonal fruit and nuts—walnuts, hazelnuts, almonds, pistachios—which signified the conclusion. Wine drinking would have thus far been kept to a decorous minimum, as votive offerings to the guardian spirits of the household were made before the *mensa secunda*. After that the amphorae were brought out, the wine filtered and decanted, and the rumpus could begin amid song, dance, and party games, and of course—more food. Sensibly, the Romans used the meal itself as the principal forum for interaction, as opposed to the after-dinner drinks phase, or *commissatio*, when the Greeks did their serious talking

Commissatio—wine and snacks
Vesperna—supper

For those who lingered about until the wee hours, another meal was served. *Vesperna* was originally the name given to the light supper served in the evening, when the main meal was served at midday. But as the main meal migrated to dusk, vesperna became a midnight repast.

Ancient authors concurred that the main attraction of communal meals was the opportunity to converse and make new acquaintances. Plutarch says in his *Table Talk*: "In fact, the man of sense who comes to dinner does not betake himself there just to fill himself up as though he were some sort of pot, but to take part, be it serious or humorous, and to listen and to talk regarding this or that topic as the occasion suggests it to the company, if their association together is to be pleasant."[76] To this end, it was common to allow in a few so-called parasites—the Greek word meaning "someone who eats at another's table"—who were supposed to be adept at jollying things along. Some parasites were one-off invitees, while others were duty bound to a single or a few patrons. Their obligation was to pay homage by kowtowing to the patron's whims, boosting his ego through adulation. One who at least sometimes adopted the role was the poet Martial, whose patron took him on in recognition of his intellectual merits. Much to Martial's chagrin, he was expected to rise at dawn and dress to perform the formal morning *salutatio* to his patron along with the other clients. He assisted in carrying the patron's sedan chair, and throughout the day showered praise upon him for everything he said and did. In exchange, he received a *sportula*, an alms-basket of food. This custom changed later to the *cena recta*, dinners organized for clients, but as patrons tended to be tightfisted on both counts, clients preferred collecting their due in cash. Juvenal describes the paltry fare of a banquet for clients as: "bits of hard bread that have turned moldy . . . sickly greens cooked in oil that smells of the lamp . . . toadstools of doubtful quality . . . a rotten apple."[77] Such stinginess may have been a tactic to keep the client in line. In the context, the voluntary annihilation of one's dignity may have seemed a small price to pay; indeed, for many, the indignity of leeching from a patron was preferable by far to manual labor.

Paradoxically, despite the emphasis placed on quantity, quality, refined preparation, and elaborate presentation, as well as novel experimentation at banquets as essential social markers, the Roman cook did not enjoy the status of his Greek counterpart. In ancient Greece, the *mageiros* was a combination of butcher, cook, and sacrificer, a trained professional "whose functional name denotes the conjunction between the slaughtering of the victims, the sale of meat, and the preparation of fleshly food."[78] The Roman professional cook was either a slave or a freedman. He learned to carry out his tasks from someone more knowledgeable, though it was not a formal apprenticeship. But despite the role he played in pleasing and impressing his master's guests, he was viewed with contempt, on the one hand because of the vile tasks he had to perform and, on the other, because of his association with luxury and excess.[79]

Late Antiquity: From Tyrannopolis to Necropolis to Theopolis

> The city of Scipio's and Cicero's dreams vanished even before the sleepers awoke.
>
> —Lewis Mumford

In the third century, Rome underwent a fifty-year crisis. The earlier imperial constitution, or principate, which mixed the personal rule of the emperor with elements of the old republican structures, was supplanted with a succession of military governments; the numerous claimants vying for emperorship had Rome teetering on the edge of anarchy. Brigandage and armed conflict had for some time been staunching the flow of goods in and out of Rome along the vast network of Roman roads, one of the glories of the empire, some dating back to the ancient kingdom. Under Aurelian (270–275), the empire united once again, though trade would continue to decline. Aurelian attempted to instill a sense of stability in the city by upping the bread dole[80] to two loaves of government-issue bread, *panis civilis*, rounding it out with olive oil, salt, wine, and pork.[81] The earlier changeover from grain to loaves stands as a significant culinary marker, insofar as the former *pultiphagi* "gruel-eaters," as the Romans were chidingly referred to by the Greeks, had been supplanted by a more sophisticated gastronomic identity. The addition of pork into the dole is also noteworthy. Previously, public distribution of meat had been limited to the results of sacrifice, and recipients were likewise limited. Governmental distribution of pork not only brought regular meat consumption into the mainstream, it shifted the power focus from religious to secular. Pork was the most loved meat in Rome, as well as being the most expensive of butchered meats, with lard and cured fatback (*laridium*) surpassing the price of lean cuts,[82] underscoring the high value of pork fat on the gastronomic spectrum.[83] From a purely pragmatic standpoint, pigs were also the logical choice, as sheep, goats, chickens, and cattle supplied humans with other products and services. The finality of pigs was meat. Eligible citizens were given an allowance of 8 and later 10 kilograms of pork per year, so gainfully employed citizens who received the dole and who might have otherwise been able to afford a bit of meat were in a position to supplement their handout further, thereby allowing them a higher consumption than has been assumed.[84]

The expanded dole put an increased strain on economic and human resources, as bread had to be prepared and distributed on a nearly daily basis, and the traffic from the throngs streaming in for their handout only added to the civil unrest. Aurelian also had a fortified wall built around the city that encompassed its new dimensions in an effort to safeguard the citizens from mounting instability. Both projects, though well intentioned, lacked economic foresight—and the people were left to pick up the tab through taxation. City life became increasingly unbearable, due to invasion, plague, war, pestilence, famine, and conscription into the army, leading both rich and poor to flee its confines. Diocletian's reforms a few decades later sought to stem the tide by making many trades hereditary, effectively blocking citizens from leaving their jobs and the city itself. Bakers were among the many to have their occupation supervised by the state and made hereditary, hampering social and professional mobility.

The availability of bread and other comestibles at accessible prices was key to maintaining public calm, and toward the end of the economic crisis of the third century CE, Diocletian established fixed prices for many basic foodstuffs. His austerity measures managed to stabilize the crisis in the short term, but the trade routes, the arteries that sustained the Roman way of life, remained impassable. The economic interdependence that had developed over centuries and was the lifeblood of the ager Romanus and the Urbs continued to wane.

While urban citizens counted on the annona to survive, no analogous welfare system assured the well-being of peasants outside the walls. Most had become dependents, the majority of the free holders having lost their land. As the ager Romanus emptied, tenant farmers, or *coloni*, steadily lost the right to move off the land, a bond that passed on to successive generations.[85] From his perch in the new capital at Constantinople, Constantine authorized landlords to put tenants in chains if they attempted to or were even suspected of planning to escape.[86] The decree issued by Theodosius (379–92) abolishing the poll tax, echoes the desperation to restrict the movement of peasants, "in case it may seem that permission has been given to coloni . . . to wander any go off where they will, they are themselves to be bound by rights of origin, and though they appear to be freeborn by condition are nevertheless to be held to be slaves of the land itself to which they were born, and are not to have the right to go off where they will or change their domicile."[87] Landowners themselves were taxed for uncultivated land, as the trade winds bringing wheat imports shifted more favorably to Constantinople.[88] To restock the dwindling workforce, prisoners of war and beggars were given to landlords as coloni or slaves, the status delineating the two having blurred considerably. But instead of being inspired to revolt, peasants settled into a soporific acquiescence. "Apathy was the characteristic mood of the peasant, for whom no prospect of better conditions was visible, and whose only object was to avert starvation for the coming year."[89]

Meanwhile, in the city, the dazed generations addicted to free food and raunchy spectacle were rudely awakened by the fizzling out of public entertainment. "Though Rome did not go so far as to invent the quiz show beloved by television audiences, people became interested in the same kind of vacuous questions: How many men rowed in Aeneas's galley? or what kind of food did Scipio have for breakfast before he conquered the Carthaginians?"[90] A mere four years after the first sack of Rome in 410, Emperor Honorius resuscitated the gladiatorial games to repair his image, repeating the gesture for the final time in 416. In an attempt to starve Rome into submission, Alaric, the first king of the Visigoths, had blocked incoming food supplies, and the precious little stock that did filter in was hoarded by merchants who had picked up the scent of opportunity. "The populace knew well what mechanism drove pricing in times like these, and with grim humor predicted in their chants at the Circus that they would be driven to cannibalism: *pretium impone carni humanae.*"[91] In a counter gesture of grandiloquence masquerading as welfare,[92] in 419 Honorius increased the free salt pork ration allotted in the annona—the games may have waned, but the spectacle of Roman largesse would continue undaunted. After the loss of Africa to the Vandals in 428, agreements were negotiated to continue to the city's grain supply and the cure annonae persevered, pork and all.

The Decline and Fall

Historian Lewis Mumford uses a food metaphor to capture the image of the declining empire:

> An oak whose wide-spreading branches hid the rottenness that was eating from within at the base of the trunk: the pigs might snout for truffles, which flourish best under diseased oaks, in the nearby earth, but more nourishing kind of food would not grow beneath those branches.

As a prelude to the second sack of Rome in 455, the Vandals damaged many of the aqueducts, thereby cutting off the main water source that not only quenched the Roman's thirst, but irrigated gardens, powered the mills that ground cereals, and filled the public baths, a fulcrum of Roman social-ization and symbol of civility. The Vandal siege lasted two weeks, making a more thorough job of it than their predecessors the Visigoths had done. A final ancient siege of Rome, carried out by the Ostrogoths in 549–50, came under the reign of the controversial emperor Justinian. During Justin's watch, undertaken from far to the east in Constantinople, the aqueducts in Rome had not been properly maintained; contrary to custom, he had not once during his reign declared a moratorium on taxes, wiping the slate clean and allowing some relief to the smallholder. But the fatal error for the city was neglecting to pay his soldiers for years on end and leaving them on starva-tion rations. Large landowners as well were choked with requisition demands that were beyond their means.[93] The principal Greek-Byzantine historian of the sixth century, writes poignantly of the hunger during the siege, "but the famine becoming more severe as time went on, was greatly increasing its ravages, driving men to discover monstrous foods unknown to the natural desires of man. . . . This was their food and necessity made it most sweet and dainty to their taste."[94] Urbanites brought whatever possessions they had to the marketplace and exchanged them for food. And when nothing remained to trade, they ate nettles. "In order to prevent the pungent herb from stinging their lips and throat, they boiled them thoroughly before eating. . . . And it happened to many that, even as they walked along chewing the nettles with their teeth, death suddenly came upon them and they fell to the ground."[95]

Procopius reports that the people were reduced to eating dogs, mice, or any other dead animals they could find.[96] And when that source was depleted, they ate each other's dung. Some, driven to desperation, killed themselves; others fled.

The *Liber pontificalis*, or *Book of Popes*, recounts that the famine in the city was such that people ate their own children,[97] fulfilling the prophetic chant from the circus of years before. When the Ostrogoths approached Rome they easily cut a deal with the famished soldiers to facilitate their entrance into the city. "And thus the Romans in general, and particularly the members of the Senate, found themselves reduced to such straits that they clothed themselves in the garments of slaves and rustics, and lived by begging bread or any other food from their enemies."[98] Although he had threatened to make Rome a pasture for cattle, Totila, the king of the Ostrogoths, did not raze it to the ground. The conquerors, too, picked up the annona as a useful instrument for securing loyalty and influence over the people. Attacks on Rome would continue, as would the famines and flight, the urban population decreasing from one million inhabitants in 210 CE to just 20,000 by the sixth century.

The last head of an empire no longer even centered on Rome was Romulus "Augustulus," a diminutive name that reflected his ineptitude and the lack of respect he elicited as a statesman, as well as bookending the *civitas romana* in everlasting irony. The events that followed his reign, between 476 and 1000 CE, are convulsant, overlapping, nonlinear, and uneven, and as such resistant to a tidy progressive metanarrative. But a sketch is possible.

While the Empire was coming undone, the few large Roman landowners who could had retreated to their country seats and formed familial networks to ward off the tax collectors. Clients found themselves increasingly dependent on the crumbs cast by the diminishing stock of solvent patrons, and clung ever more tightly to their meal ticket, abandoning whatever vestiges of independence they might have had left. The Roman villa system would in some cases evolve into various forms of manorialism, self-governing, insular "house-economies," although this phenomenon developed differently in what had been the ager Romanus than it did in other areas throughout Italy. Food imports gradually slowed during the seventh and eighth centuries, coming to a near halt in the ninth.[99]

Under the emerging seigniorial system, tools, textiles, handicrafts, and other necessities were produced principally from within the estate itself and agricultural practices reverted almost exclusively to subsistence farming. This led to local surplus that could be stored or occasionally traded with neighboring communities. Alternatively, it could be sold to soldiers who had to see to their own provisions.[100] Previously, commercial trade was a viable choice only for farmers who lived along direct routes by land or sea to major urban areas, recalling the characteristic lament, "But those of us who dwell far from the sea derive no advantage from those things in which we abound, nor can we obtain what we lack, as we can neither export what we have nor import what we need."[101] Insular production diminished the quality and variety of some goods, and trade devolved from a monetary system to one of barter in kind, as coinage had bottomed out.[102]

Germanic migration or *Völkerwanderung*, better known as the Barbarian Invasions, has been widely discredited as the cause of the fall of the Roman Empire.[103] The popular notion of uncivilized hordes pouring into Italy and simply laying waste to everything in their path in a murderous slash-and-burn rampage, while theoretically convenient and affectively promoted,[104] ignores the human propensity toward integration and the need to return to the cooperative business of producing and selling food. While some members of the various Germanic peoples undoubtedly reveled in the sport of war, and destruction was often gratuitous, a more apt description is that they infiltrated, displaced, and assimilated rather than conquering and taking over; indeed, the despoiling was sometimes a collaborative effort between newcomer and native.[105] Eventually, the dust of conflict settles—if not through agreement then through exhaustion or forgetting. Novelty becomes commonplace, and everyone gets on with the matter of living, recognizing the mutual benefits of taming the volatility. Over time, the curious practices and erstwhile loathsome customs that had raised the collective xenophobic eyebrow of the natives intermingled with local traditions to forge new combinations.

The Rise of Christianity

Constantine, the first Christian emperor, began the process of establishing the Church as a major property holder and beneficiary of patronage, setting a trend imitated by other individuals and families of means. In 380, under Theodosius, Nicene Trinitarian Christianity was codified as the official imperial religion. Most of the properties absorbed into the Patrimony of St. Peter came from the ager Romanus, hence, the latifundia, reinforcing Rome as the seat of Catholicism. But in due course, Church holdings would stretch across the girth of Italy forming the Papal State, which strategically divided northern and southern Italy until the mid-nineteenth century. As ecclesiastical power grew, new networks of dependence were set up to replace the old through all levels of the social strata. Ostentatious spectacle bearing a family surname was replaced by religious ceremonial opulence in the transference of patronal power from the aristocracy to the Church. Euergetism, the civic obligation to share one's wealth for the betterment of the community, embodied in the *patronus-cliens* relationship and through donations to public works, shifted from the plutocrats to the Church.

In order to keep the steady accumulation of territories from becoming unwieldy, the Church adopted the Roman land-distribution policy based on emphyteusis, extending land leases in exchange for a modicum rent on the condition that the land be put to productive use. Under Pope Zacharias (741–52) while the Church was grounding its temporal governance, this concept developed further into agro-towns called *domuscultae*. These aggregates of dwellings clustered near a main roadway and a common water source. They were often situated in an elevated area that offered some protection from malaria and marauders. Here too, the emphasis was on creating self-reliant communities, whose agrarian and meat products would supply their direct landlords—the local clergy—as well as stocking the larder and pantry of the central papacy.[106] Self-sufficiency meant local production of cereals, notably wheat and barley, though the Church also assumed the responsibility for importing supplemental wheat, wresting the scepter from the goddess Annona. Monasteries, hospitals, and *diaconiae* (deaconries) also vied for large estates to populate with peasant farmers who would supply them with foodstuffs—cereals, legumes, wine, oil, and pork—and services.

By this time, the Church had become law in Rome and largely taken over the helm of the Roman tradition in the West. Foods like the Graeco-Roman trinity of bread, wine, and oil were subsumed into the Catholic liturgy already charged with cultural significance from pre-existing systems, thus fortified in advance with meanings and associations that allowed them to immediately assume a central position. In the Eucharist, bread and wine would take over the role once held by sacrificial meat, representing the ultimate sacrifice, not *to* the gods, but *of* a god. The distribution of bread as the symbolic body of the Savior would in perpetuity remind believers of the end of the Roman sacrificial rite and yet maintain the suggestion of communion with the godhead. Participation in the Eucharist, ingesting the blood and body of Christ, "permits men to take communion with a divine power through the same flesh and thereby commemorate their natural kinship."[107] Oil, though not used for alimentary communion, was essential for the various unctuous rituals requiring anointment, and imbued with the power to unite one with the Holy Spirit and ward off threats of Satan. Chrism is, in essence, olive oil that has been blessed and mixed with a balsam, generally made from the resin of terebinth trees.[108] The odiferous essence is a legal component of chrism, although theologians disagree as to whether or not a sacrament carried out with pure olive oil could be considered valid. The smooth quality of the oil represents the outpouring of grace, while the balsam's agreeable fragrance preserves one from corruption; combined, they embody Christian virtue. "For we are the good odor of Christ unto God" (2 Corinthians 2:15).[109]

The consumption of *sus scrofa domesticus*, or swine, metamorphosed into a high profile dietary marker that fundamentally divided Christians from Jews. The dietary taboos of the Jews had been parodied by the Romans, in particular their abstention from pork. The Christian dietary identity adhered to Roman values by allowing pork; however, the Church used meat consumption in general as a religious vehicle, profiting from two existing conflictual forces that Romans were bound by tradition to be wary of: luxury and barbarian foodways. Through the institution of obligatory meatless days into the Christian dietary calendar, believers were reminded daily of their tie to ancient Roman values, the nobility of parsimony and civility, and the disdain for gratuitous excess. Christianity would take that a step further by spotlighting the lascivious nature of flesh, an appetite that, if left untamed, would surely lead to eternal damnation. While it is true that society was divided by what one could and couldn't eat in terms of quality, there had been no Roman tradition by which ritual fasting or abstinence from meat had been imposed on the population at large. The attraction in this case was renunciation as a moral imperative whose compensation was salvation; indeed, without trials to endure there can be no religion.[110]

Fasting has a long history of antecedents, but Christianity settled on defining their form of dietary self-abnegation in terms of "fat" days and "lean" days, the latter allowing eggs, cheese, and fish, whereas fat indicated meat. Strict fasting, for example during Lent, restricted followers to one meal per day and did not include eggs or dairy. Meat-eating, in and of itself, not to mention the spectacle of blood involved in sacrifice or butchery, inflamed carnal passions, the antithesis to Christian humility. Meatlessness, which "extinguished the fires of concupiscence,"[111] was a stark rejection of and departure from the Roman "cuisine of sacrifice." Sacrificial meat, prepared and eaten in the temple directly or apportioned and distributed for takeaway, was often the only opportunity for the poor and lower classes to indulge in meat. Ritually prepared meat was also sold in the marketplace, putting Christians in a quandary. What if the meat had been procured from a pagan rite? Paul the Apostle's advice was that what you don't know won't hurt you. If you know it has just come from a pagan temple, avoid it; if not, no one will be the wiser.[112] The association of meat and idolatry led some Christians to refuse it altogether as an expression of dietary dissent; they would await their rewards in heaven. Others reasoned that if the pagan gods were not real, why not indulge?[113] As the vine of Roman Catholicism climbed through Europe, entwining its tendrils into the nascent countries, the Graeco-Roman/Christian culinary directive brought with it not only the foodstuffs that companioned sacrality, but also sobering concepts of temperate self-consciousness like gluttony, guilt, reverence, renunciation, and humility.

CHAPTER THREE

Cooking from Books

Treatise, Philosophy, Literature, Cookbooks

Classical Authors

The entire historical trajectory of Rome from the ancients to the present is punctuated by texts of various genres that deal with food. Out of Rome have come some of culinary history's finest and most venerated works. However, rather than defining Roman cuisine per se as an index of "typical" recipes, they should be approached as nodes on a continuum, documenting the ever-evolving trends, tastes, mind-sets, approaches, and tendencies emanating into and out of the kitchens of Rome, insofar as they can be discerned from surviving literary sources. The earliest texts discussing Roman food are agricultural handbooks written for the elite rural estate owner. *De agricultura* (c. 160 BCE), by Cato the Censor, covers a broad spectrum of farming advice: details on how to organize the barns and workers, veterinary and human remedies, fattening fowl and livestock, planting and harvesting, as well as rituals to insure robust crops. Notorious for his rigidity regarding tradition, Cato's aim was to pass on his erudition and years of experience so as to guide men to a life of true virtue as farmers.

The somewhat haphazard organization in the treatise gives the impression that the various points of interest had been jotted down as they came to mind. There is a brief departure in which Cato ventures away from farm management and into suggestions for food preparation, offering up a few recipes. He begins with an unleavened flatbread, and moves on to eight recipes that are variations of cheese cakes. The first, *libum*,[1] is two parts cheese that has been pounded to a paste, and one part wheat meal or flour. An egg is worked in and the dough is placed on a bed of laurel leaves. A hot flat stone is then positioned on top and the bread is left to cook at length in the hearth. The second recipe, *placenta*,[2] is a massive twenty-five pound encrusted block concocted with cheese, flour, and honey, the ratios 14 to 2 to 4. It too was placed on laurel leaves to bake, but with an inverted hot earthenware crock heaped with coals serving as an oven, a cooking method that would continue to be used in Italy until the twentieth century. Both of these cakes were sometimes used for ritual purposes, particularly the latter, which would have fed quite a crowd.

The six recipes that follow are variations on the placenta theme, after which the motif shifts suddenly to the meat sacrifice offered in the woods to ensure healthy livestock. For each head of cattle, one was to immolate nine pounds of meat, some wheat meal, and wine. The lot of it was to be consumed on the spot by the participants, be they slave or free men, but women were strictly excluded from both the ritual and the feasting. Curiously, the last recipe Cato passes on is for a simple preparation of whole-grain *puls*. It is boiled in water until soft. Milk is added toward the end for a creamy effect. In all cases, Cato's objective was passing on culinary traditions tied to the culture, rather than imparting tempting dishes.

In his *De re rustica*, written over one hundred years later by the second of the three great agriculturalists, Marcus Terentius Varro gently chides his mentor, Cato, for the unseemly inclusion of recipes and undignified anecdotal advice, such as eating cabbage with vinegar as hangover prevention. Unlike Cato's haphazard text, Varro's is a meticulously constructed work of scientific prose, although he does give the gods their due:

> And I do not mean those urban gods, whose images stand around the forum, bedecked with gold, . . . but those twelve gods who are the special patrons of husbandmen. . . . Jupiter and Tellus, who, by means of the sky and the earth, embrace all the fruits of agriculture; . . . they are the universal parents; Jupiter is called "'the Father,'" and Tellus is called "'Mother Earth.'" And second, Sol and Luna, whose courses are watched in all matters of planting and harvesting. Third, Ceres and Liber, because their fruits are most necessary for life; for it is by their favour that food and drink come from the farm. Fourth, Robigus and Flora; for when they are propitious the rust will not harm the grain and the trees, and they will not fail to bloom in their season. . . . Likewise I beseech Minerva and Venus, of whom the one protects the oliveyard and the other the garden; and in her honour the rustic Vinalia has been established. And I shall not fail to pray also to Lympha and Bonus Eventus, since without moisture all tilling of the ground is parched and barren, and without success and "'good issue'" it is not tillage but vexation.

The third great agricultural treatise, *De re rustica* (c. 4–70 CE) by Lucius Junius Moderatus Columella, acknowledges the farmers' debt to the substantial corpus of "ancient" writings on husbandry from Greece and North Africa, as well as to their Roman predecessors, and bows humbly to their erudition, but Columella believed that successful tillage of Roman soil in his day and age required a modern, local reexamination. He postulates that fluctuations in the climate, possibly due to astronomical shifts and the changing position of the poles, had altered the growing season, thereby affecting the crops and agricultural methods that should be applied for an optimal harvest. Columella's work is a professional treatise about the business of farming, the main thrust of which is olives and grapes. His tone is managerial, imparting his wisdom about purchasing, setting up and operating a profitable farmstead estate. In the spirit of a CEO, he discusses the handling of workers, favoring a decidedly strict but not cruel hand in the management of slaves, advising the master to personally try their food and drink and see that their clothing and accommodations are adequate but stark. Speaking from experience, he suggests asking their opinion on occasion to make them feel valued. He also recognizes the burden of prolific women and proposes that those who have borne more than three children be exempt from work or even freed. In spite of an abiding preoccupation with curtailing idleness, he concludes that being feared or despised by one's slaves was not conducive to prosperous farming. In the very last section, book 12, he discusses food: preserving, pickling, fermenting, drying, salt-curing, and wine and cheese making all under the supervision of the overseer's wife.

The final entry of book 12 is a stand-alone recipe for "salad" an intensely aromatic paste (or pesto, if you will) of herbs, vinegar, cheese and crunchy bits of nuts and seeds, most likely enjoyed with bread or a flat cake of coarse grain:

Put into a mortar savory, mint, rue, coriander, parsley, leeks or, if you have no leeks, a green onion, leaves of lettuce and of rocket, green thyme or calamint. Also green pennyroyal and fresh and salted cheese: pound them all together and mix a little peppered vinegar with them. When you have put this mixture in a bowl, pour oil over it.

When you have crushed the green stuffs detailed above, rub into them walnuts, well cleaned, in what seems a sufficient quantity, and mix in a little peppered vinegar and pour oil on the top. Crush up some slightly parched sesame with the green stuffs detailed above; also mix in a little peppered vinegar and then pour oil on the top. Cut Gallic cheese, or any other sort you like, in minute pieces and pound it up; take pine-nuts, if you have plenty of them, but, if not, toasted hazelnuts after taking off their shells, or almonds and mix them in the same quantity over the herbs used for seasoning and add a little peppered vinegar and mix it in, and pour oil over the compound thus formed. If there are no green seasonings crush dry penny-royal or thyme or marjoram or dried savory with the cheese and add peppered vinegar and oil; but any one of these herbs when dry, if the rest are not available, can also be mixed by itself with cheese.[3]

Many other ancient authors have left a record of foodstuffs and food-ways, with occasional mentions of preparation. Of note is the encyclopedic *Naturalis historia* (77–79 CE) by naturalist philosopher Pliny the Elder, ten volumes containing thirty-seven books covering myriad topics from the cosmos to medicine. He gives detailed advice about foods and foodways but steers clear of actual recipes. One well-intentioned pointer that persisted in many forms over the centuries regards the powerful effects of the menstrual cycle: "Contact with [menstrual blood] turns new wine sour, crops touched by it become barren, grafts die, seed in gardens are dried up, the fruit of trees fall off, the edge of steel and the gleam of ivory are dulled, hives of bees die." But the devastation could also work to a good effect, "If the women walk naked through a field, worms, beetles, and other pests fall down. This was discovered in Cappadocia during an infestation of cantharid beetles, for which women walk through the fields with their dresses hiked up above their buttocks."

The medicinal work of Galen, whose patients ranged from the illustrious Marcus Aurelius to the peasantry, focused specifically on food and diet. Taking his teachings from Hippocrates, Galen believed that health was a question of maintaining the balance of the four humors (blood, phlegm, and black and yellow bile) through diet and lifestyle, for which he compiled a catalog of all of the foods available in the Roman farm and market, elaborating a detailed description of each in accordance to their potential to tip or balance the equilibrium of the body, "salty or sweet, good or bad for the stomach, promoting one or other of the humors, sharp or bitter, sour or watery, easy or difficult to digest, slow or quick to pass through the body, costive or laxative, composed of fine or thick particles, cooling or heating."[4] Galen felt that a good doctor should also be a good cook: unpalatable or improperly prepared foods were not conducive to healing. In *On the Powers of Foods* (c. 180 CE), he expounds on the preparation and ministration of barley soup, explaining the efficacy of his recipe thus: "Everything flatulent is removed and its thick mucilage is smooth, clinging, soothing, slippery, moderately watery, quenching of the thirst, laxative and easy to excrete . . . and without astringency. It neither disturbs the other foods nor does it swell up in the bowels."[5]

In proportion to its importance in the Roman diet, the details on bread in Galen are dizzying. In his lengthy exposition, he makes mention of what seem to be the ritual cheese breads that were of such great importance to Cato, giving us a window onto the Galenic sociology of digestion:

> If you add some cheese, as is the habit of the farmers who live round me when celebrating a festival, and these breads are what are called unleavened, then everyone is harmed, even if they are the most healthy of reapers and diggers, and yet these people seem even better than sporting heavyweights at digesting unleavened bread. . . . It is partly habit that contributes to their digestion, partly and not negligibly the small quantities that are eaten, and the hollowness of the whole body that is an inevitable consequence for those working the whole day in their own areas of activity. For the empty flesh seizes from the stomach not just partially digested juice, but also on occasion completely undigested juice, whenever it is struggling for food, and as a result these people later catch the most intractable diseases and die before they are old.[6]

Sources that give us a glimpse into the diet of the humble home are few, and are invariably written from an outsider's viewpoint. Ovid in his *Metamorphoses* (8 CE) sets a scene in which an old country couple is visited unexpectedly by Jupiter and Mercury disguised as mortals. They have been turned away from every house they visited but are taken into the humble home of Philemon and Baucis. Ovid was from an important equestrian family, for which his vision of country folk may be somewhat romanticized, but the excerpt is a poignant study of country generosity:

> The old woman, her skirts tucked up, her hands trembling, placed a table there, but a table with one of the three legs unequal: a piece of broken pot made them equal. Pushed underneath, it countered the slope, and she wiped the level surface with fresh mint. On it she put the black and green olives that belong to pure Minerva, and the cornelian cherries of autumn, preserved in wine lees; radishes and endives; a lump of cheese; and lightly roasted eggs, untouched by the hot ashes; all in clay dishes. After this she set out a carved mixing bowl for wine, just as costly, with cups made of beech wood, hollowed out, and lined with yellow bees' wax. There was little delay, before the fire provided its hot food, and the wine, of no great age, circulated, and then, removed again, made a little room for the second course. There were nuts, and a mix of dried figs and wrinkled dates; plums, and sweet-smelling apples in open wicker

baskets; and grapes gathered from the purple vines. In the centre was a gleaming honeycomb. Above all, there was the additional presence of well-meaning faces, and no unwillingness, or poverty of spirit.[7]

The First Roman Cookery Compilation

The first Roman recipe compilation in Latin that could indisputably be called a cookbook is enveloped in mystery. The first and most basic question regards authorship. Who is the Apicius who wrote the collection of recipes that would be called *De re coquinaria*? The name Apicius has been interpreted as a character cognomen applied to gourmands, *buongustai*. Three likely candidates who fit the bill have been proposed, the most significant of whom is the infamous gourmand M. Gavius Apicius, active in Tiberius's time. Such was his obsession with fine dining that after having squandered the better part of his fortune on his appetite, he reportedly poisoned himself at the prospect of having to eat humble fare. Apicius was an upper-crust gastronome (the word gastronomy is supposed to have originated from Archestratus, a Sicilian Greek poet/gourmand writing in the mid fourth century BCE, author of the first substantial cookery book *Hedupatheia* (Life of luxury). But because the surviving *Apicius* compilation of four hundred and seventy recipes seems to derive from different sources and addresses a spectrum of interest groups from the practical farmer (how to doctor bad honey to make it viable on the market) to the eccentric thrill seeker (the layered dish featuring sow's udder, fish fillets, chicken, fig-peckers, breast of turtle-dove "and whatever good things you can think of")[8] it is probable that there were multiple authors. And finally, although much of the work is believed to be by a single author, the compiler has included dishes named to honor illustrious figures that postdate the historical Apicius. Indeed, a case for multiple compilers can be made by virtue of the fact that some recipes appear twice and the chapter headings are not faithfully carried over into the table of contents.

Given the class and proclivities of the original Apicius, not to mention the composite nature of the work as we have it, historians differ as to how far *De re coquinaria* can be considered a reflection of the Roman diet. Defining a dish as luxurious was indeed relative against the ubiquitous backdrop of coarse bread, dried beans, base vegetables, figs, and rotgut wine. The very fact of its written form takes for granted a literate public and, as such, a person of exceptional means.

There is an unmistakable nod in *De re coquinaria* to Greek cuisine, but the Romans had for centuries been refashioning Greek culture in their own image, and did no less with cooking. In spite of the value placed on restraint, they would not kowtow to the culinary dictates of others, nor be outshone by anyone, certainly not with the wealth of ingredients in circulation in the Urbs. Roman aristocrats lived lavishly, and ostentation was an important expression of social power, but there were established limits. Excess taken to the point of vulgarity was vile. Rather than excess, it could be said that food-stuffs were given a rigorous makeover. One of the most notable characteris-tics, in keeping with the civilization of food, which the Romans felt elevated and distinguished them, is the reconceptualization of foods so that the main ingredients defied recognition. "The Romans abhorred the taste of any meat, fish, or vegetable in its pure form. There is hardly a recipe which does not add a sauce to the main ingredient which changes the original taste radically."[9] Indeed, the recipe "'Patina of anchovy without anchovy" at the end boasts: "At table, no one will know what he is eating."[10] Myriad herbs and spices were used to alter or rather create the character of each dish, the latter be-ing an open display of wealth. The most prominent spices were black pepper and cinnamon along with the sweet spices ginger, nutmeg, and cloves. The enigmatic silphium was a popular flavoring, but if it is true that Nero was gifted the last known stalk, then it would not have survived much after the original Apicius's time. It was substituted with the cheaper asafetida, which may give an indication of its unique flavor.

Other notable culinary devices were lovage, coriander, cumin, oregano, fennel, mint caraway, mustard, celery and mustard seed, chervil, parsley, thyme, sage, and saffron. In his play *Pseudolus*, Plautus leaves us with his own pithy observations on such practices: "I don't season a dinner the way other cooks do, who serve you up whole pickled meadows,—men who make cows their messmates, who thrust herbs at you then proceed to season these herbs with other herbs."[11] Later, as Christian asceticism blended with Roman *mos maiorum*,[12] fanciness or even tastiness became a vice, but the legacy of herbs and particularly spices would be passed on into the culinary style that characterized the Middle Ages, not because (as is popularly thought) they overpowered the fetid taste of rotten meat, but because it had become part of a revered gastronomic tradition. Freshness was a priority for those who could afford the best, and for those who couldn't, spices would have been too costly.

A discussion of the tastes that marked ancient Roman cookery cannot be left without mentioning *garum*, the ubiquitous fermented fish sauce. A Western sensibility may disparage the thought of putrefying fish matter rendered into a highly salty condiment (notwithstanding the current in-terest in East Asian foods), but for the ancient Romans it was an essential ingredient and can be found in some form in the vast majority of Apicius's recipes.[13] Although it could be made at home, most of it was produced commercially, Spain being the greatest producer of garum, given the high quantity and quality of the fish in those waters. To every ten liters of fish, one liter of salt was added. Some also threw in a liter of old wine for good measure. It was left over night and then put in the sun in an earthenware vessel for two to three months and stirred with a stick every now and again. Once it was ripe it was covered and stored.[14] Garum was found on the tables of the rich as well as the poor and came in varying qualities, *muria* being the lowest grade of brine. Its appeal may lie in the fact that fermented fish sauces are a source of naturally occurring glutamate, which excites the umami sensors of the tongue. The solid remains were a sort of fish pickle, called *hallec*, which Cato recommended giving to farmhands, perhaps as a condiment for bread.

Ancient recipes can only be replicated with a margin of approximation, and while many foods carry the same name as those that are commonly eaten today, they may have been quite different. Industrial farming has produced far larger, less gamey and meatier sheep, pigs, and chickens than would have been available to the Roman consumer; fruits would have been more pungent, greens coarser, and the spices would have arrived after months of travel.[15] The glaring lack of sweet desserts and any sort of recipe for the main staple, bread, could be an indication that the version of *Apicius* that has come down to us is incomplete, although bread recipes also seem to be conspicuously lacking in cookery books from other countries through the Middle Ages, denoting deferment to the professional bakery.

The written history of pasta has been fraught with anxiety, given its importance as a culinary marker for Italian cuisine. A thorough combing of *De re coquinaria* reveals two consecutive recipes in the *Pandecter* (Many Ingredients) section that could, with only a gentle stretch of the imagination, be construed as precursors to lasagna. The first is the aforementioned multi-meated sow's udder extravaganza. Various precooked meats are layered in a baking tray between sheets of *lagana*, rolled-out swaths of dough that are duly moistened with broth to provide the necessary liquid to cook them. Cato's *placenta*, described above, was also constructed with alternating layers of cheese mixture and unleavened dough called *tracta*. In both cases, the final product is sealed in dough and baked, leaving purists hesitant about referring to these early assemblages as pasta dishes, rather than savory pies, whereas enthusiasts place them firmly within the annals of pasta history. Further mentions of pasta would remain sketchy and sparse for the next one thousand years.

Medieval Foodways: The Backdrop

Greek and Latin prescriptive food recommendations had revolved around an individual's humoral profile, present state of fitness, age, sex, living conditions, and so on. Over the course of the Middle Ages, social and religious dietary dictates came into play, the two frequently overlapping. Socially delineated foods were justified by the obvious fact that the Christian God had himself arranged all things in nature (as in heaven) hierarchically as part of the Great Chain of Being. Foods were classified on a scale from more to less noble, and consequently, more to less suited to a person's table or digestive tract in accordance with their "natural" social status. The *Ruralia commoda* (c. 1305), an agricultural treatise based largely on Columella's *Res rustica*, acknowledged wheat as the noblest of grains, but claimed that the nutritional needs of peasant laborers could also be satisfied with the "inferior" grains more generally allocated as swine, oxen, and horse fodder.

Food consumption was a physical necessity that separated man from the godhead. Early Christian theorists classified gluttony first and foremost among man's tendencies toward sin, even singling it out as the primary catalyst for the others—once one had succumbed to this fundamentally base desire, the rest of the sins were sure to follow, particularly lust, handmaiden to gluttony. After all, had it not been proscribed eating that led to sexual awakening and then banishment from the Garden of Eden? According to Tertullian (160–220 CE) one need look no further than man's anatomy for proof of the irredeemable connection between lust and voracity: "These two are so united and concrete, that, had there been any possibility of disjoining them the pudenda would not have been affixed to the belly. . . . The region of these members is one and the same." The prolific Pope Gregory the Great (540–604) concurred, affirming further that enjoyment of food was a catalyst for concupiscence, "But it is plain to all that lust springs from gluttony, when in the very distribution of the members, the genitals appear placed beneath the belly. And hence when the one is inordinately pampered, the other is doubtless excited to wantonness."[16]

In order to curb sinfulness, the calendar was divided into feast days and fast days, in total over a third of the year dedicated to the latter, including the lengthy trials of Advent and Lent. Fasting for the most part did not mean going without eating, but limiting the number of meals and forgoing meat, eggs, dairy, and luxury items, excluding marine creatures. Lean days, on the other hand, included eggs, and dairy. But despite the dangling carrot of eternal salvation, the faithful complied reluctantly. Indeed, Martin Luther complained that the oil substitute for butter was of such poor quality that "people in Rome would not use [it] to grease their shoes."[17] To allay their cravings, the wealthy could apply for dispensations, whose revenue the Church welcomed as charitable donations.

The desire for a strict sense of order and propriety took on a more imperative tone during the peak years of the Black Death (1346–1353), one of whose entry points into Italy was Lazio. The plague years coincided with devastating famines brought on by a series of situations: climactic conditions, like the effects of the intermittent Little Ice Age, mercenary troops ravaging the resources of the countryside, and the inevitable consumption of the grain seeds meant for the next year's harvest, an unnerving combination that served to heighten religious intolerance and set off a witch hunt in order to right whatever wrong had upset God and thus afflicted humankind. Hence, a frenzy of executions accompanied the list of causes decimating Europe alongside disease, war, and starvation, prompting the prayer *Libera nos Domine a fame, a bello, a peste*.

The Late Middle Ages and the Pleasure of the Table

In 1377, the papal court took up residency once again in Rome, after nearly seventy years in Avignon.[18] Under the third pope, Boniface IX (1389–1404) the Church assumed total temporal control over Rome and would maintain it until 1870 when the last remaining fragment of the Papal States had succumbed to a unified Italy. Under Pope Martin V (1417–1431) and his six successors, the Roman Renaissance, a total revitalization project, restored the derelict wasteland that Rome had become to its former glory as *caput mundi*, the Eternal City. This backdrop of sin, salvation, pestilence, culture, and social stratification was the context that set the stage for the next milestone in Roman culinary literature: *De Arte Coquinaria* (*The Art of Cooking*), by Maestro Martino. Published in c. 1465, it was a product of its time, recalling the sophistication of the courtly International Gothic period while reflecting the tastes of the High Middle Ages. He borrows freely from the extant works of other authors, and they from him, an exchange that is perfectly in keeping with the evolution of cookery texts. Lifting texts, even verbatim, from a revered author was an homage that lent authority to your own work. A distinct salute is given to Catalan cuisine, the tradition in vogue at the time, whose influence emanated from the nearby Catalan court in Naples.[19] The increasingly international makeup of the high clergy, arranged aristocratic marriages, and the constant flux of political alliances, promoted the trafficking of courtly cuisine, resulting in a standardized repertoire of international fare and the refinement of cooking methods.

Biancomangiare is probably the ubiquitous dish *per eccellenza* that more than any other permeated culinary literature throughout Europe.[20] "White-dish" heads up the recipes in Martino's second chapter, titled, "How to Make Every Type of Victual." His version combines soaked crushed almonds, capon breast, crustless white bread soaked in broth, verjuice (an acidic juice derived from unripe grapes or other sour fruit, though less imposing than lemon juice or vinegar), ginger root, and a significant amount of sugar. After pounding it to mush, it is further refined by passing it through a sieve, a common technique. Simmer one half hour on a pile of embers, add rosewater and serve. He follows this up with the Catalan version, basically a goat's milk pudding thickened with rice flour into which threadlike strings of capon breast and sugar are added to the thickened mass. It too is finished with the ever-present rosewater and topped with sugar sprinkles. Rosewater was included almost ubiquitously, perhaps because in addition to its heady taste, it was categorized as "cooling," particularly important in the Roman clime.

Lenten versions of dishes that allowed the well-to-do to continue eating in style without guilt was becoming a standard feature of cookery books. Martino's "Lenten Whitedish" has the bread soaking in white pea broth; instead of capon, fish is used; the ginger is increased and the sugar reduced by half; the pungent verjuice is substituted with orange juice (but if unavailable a little verjuice/rosewater mixture will do). Other recipes suggesting alternatives for fast days simply stated what to leave out; for example, instead of frying apple fritters in lard they should be fried in oil, and the batter should not contain eggs. Some suggestions are less convincing, like fake butter for fasting days consisting of almonds reduced to a paste, moistened with pike broth, thickened with starch and flavored with a modicum of sugar and rosewater, plus saffron to tinge it yellow. Shape the resulting mass into a loaf and let it solidify overnight in a cool place.

The *Art of Cooking* has been called the "First modern cookery book."[21] It does fall within the broadly defined "early modern period"[22] but is untouched by key culinary events of the age, such as the Columbian Exchange, which witnessed the slow influx of foodstuffs from the Americas. Modernity in this case manifests in the way Martino approaches the tastes of his contemporaries and the established conventions of his profession, building upon them and innovating, pushing the boundaries in synch with the unprecedented cultural wave that was sweeping through fifteenth-century Rome. His readership would have been professional cooks practicing at the tail end of the International Gothic, which witnessed the first significant burst of culinary

exchange at court. Had he followed the trend of previous cookery compila-
tions, the recipes would have been mere sketchy outlines, leaving much to
the imagination and experience of the cook. In this regard, Martino is more
thorough than his predecessors in attention to details, almost to the point
of nervous apprehension ("this should be done when the partridge is still
hot, and not over-cooked, but rather green and almost bloody, that is, not
well done but very hot, turn it over quickly, not slowly"),[23] whether about
the grade of chopping, how long and in what way a dish should be stirred,
alternative ways of serving, as well as emphasizing quality ("good oil"), texture ("so that it comes out spongy"), density ("not too thin"), appearance
("once fried they will resemble fish"), remedies ("remove the burnt taste as
follows") not to mention cleanliness ("clear water"; take some white cloth";
"in a clean pot"). This penchant toward precision was a precursor in the
evolution of the standardized culinary terminology that would develop over
the next few centuries.[24]

Modernization, or rather the move from medieval to Renaissance cookery,
can also be inferred through his tendency to exalt the flavor of the main
ingredients through herbs, as opposed to elaborating ways of rendering them
unrecognizable with excessive use of spices and other artifice. Whereas pepper graces nearly every dish in Apicius, Martino shows more restraint: "if
desired you can add pepper" or "enough pepper as is necessary." To this same
end, he also favored local products over exotica. Perishable goods, by their
very ephemerality, and Martino's use of sugar as a main ingredient[25] also
served as expressions of affluence.

Although Martino was not Roman per se, and information about his time
in Rome is speculative, he was employed as the cook to Cardinal Ludovico
Trevisan, Patriarch of Aquileia, who was infamous for his sumptuous (by
some considered outright licentious) banquets, which led to Martino's ascent to fame. True to the appetites of his diners, *mirabilia gulae*, spectacle
dishes intended to amaze and entertain the upper echelon, are not lacking,
for example the self-descriptive "How to dress a peacock with all its feathers so that when cooked, it appears to be alive and spew fire from its beak."
Showcase pieces date back to ancient times and would continue through
the coming centuries to be an important medium to impress guests, but the
peacock trick was signature medieval. Even thrill seekers had to eat, however, and Martino proposes an extensive variety of vegetable and legume
dishes with complete disregard for what might have been suggested by the
Great Chain of Being. Indeed it is not pageantry that characterizes most
of his fare, but hearty food meant to satisfy both the discerning palate and
hungry stomach:

Frying Fava Beans
Take some fava beans, and sage, and onions, and figs, and some apples, and some good herbs as well, and mix together and fry in a pan with oil. When prepared, remove and top with spices.

The recipe for the Roman cabbage soup is another example of home-style cookery that would go on to be replicated in nearly every cookery book in his wake. The dish celebrates Rome's long-standing peasant tradition of cooking in pork fat, the appreciation of a comfortingly caloric broth, and unembellished simplicity:

How to make Roman-style cabbage soup
Break off the cabbage leaves with your hand in the usual way and put them in boiling water and when they are about halfway done, discard the water and take a good amount or at least enough of some finely minced good quality lard and put the drained cabbage in turning them well with a spoon. Then add some good fatty broth and simmer on the fire for a few minutes.

But most significant for the development for the Italian culinary identity is the inclusion of three recipes that are unmistakably pasta as we understand it: a flour and water preparation that is rolled out, cut into shapes, boiled and finished. "Roman-style Macaroni" may be the very first Italian recipe explaining how to make pasta from flour to plate. It calls for a simple flour-and-water dough that is then rolled out as one would a sheet of lasagna—but a bit thicker, and up to here can look back to *lagana* as antecedent. The sheet of dough is then, however, to be rolled around a stick; remove the stick and cut the rolled dough into ribbons the width of your little finger. Although not mentioned by name, here we are most certainly talking about fettuccine—the base word meaning "ribbons," a pasta shape that would make international history in the 1950s as Fettuccine Alfredo. In fact, Martino suggests serving them simply with fresh butter, salt, cheese, and sweet spices. Perhaps he was on to something.[26]

In the summer of 1463, Bartolomeo Sacchi, better known by his sobriquet "Platina," is believed to have met Maestro Martino and acquired a manuscript copy of *Libro de arte coquinaria*.[27] Like Martino, Platina was a man of humble birth, but in the great client/patron tradition, he ingratiated himself into the embrace of the nobility, the high clergy, and exclusive intellectual circles through wit, intelligence, and cultural acuity, not to mention the necessary dose of sycophancy. As a reputable scholar, he became a leading member of the Roman Academy and the College of Abbreviators, the former a humanist group seeking to revitalize the cultural sphere by resuscitating the ideals of ancient Greece and Rome, and the latter an exclusive society of literati funded by the Church. His talents were offset by an unwieldy ego and a tendency toward irascibility, which found him imprisoned in the summer of 1464 by the newly elected Pope Paul II for an insolent letter sent when the pope dissolved the College of Abbreviators.

In accordance with Renaissance humanism, Platina believed that a man of learning should be acquainted with various spheres of knowledge spanning the arts and sciences, but that the secret to total fulfillment lay in balancing scholarly pursuits with a regimen specifically aimed at health and well-being: *mens sana in corpore sano*. To his contemporaries he advocated the Epicurean ideal of seeking pleasure and avoiding pain, which smacked of paganism, wantonness, and sin, not only to the clergy and the masses, but also to some humanists.[28] Therefore, while voluptuary banqueting was abloom in high Roman society, deriving pleasure from eating was a difficult topic to broach openly, even when presented as a way of honoring nature, and thereby the Creator. But in *De Honesta voluptate et valetudine* (*On Right Pleasure and Good Health*), Platina took on the challenge of systematically compiling and formulating a holistic life manual whose aim was to encourage a temperate albeit pleasurable lifestyle that would nurture body, mind, and spirit.

The preamble, which takes the form of a direct dedication to Cardinal Roverella, is a long explanatory apologia preempting the attack of inevitable detractors: "Far be it from Platina to write to the holiest of men about the pleasure which the intemperate and libidinous derive from self-indulgence and a variety of foods and from titillations of sexual interest."[29] He backs his cause with an impressive list of the great Greek and Roman philosophers and rallies them in defense of Epicurus. "For pleasure that derives from right action leads to happiness, as a doctor's skill leads a sick man to health."[30] In an effort to embed his work solidly in the Roman tradition, Platina declares that he has followed in the footsteps of Cato, Varro, and Columella, although in truth, he has little to say about agricultural practices. He fails to acknowledge Pliny, Galen, and the great body of Arabic medical advice that was available to him in Latin or Italian and from which he borrows liberally.[31] The recipes comprise 95 percent of Martino's total opus, whose achievement he recognizes with gratitude and admiration, "What a cook you bestowed, O immortal gods, in my friend Martino of Como, from whom I have received in great part the things which I am writing!"[32] As a classicist he attempts to reference Apicius, but concedes that with regard to cuisine, the ancients leave something to be desired. True to his intention, *On Right Pleasure* imparts instruction on a wide range of topics from choosing one's living space to getting proper rest and exercise to the importance of a pleasurable dining atmosphere (table settings, manners, cleanliness), in addition to a detailed description of the health properties of foods in accordance with the humoral theory of medicine, the undercurrent through the whole of the book.

Platina had no training as a physician, agriculturalist, or cook. His aim was to celebrate the culinary arts as part of a philosophy of healthful living, of which satisfaction at the table was paramount. Hence he has been referred to as the father of gastronomy, for he had taken Martino's work from the ambit of the kitchen and elevated it into a topic worthy of the academic salon. In and of itself, the *Libro de arte coquinari* received little attention beyond its own insular group of practitioners. *On Right Pleasure*, on the other hand, had an altogether different audience, the upper-middle class, the bourgeois elite, a public who could read Latin for pleasure and who might not have otherwise bothered with a simple cookery book; this served to bring Martino's work to a wider, more erudite readership.

The manuscript version is thought to have been drafted in the summer of 1465, following Platina's imprisonment.[33] The earliest extant printed edition dates to 1468, the same year in which Platina was imprisoned for a second time. On this occasion, it was the Roman Academy that had come under fire. Given their common obsession with ancient Rome, members were suspected of carrying out pagan rites and worshipping pagan gods. Detractors conveniently combined these rumors of heresy with a conspiracy to assassinate the pope. After a torturous imprisonment, Platina was released in early 1469, but all traces of any written account of the accusation have mysteriously been lost. The information may have been buried by Platina himself during his years of service as Vatican librarian[34] under Sixtus IV (1471–1484), so one can only speculate as to whether or not *On Right Pleasure* had sparked the controversy.

Despite protestations of moderation, Platina kept close company with notorious voluptuaries like Pietro Riario, Pope Sixtus's favorite nephew (or son), whose opulent and decadent banquets had few rivals, indeed, outdoing himself seemed his greatest challenge. In a gala dinner Riario hosted in honor of Eleonora of Aragon, the first course (before the first of four table cloths was removed) is described as follows:

- After we were seated at table, knives were placed around and gilded salt-cellars made of sugar and bread-paste and cups and glasses for wine.
- Then a page arrived with a plate that contained ten little birds [*cotignoli*] very small, one for each. They were beautiful and well prepared and were the antipasto.
- Five plates of two capons each, covered with white sauce and gilded pomegranate seeds, and ten bowls with ten small chickens covered with *sapore pavonaza*,[35] *garbo* and wine was poured.

- Two whole boiled veal in five large platters and then each person was served with five pieces of veal and five of castrated mutton, three of *senguato*, three whole kids, six small chickens, six capons, *tete-de-veau*, and with the boiled meats, five plates of sausage [*salsume*], and the milk-filled teats of a pig [*presucti somete salsusole*] and ten plates of agnolotti filled with pumpkin.
- Five large plates of roasted meat, on each of which were six pieces of veal, three whole kids, and ten small *peguni*, ten chickens, four rabbits, and a peacock, cooked and dressed in its feathers, with *camelina* sauce in sauce dishes.
- During this serving, a youth came in wearing a garland and carrying a viola in his hand [Orpheus] and when he had arrived, he sang the following verses: "My father wishes he could descend from airy Olympus / In order to enjoy these verses: / Do not be astounded by our heavenly revels / Jupiter is wont to celebrate his festival at this time."
- Then came four men carrying a mountain on their shoulders, and on this mountain there were three whole *paghi*, a peahen with her babies, two pheasants, a wild cat [*gena*], two great birds [*drongne*], two whole goats, and a live bear. All of these animals were placed around on the mountain, and on top of it someone [Orpheus] sang the following verses: "In Heaven the disposition of the mighty thunderer is sweetened / because of Orpheus's brilliance in the art of music. / Enjoy our fountains and look with pleasure upon our woods. / For your feast we offer game newly caught. Hercules has better luck than Orpheus / Instead of Eurydice he has been given Leonora."
- Five plates of galantine of capon and gelatin shapes [*mollume*]; under the gelatin were drawn the arms of the cardinal, certainly very well made.
- Five plates with white tarts, gilded and also with junkets of meat and muscatel pears in crust.
- We washed our hands with water of lemon blossoms, and the uppermost table covering was taken away along with the cups and the drinking glasses.[36]

As a testament to the detriments of high living, Pietro (Cardinal Riario at that juncture) died at the age of twenty-eight, allegedly poisoned after fleeing some scandal he had stirred in Venice.

At the same time that Platina was writing *On Right Pleasure*, he was composing a parallel treatise entitled *De amore*, thus tackling gluttony and lust in one fell swoop. In their own way, both texts were meant to guide wandering souls toward the path of cultured self-restraint. *De amore* seems to have influenced some of Platina's culinary observations in *On Right Pleasure*, alerting the reader time and time again that consuming certain foods like pine nuts, chickpeas, broad beans, onions, and of course oysters would excite passions. As a strong-smelling root vegetable, onions ranked low on the Great Chain of Being, associated with rough appetites, literally and figuratively. On the dual nature of the onion, Platina offers these cagey observations:

Doctors agree for the most part that inflammations are clearly kindled by them, the head made to ache, brain and memory impaired. [. . .] Some, however, think they are healthful when used moderately because they soften the bowels, induced dreams, create an appetite, especially arouse sexual appetite, and increase its foment with lustful dampness.[37]

Onion breath notwithstanding, such circumspect tips had a puzzlingly ambiguous ring.

On Right Pleasure has the distinction of being the first printed cookery book. In 1475, two days before his installation ceremony as Vatican librarian took place, the book underwent a second printing in Venice; all subsequent printings are based on this edition. On September 21, 1481, at the age of sixty, Platina died of plague in Rome.

Rome-Centric Culinary Renaissance

Nearly one hundred years would pass before the next significant culinary opus reached publication. Bartolomeo Scappi, like Platina and Martino, was originally from northern Italy, and the knowledge, experience, skill, and reputation he acquired in various cities cooking for prelates would, like his predecessors, bring him to Rome under the papal wing. His cookbook, succinctly titled *Opera* (1570), literally "Work," is considered the most complete and definitive text reflecting the practices and tastes of the Italian Renaissance upper classes, aristocracy, and papal court. Despite the shadow of the 1527 Sack of Rome, the threat of Luther's protestant movement, and the schism between Henry VIII's England and the papacy, Rome was still a point of arrival. Rome meant you had made it. Scappi proudly identified himself as belonging to the corps of Roman cooks, despite his extensive experience in other cities, particularly in Venice and Milan. Indeed, to qualify as cook for the papal court, the center of the Christian world, one had to have accrued an immeasurable body of gastronomic expertise that reflected the cosmopolitan current of Roman society, and this could only be achieved through study and exposure to various kitchens, practitioners, and markets over an extended period of time. The papal chef had to satisfy finicky traditionalists, as well as gastronomic adventurers, produce opulent display that showcased the master's wealth and power—without crossing the line into gaudy or yesterday's news—and cater to the prelate's personal taste, including his religious tolerance for lavishness. Amid the profusion of political, familial, economic, and religious controversy, the head cook also had to be incorruptible, as he was a direct line through which poison could find its way to the Holy Father.

The pecking order of the aristocratic/papal household staff was headed by a steward, or *scalco*, who oversaw all of the details of the meals, from menu planning to stocking the kitchen to table settings and serving. The most thorough text outlining the duties of the steward, *La dottrina singolare*, was published in 1560, about the time that Scappi would have been compiling materials for his own volume. Early in his career, the author, Domenico Romoli, had been in the service of the Medici pope Leo X (1475–1521), whose grandiose banquets set the bar for stately luxury among the aristocracy. Although he was not a cook himself, as steward Romoli was uniquely positioned to build upon the previous works by Martino and Platina. The book is divided into twelve sections, the first detailing the duties of the various household servants under him from the buyer to the carver to the sommelier to the waiters; the second lists the best season for meats and fowl among which he lists the New World novelty *gallina d'India*, or turkey;[38] the third does the same for fish and seafood, mushrooms, and truffles. Section four presents a menu for the afternoon and evening meals for an entire year, beginning with the first day of Lent. The meal proposed for Ash Wednesday, directly on the heels of *martedì grasso*, is rather substantial for an exercise in mortifying the flesh:

Antipasto
Figs, nuts, lettuce salad, Florentine mint and capers, tench, marinated grey mullet, grilled red mullet
Poached course
Umbrine, potage of *macarelli*, white chickpea soup, red tuna belly, white almond pudding
Fried course
Wild strawberries, baby calamari, small clams in shell, Florentine spinach, olives and thinly sliced lemons
Fruit course
Cold nun's fritters, artichokes, almonds soaked in rosewater and sugar, walnuts soaked in red wine and salt, grilled Florentine fennel

The entire period of the *Quadragesima* witnessed a veritable parade of fish, shellfish and crustaceans: sturgeon, shrimp, oysters, tuna, eel, salmon, snails, turtle, lamprey, carp, *laccie*, squid, herring, and brill. Lack of refrigeration meant the fresh fish trade at the Roman market was brisk, as might be expected when the entire population was forced to abstain from meat and the *Roma bene* consumed conspicuously. As can be discerned from some of the menu items above, our author is Florentine and did not hesitate to bring that to bear in his service in Rome.

Menu planning was the creative space of the steward, an activity that many cooks, including Scappi, felt should have been their domain, in fact the two roles were interdependent. In the fifth section, Romoli ventures into the cook's territory by presenting a few hundred recipes, packing in everything from German-style brain to cordials. It is at once an attempt at logic and order and yet bulging with a plenitude that verges on the bizarre, recalling the mannerist food portraits of Giuseppe Archimboldo. Sections six through twelve are dedicated to health, balancing the humors, and the properties inherent in food, and like Platina, Romoli has an abiding preoccupation with foods that stir the passions. He concludes with a treatise on the fundamentals of health: rest and exercise, the four elements (earth, wind, fire, water), the four ages of man, the four seasons, the four complexions and so forth.

Normally a cook would enter into a household as an apprentice and work his way up through the ranks acquiring skills and a repertoire of recipes. For the most part, the recipes were committed to memory, though informal records were also kept. Often the master of the house had the scalco or the *cuoco segreto* (the personal cook—just as a secretary is a personal assistant) keep a formal register of meals for which detailed descriptions were on hand, and which were most likely used as source material for cookbooks. It is therefore assumed that Scappi started compiling content for his *Opera* long before the publication date of 1570, having arrived in Rome in the late 1540s. The increasing complexity of the modern kitchen, the instruments, ingredients, techniques, and the demand for artistry and craftsmanship, raised the status and respectability of the cook. Scappi saw the passing on of such a wealth of knowledge as an affective or even poignant exercise, tending away from the terse, arid cataloging of recipes that characterized works before his. The book is framed as a passing-on of teachings from the *maestro* to his actual apprentice, Giovanni, thereby providing the human element as a sort of rhetorical device that creates purpose behind his efforts. Thus, in reading, we all become Giovanni, and Scappi our personal instructor.

Scappi was not in the employ of a flamboyant Medici pope whose life was a cascade of parties, but of two sober inquisitors, Pius IV and V, the latter a hellfire and brimstone, ascetic vegetarian who spent his last years on a diet consisting mainly of goat's milk.[39] Perhaps because his potential was stymied, Scappi includes an elaborate section of menu proposals of his own, many of which had never come to fruition but demonstrated his inherent talent as a steward. For a man of this time, his awareness of foods, much of it firsthand, spanned extraordinary distances, both in Italy and abroad, and in minute detail, all of which formed his contribution to the Roman culinary melting pot. Lombardy and Milan exert the greatest influence on Scappi's cooking style, but he also showers praise upon the foodstuffs of his adopted home, commending the quality of Roman veal and cherries, as well as the freshwater catch from nearby lakes and streams: smelt, tench, pike, eel, trout, crayfish, and shad.

In addition to recipes and menus, his purpose in writing *Opera* was to convey the probity and dedication that a cook had to have in order to be worthy of the position and responsibility that came with it. The serenity of the household and guests depended upon a well-functioning kitchen. Whatever the sociopolitical upheavals, the food service had to remain a reliable and steady constant. In a book whose intent is to provide thorough instruction to the neophyte, Scappi adheres to the expectations of the cookery book genre in the standard division of the sections (meat, fish, vegetables) and the expected subgenres (soup, sop, broth, etc.). Likewise, he includes his version of the classics (several variations on whitedish and the standard "Roman-style" dishes) as well as alternative suggestions for lean and fast days. While much of the work recopies, recycles, and revises the canon of current practice, he also offers a plethora of wholly original recipes, more than half of the total output, a daring move that only an assured professional could achieve successfully. Much of this original work is in Book V on savory pies, tarts, fritters, and pastries and in Book VI, dishes for the convalescent. These were standard categories, but Scappi's assortment of tortes and sickdishes went far beyond the achievements of his rivals.

Whereas Romoli and Platina donned the physician's hat regardless of their lack of expertise, Scappi did not presume to wax on about the medicinal properties of individual foods, their effects on the humors, or their potential as aphrodisiacs. For the sickly or finicky eater, he created comforting, easily digestible dishes, recommending that they check with their doctor if in doubt, thereby relieving himself of any responsibility for unbalanced humors. He derived his assurances not from the corpus of ancient medical literature, but from the approval of his illustrious patients, as in recipe 6.19, titled, "To prepare a chicken broth of great nourishment reduced down to a jelly," for which Scappi proudly records the accolades received in 1551 from the most illustrious and most reverend Cardinal Andrea Cornaro. His patron, Pius IV, was partial to the Galenic barley soup as his comfort food of choice when feeling under the weather.

Sugar, a high-energy substance, was added liberally in sickdishes as the optimal nutrient for rebuilding one's strength. Still considered a spice, it was used indiscriminately, regardless of whether the dominant taste was sweet or savory. Cinnamon and pepper are the most frequently used spices (albeit second to sugar) followed by saffron and cloves.[40] Scappi would have had his own generic multipurpose spice mix, like a signature garam masala; he is therefore respectfully vague about the addition of spices, leaving it to the discretion of the cook.

The context of the courts allowed Scappi the luxury to experiment, which honed his craft. He had funding for the best in foodstuffs, staff, and equipment, as well as diners with cosmopolitan tastes. Indeed, at the beginning of Book 3, he declares that the bulk of recipes in Book 2 "had been tested by me in the bountiful City of Rome." The burden of such a superabundance of dishes required for one meal was relieved by the presence of a *credenziere*, who was in charge of the credenza, or sideboard of cold dishes, ready to be served when diners were seated. By Scappi's time, this course was already referred to as the antipasto and consisted of sliced meats, biscuits soaked in wine, savory pies, marzipan, fruit or vegetable salads, dishes in aspic, fruit preserved in spirits, caviar, cured salmon, and the like. This allowed the kitchen to coordinate the courses of hot foods, or *servizio da cucina*, which followed. The main feature was meat prepared in various manners: roasted, fried, stewed, stuffed, and boiled, all in the same sitting. Any number of meatballs, fricassees, soups and pottages, savory tarts or pies, rice and pasta dishes, or dumplings were also part of the servizio da cucina, but not served in any particular order.[41]

The meats and other foods were skillfully carved or otherwise portioned in the presence of the diners and artfully plated by a figure called the *trinciante*. The household carver was a prestigious position and complex enough to merit a section in every book on stewarding, as well as a monograph on that topic alone by the distinguished Roman trinciante Vincenzo Cervio. The choreography of gestures, postures, and handling of the serving implements lent an air of sophistication that was an integral part of the enjoyment of the meal. Once the penultimate tablecloth was removed, the meal would conclude with another round of *servizio di credenza*, the "postpasto" course, with items such as fruit pies and tarts, salads and cold vegetables, fruit, cheeses, whipped cream, ring-cakes, fried cakes, wafers, olives, roasted chestnuts, blood pudding, and oysters. At the end of the meal proper, the last tablecloth was removed, the guests washed their hands in bowls of perfumed water and the confectionery was brought out consisting of candied fruits and jellies.

Scappi gives less space to game meats than had been afforded in the past, which may indicate that their distinct gamey tastes were becoming less popular. Even in domestic meats, he specifies castrated animals whose meat would have been milder. Pork was still highly prized in Rome. Fresh or salt cured, nose to tail it provided a variety of flavors and textures. Pork and

Figure 3.1. Depiction of the papal serving staff at a formal meal. Engraving in Opera, by Bartolomeo Scappi, 1570

other animal fats were fundamental as a cooking medium, although Scappi had a penchant for butter, a fat little used in the Middle Ages but which would come to be identified as a healthy option, as well as the fat choice of the upper classes in successive centuries. Veal reigned as Scappi's preferred meat, owing perhaps to the statement of wealth that it made for his patron. A young or even suckling calf prepared for the table represented an animal that would not provide traction to pull the plough, or supply milk for dairy products. Such carefree waste was an important form of conspicuous consumption.

The Roman food of the upper classes was not characterized by insular regionalism, chauvinistically based on its own products and coveted recipes. Theirs was more accurately Roman-style International Cuisine. Even a few foods from the Columbian Exchange made it into *Opera*, notably the *gallo d'India* (turkey) the *anatra d'India* (Muscovy duck), and the *coniglio d'India* (guinea pig), the names originating from the idea that Columbus's mission had been to find a maritime passage to India.

Three New World products significantly missing from his book are *granturco* or maize, originally also called *grano d'India*, potatoes, and the tomato. Antonio Latini, who had done his apprenticeship in Rome and served as scalco to Pope Urban VIII's nephew Cardinal Antonio Barberini, has the distinction of recording the earliest surviving recipe for tomato sauce in his book *Lo scalco moderno* (1692).[42] "Spanish Tomato Sauce" was in essence a roasted tomato salsa mixed with fresh chopped onion, herbs, salt, oil, chilies, and vinegar, recommended as a condiment for boiled foods. It would take more than a century, however, before Romans would warm to tomatoes. And Italy was even more reluctant to adopt the *pomi di terra* than the *pomi d'oro*. In a treatise published in Rome in 1784, Father Giovanni Battista Occhialini pleads the case for the humble yet wondrous potato with Cardinal/Governor of Rome, Antonio Casali, encouraging him to invest in it as a way to feed the poor. "As soon as you have tasted its delicate flavor you will not just love it, you will crave it."[43] Recalling the famines that devastated Rome in 1764, 1765, and 1782, he promotes the potato as a toothsome solution to such crises:

> You can eat these roots raw, like the Negros in America do, or boiled. They taste like chestnuts and because they are floury, sweet, and filling in that same way, they are very tasty. If it should happen that the poor lack bread, they could sustain themselves with these roots alone, and not fear the horrible whip of starvation.[44]

He claims that some enterprising entrepreneurs had already successfully experimented with the potato in Roman soil, producing them in various colors: yellow, white, red, green, and blackish. They grow just as well in heavy wet lowland soil, as they do in the woods, or on hills, making them ideal for Rome, he claimed. In his own overzealous promotion, Occhialini even proposes that the leaves of the potato plant can be dried and smoked like tobacco.

After about 1,500 years had passed, Rome was ready for *The Modern Apicius* (1790), a rather presumptuous title but by an author who more than fit the bill. It is encyclopedic in scope and fills six volumes. Unlike the other authors from northern Italy, whose main experience played out in Rome, Leonardi is Roman, but because of the involution of Italian cuisine, having been eclipsed by French cuisine since the time of Scappi, he gained his experience initially in Paris and moved on to various positions in the courts and embassies of Europe. Along the way, he acquired knowledge about food in Poland, Turkey, Germany, England, and Austria. The pinnacle of his career was as scalco and chef to "Her Majesty Catherine II, empress of all of Russia." Unable to tolerate the cold weather, however, he returned to Rome and published his masterwork.

Despite his far-reaching experience, he is a strong defender of the potential of Italian gastronomy. He waxes poetic for several pages about the food of ancient Rome and the important role of the Roman cook, and true to his title, showers his praises upon the original *Apicius* as the foundation of Italian cookery. Leonardi attributes the rise of French culinary hegemony to the arrogance of his Italian contemporaries who do not want to study their craft, and who cannot be bothered to open a text and undertake the arduous study of cooking. Furthermore, they do not trouble themselves to go abroad to observe the practices in foreign kitchens. The final blow sealing the decline of Italian cooking was dealt when Catherine de' Medici married and relocated to France, where, as Leonardi would have it, she was followed not only by fine cuisine but also the sciences and many other professions. "This was the age of the fall of the culinary arts in Italy, when taste and refinement transferred to France, precisely when Italians had brought the pleasures of the table to the height of perfection, as can be seen in the number of Italian cookery treatises published in the fifteenth and sixteenth centuries."[45]

Although he praises his Italian predecessors, Leonardi moves away from the decisive flavors of the Renaissance, advocating for simple and natural preparations, "broth that is not too meaty; sauces without too much lard, prosciutto and butter; salt, pepper, spices, and all other condiments in small quantities."[46] As for drink: "Wine should be drunk in moderation, and at the end of the meal, a glass of something from Capo or Tokaj or Cyprus or the like," and in the morning: "some good mature fruit, a few cookies, some fruit compote or in syrup, gelato, a cup of not too bitter coffee, good bread and an excellent hot chocolate."[47]

The Modern Apicius is the first instance in which an Italian cookbook overtly acknowledges the existence of an ongoing Italian culinary tradition and encourages its rebirth. Leonardi leads by example, liberally using tomatoes and documenting their use as a condiment for pasta. Alongside the vast output of international and classic recipes, Leonardi posits various local and regional dishes from Italy. Thus he not only dignifies them, but foreshadows the political move toward unity that would sweep through the peninsula from the 1820s to1871, when Rome would become the capital of the newly formed Kingdom of Italy.

The Kingdom of Italy:
From Roman to Romanesco

Following Leonardi's lead, "modern" was the keyword of the nineteenth-century cookbook—cosmopolitan, but regardless, following the lead of French cuisine. This new generation of cookbooks was no longer addressed to cooks of the aristocracy but to the up-and-coming Third Estate market, the masses of *piccolo borghese* moving into the network of petty office jobs and professions proliferating in the neophyte nation. Thrift was paramount, but more important was keeping up with the Joneses. A flurry of cookbooks were published with recipes tailor made to advise those climbing the social ladder how to eat, behave, and entertain in accordance with their new station. The word "modern" was in nearly every title as the Risorgimento swept through the country, and as unification and the Kingdom of Italy became a reality, the focus of cookbook titles shifted to the royals.

The choice of Rome for the capital was not merely owing to its past glory. Indeed the capital had moved from Torino to Florence before ending up in the Eternal City. Heavy-handed assumption of political power in the spiritual capital of the country and former heart of the Roman Empire sent an unmistakable message to the population about the presence of the new order. The House of Savoy established residence at the Quirinal Palace with King Victor Emanuel I at the helm. In 1878, he died and was buried in the Pantheon, and his son, Humbert I, ascended the throne. Cookbook titles reflected the enthusiasm for the royal family: *The Queen of the Cooks*, multiple versions of *The King of the Cooks*, followed by clever titles like the *King of the King of the Cooks*, *The True King of the Cooks*, and *The Modern King of the Cooks*. All were trumped at the end of the century by *The Emperor of Cooks* (1894–1895), Rome's claim to the cookbook throne.

Originally published in the form of a weekly serial over fifty-seven weeks, each issue had eight pages and an illustrative lithograph. *The Emperor* was "compiled" by Count Vitaliano Bossi and his head chef, Ercole Salvo, a common authorship formula in the nineteenth century denoting status and credentials. The byline of the book is "Homestyle cooking and haute cuisine," again, appealing to a public whose aim is pretension, but whose pocketbook is light. "The author" (as the preamble is signed) addresses himself to "good housewives, ladies whose intent is to honor their guests, the cooks of private families and public Hotels." The book is not a single collaborative effort but one book divided among two authors. The Count begins with meticulously divided chapters, but three-quarters of the way through creates a catch-all chapter (22) called "Other Miscellaneous Recipes and Preparations Dealing with the Kitchen," a haphazard deposit of everything and anything else that came to mind as the serial continued.

The recipes are all in the French-International style with an occasional lean toward Italy. For example, the first recipe in the Soup section is a heavy northern-style risotto, called simply *risotto da grasso*—meaning risotto for "fat" or feast days. It is unctuously rich with butter, bone marrow, and an unspecified animal fat, tempered with wine and broth as the rice cooks. In keeping with the Lombard style, saffron is added, making this nearly a *risotto alla milanese*. Shavings of white truffles and a sprinkling of cheese finish the dish, a Piedmontese touch. First-course starch dishes, whether or not they were served in broth, were called "soup," as they had not yet acquired a distinct category of their own, the logic being that they had been prepared in a boiling liquid. This concept persisted until after World War II, when pasta, rice, and polenta asserted dominance over soup proper.

There are only three recipes for pasta in this section: *ravioletti di grasso*, *ravioletti di magro*, and *ravioletti di verdura*, respectively, meat, fish, and vegetable ravioli. In general in the nineteenth-century Italian cookery book, aimed at helping the up-and-coming middle classes adjust to their new status, there is a glaring lack of pasta recipes. Could it be that pasta was considered a task that did not require explanation? Or was it because, unless filled and/or used as filler for a timbale, pasta was not up to standard for the dining table? Recipe #71 sheds some light on what appears to be a general lack of enthusiasm for pasta:

> Even a mediocre cook knows how to make pasta, besides that there are pasta makers everywhere that one can turn to save time. One makes pasta at home when one wants to add some ingredients that the pasta makers do not use, like eggs, butter, etc., etc. In this case, the whole art lies in mixing and kneading it well, in rolling it out evenly and thinly, and in cutting it into the proper shapes. . . . In general any pasta that has to be boiled requires a lot of attention as it cooks. All it takes is a few minutes too many to make it mushy . . . whereas too little time will leave an unpleasant floury taste. On meat days chicken broth is excellent for cooking pasta. On lean days, it should be livened up with some sort of sauce or at least with browned butter and chives, and a few sage leaves.[48]

One dish of note is the monumental homage to frying promoted as being "the favorite dish of the Romans." *Fritto all'Italiana* is a composition of brain, sweetbreads, liver, lamb testicles, various types of croquettes, and *supplì*, rice croquettes that are a signature food of *romanesca* cooking. The vegetables are cauliflower, broccoli, artichokes, squash—all framed in a crown of *provatura* (mozzarella) cheese or prosciutto. "The Romans prefer to fry it in a pan of pure pork lard and serve it hot." The illustrative lithograph suggests mounting it onto a dome-shaped base support made of cold, solidified pasta and separating each food from the other with crouton barriers: a showcase piece to sink your teeth into.

While this dish specifies the Roman preference for frying in lard, the main cooking fat throughout this cookbook is butter, seconded by pork and other animal fats and only occasionally oil, though never specified as being olive. Even the tomato sauce is made with a butter and minced onion base.[49] Butter was the fat of upper-crust society; and its ubiquitous use here is exemplary of a cuisine that delineates itself by social class rather than region.

The second book is purportedly the home-cooking section, and while it does include some local Roman specialties—the *coratella*, peas *alla romana*—most of the recipes follow the fashion of sporting place names, mainly European countries and Italian and French cities, although the preparations themselves have been filtered through French inclinations. One oddity is beef filet—curiously—*alla indiana*—cooked whole on a skewer until rare, and served with an equally curious *salsa all'indiana* (butter, prosciutto, celery, scallions, thyme, parsley and the enigmatic "Lary powder").[50] Another surprising entry is recipe #409 entitled, simply, Cat. "Although we are not much in the habit of eating it, those who are not disgusted by its meat find it as pleasant as rabbit and ruthlessly hunt them out, especially in winter." Salvi recommends roasting them with plenty of fatback, garlic, and rosemary—and a splash of good red wine.[51]

Twenty-five years after Rome had been reinstated as the capital, the population exploded. There was a constant influx and outflow of dignitaries, and Rome, already dense with noble families, many of them interrelated several times over, squeezed in even more once the Savoys had taken up residency. *The Emperor* was exemplary of the sort of cookbook that reflected the expectations of the cosmopolitan mix of aristocrats and gentry now occupying the finer dining rooms of Rome. However, it would be the last cookery book title boasting claims to royalty. In 1898, with the approval of King Humbert I, General Bava-Becaris gave the call to open fire on a crowd of protesters in Milan, among whom were women, children, and the elderly, who had gathered in a piazza to rally for *pane e lavoro*, bread and jobs. After killing over one hundred unarmed protesters, the general was given a medal of honor for his handiwork. Further celebratory associations of food with the royal family would only have inflamed public sensibilities.

Feeding the Multitude

The sudden rise in population took a toll on the Urbs and particularly on the lower classes. *How the People of Rome Live*, by Domenico Orano (1912), is one of the rare texts that sheds light on the living conditions and eating habits of inner-city dwellers, who did not use cookbooks or frequent restaurants. It was intended as an in-depth report on the demographics of Testaccio, the poor quarter in the heart of Rome, but the enormous tome reads like a heart-wrenching manifesto pleading for social reform through the very facts and figures that it unearths.

Regarding housing, he reports that a standard home was one room and a kitchen. The renter slept in the kitchen so that he could sublet the room to another tenant. Pensione housing packed up to ten beds or pallets in a room, where the exhausted and oftentimes drunk laborer laid his body down at sundown and rose at dawn for another day of toil. These shelters housed the seasonal farmhands as well, and in comparison to sleeping outside in the fields exposed to mosquitoes and the elements, the pallet, even when shared with a coworker for economy's sake, was a godsend. "Looking for a home is like begging for alms. When you get one, it feels like someone has done you a great favor."[52]

The kitchen, generally a two-by-three-meter space, "which should be the cleanest room in the house becomes a sort of garbage dump, full of bedding and other objects; it is used as a bedroom, kitchen, and eating area wherein there is no possibility to clean. The sink harbors an infinite number of insects and rodents that traipse in and out freely though the drain, because of which bread is wrapped in filthy bedclothes."[53] Communal meals were served on one huge plate, and like a trough, it was placed in the middle of the room where famished diners swooped down on it. Forks were few, so some went without or they shared. Hunger was such that no one commented on the taste of the food.[54] Men would often repair to the osteria to escape the deplorable conditions at home. The wife would bring her husband's food down, and if the osteria had a working kitchen they would prepare it; otherwise she simply brought him his dinner while he got his fill of wine.

For working-class families, the standard breakfast was coffee or a surrogate, milk and bread. In autumn, there were also chestnuts, a good source of calories, and in winter ricotta. Less frequent additions were *salumi*, cheese, and fruit. The midday meal was the main meal of the day. For the 1,340 families Orano interviewed, watery meat broth was a daily standard. On Sunday, the predominant dish was dried pasta (spaghetti or short pasta) with meat sauce. The most common everyday pasta dish was dressed with *lardo* (cured fatback) mince, herbs, onion, and tomato paste, sometimes with the addition of potatoes or cabbage or more rarely beans. Otherwise, the pasta was eaten with "fake sauce"—just tomato paste and lardo mince. Again, writing in 1912, he notes: "The working class consumed large quantities of pork fat, although it does not assimilate as easily as butter. Even the ancients were mad about it. I don't know if the soup and pasta with lardo that is so often eaten among the people of Testaccio is as succulent and healthy as the one that Horace ate, inspiring him to exclaim: 'O when will Pythagoras's beloved beans and greens with lard be put before me?'"[55] The less fortunate among the indigent were dependent mostly on legumes loaded with onion and garlic.[56] Between 1906 and 1911, the price of the few vegetables that the lower classes could afford—broccoli, cabbage, potatoes, turnips—doubled, making them a less attractive option.[57] On the rare occasions that meat was eaten, the four most common dishes were boiled ham hocks dressed with oil and vinegar; lamb sautéed or roasted; pork roasted, stewed, or chops with a legume side dish; or pig's blood fried in a skillet with lard and a side dish of onions. Of the families who imbibed on Sundays, 481 said they drank at home, while 840 went to the osteria. No considerations were made for growing children who, our author asserts, should be getting more milk, eggs, meat, butter and legumes. "Wine is the true food of the people. . . . The three dairy outlets in Testaccio together sell 475–500 liters per day. . . . [By comparison,] at the 38 osterias and trattorias wine consumption is on average 11–12,000 liters per day."[58]

Long after unification, the nation called Italy remained little more than a geographic expression, whose common bonds were religion and hunger. World War I, referred to in Italy as '15–'18, was the first time that men from diverse regions would leave their hometowns en masse and come together for a common, national cause. Many were lured in by promises of jobs upon their return but found themselves empty-handed and angry. The recently won universal male suffrage gave them a voice, and they were determined to use it. Riotous unrest, rampant hunger, and general misrule made Mussolini and his fascist party seem like a ray of hope that would bring about order and much needed change. In 1924, he took up residence in the capital, becoming de facto dictator, and envisioned a new era of glory for Italy—The New Roman Empire. An unprecedented wave of nationalism swept through Italy, part of which included a decisive turn away from French influence and an exaltation of all things Italian. The consensus of women was necessary if he was to carry out his ambitious plans, and they responded with alacrity.

To that end, fascist proponent and native Roman Ada Boni compiled a massive tome, *The Talisman of Happiness* (1926), which would see multiple reprints and editions. It was aimed at the middle-class housewife, very much in line with the new home economics movement, which brought women to the forefront in a sector where they encountered little competition or resistance from men. *Talisman* was more than a cookbook. It used the genre as a means to unite women in the celebration and creation of a national cuisine, Italian cuisine, in line with the dictates of the fascist party. In her introductory "Praise for Italian Cuisine," she speaks of her nation's food as being a patrimony that is barely taken into consideration by us, and utterly unknown by foreigners. . . . Much has been done, but much remains yet to do to complete the emancipation of our cuisine from the track we are stuck on behind French cuisine. . . . But all of this will come about spontaneously and resolve itself when we renounce following the technical methods of others and we double up on our mission to spread only our own fine cuisine, whose dishes have their own names, consecrated by tradition and use.[59]

She herself was a personal friend of Escoffier, but true to her mission, the recipes in *Talisman* are distinctly part and parcel of the modern Italian table, and do not read, linguistically or gastronomically, like mere French translations.

However, it is her book *La cucina romana* (1929) that finally recognizes and pays homage to regional Roman cuisine, *la cucina romanesca*, an act of love dedicated to her native city. After Rome had become the capital, the political life and cosmopolitan atmosphere left the old Roman families in the minority and traditions began to disappear. Boni was from a well-to-do family, by no means part of the urban working class, or even the lower-middle class. But she recognized that the heritage of old Roman culinary traditions was fading fast; indeed she felt that the honest yet modest food of the osteria, the cradle of popular Roman gastronomy, had all but vanished. "Few regional cuisines can rival Roman cuisine for taste, variety, health, and nutrition. Many speak of it, but very few really know it."[60] She rigorously selected recipes that faithfully represent the canon of Roman regional cuisine as well as "saving" recipes that were falling or had fallen into obscurity. From the very start, she begins by singing the praises of pork fat: lardo, *guanciale* (cheek), belly, and prosciutto fat. Oil is reserved for dressing raw vegetables and for frying fish. Her style is conversational; there are no lists of ingredients, rarely does she dictate precise quantities, and options are often left for the cook to decide. Many of the recipes are prefaced with lore about Rome and laced with snippets of poems and local sayings as well as prints of commoners and food.[61]

One of the recipes that has faded from the standard repertoire in Rome is hops soup. Wild bitter greens like these hops are highly perishable, and, although they are a fundamental part of the *cucina romanesca*, they have been overshadowed by vegetables that are more durable and accessible to the modern palate. "Hops, which are in some way distantly related to asparagus, are called *lùpari* in Rome and sold by wandering merchants, who hawk their wares with the characteristic sing-song "*lùpari, lùpari . . .*" Like many of the recipes, this one truly originates from the poor kitchen or *cucina povera*, another overly promoted and highly misunderstood sector of Italian gastronomy. The hops fronds are sautéed with garlic and a few bits of prosciutto, and once they have softened, "enough" water is added to make a broth—"enough" generally meaning in accordance with how many mouths there are to feed. The broth is then poured into a soup tureen over toasted bread or can be enriched with an egg or two off heat. Other former favorites have also become obsolete, like pan-fried larks, once much awaited in October, and the quick, money-saving pan-fried chicken blood. In Rome, fowl mongers collected chicken blood in an open tin, solidified it, and sold the coagulated disks of blood. At home, these were carefully sliced with thread into thin strips and fried in lard with minced onion. Dress with a squeeze of lemon and a pinch of fresh parsley and serve.

Her section on fried foods is completely dedicated to *Fritto alla Romana*, which *The Emperor*, interestingly enough, preferred to call *all'Italiana*. She explains that it is in essence a refined dish, a veritable buffet of fried foods. In its adoption into popular cuisine the number, quality, and type of food was pared down and altered in accordance with the venue and the public. While the *Fritto* often ends up a question of battering up whatever is affordable and on hand, there is a precise list of classic ingredients whose preparation for the *frittura* she lovingly details item by item.

Boni includes "classics" that had hitherto been ignored by her predecessors: *Spaghetti alla "matriciana," spaghetti alla "marchiciana"* (better known now as *la gricia*), *cacio e pepe, abbacchio* prepared in various ways, the *coratella, pagliata, coda all'vaccinara* and an extensive list of recipes for offal.[62] Notably missing are the highly mythologized *carbonara* and *fettucini Alfredo*.[63]

One dish with a longer history is the *coppiette*, or *polpette*, Roman meatballs.[64] A recipe appears in Martino called *coppiette*, although his are chunks of meat that are skewered and cooked directly on the fire. The same recipe is copied by Platina, personalized by Romoli, spiffed up by Scappi, but regardless, left as pieces of beef. Antonio Latini, a contemporary of Scappi who operated mainly in Naples, included many recipes in his book on stewarding with the tag *alla Romana*. He approaches the modern version of this classic of the cucina romanesca by using ground beef that is mixed with soaked bread, candied citron, lardo, grated cheese, bone morrow, garlic, pine nuts, herbs and spices. However, it is cooked in broth and served accompanied by marinated veal chops and small stewed headless birds.

Although meatballs by their nature resist codification, Boni's recipe is considered a go-to for authenticity:

Coppiette:
Meatballs have a wide application in everyday cooking and can be made either with raw meat, or more economically with boiled meat.

The first way is undoubtedly better. Put some lean beef on a cutting board (600–700 grams, enough for 6 people), add a good chunk of lardo or prosciutto fat (or both together), one garlic clove, a bunch of parsley, a pinch of marjoram, and mince it all as finely as possible. . . . Gather up the minced meat in a terrine and add salt, pepper, nutmeg, and a piece of bread (the size of an apple) that has been soaking in cold water and they squeezed dry. To get a good homogenous paste, it should be pounded in a mortar, but generally one is content to just mix it by hand. Once it is well mixed, add a couple of whole eggs, a couple spoonfuls of grated parmesan, a handful of raisins and a handful of pine nuts. Mix well and form into balls about the size of an apple, but pressed down a bit. Some people flour the balls, but the real Roman way is to coat them in breadcrumbs. After breading, put them in a pan with plenty of lard and fry them until well browned. In the meantime, make a tomato sauce or "fake sauce" (tomato and lardo). Put the meatballs in the sauce in a single layer and let them simmer for a few minutes so they are flavored with the sauce. They could also be eaten without sauce, but the real Roman recipe calls for sauce. As said before, this can also be done with boiled meat to save money, but the result is notably inferior.[65]

The magazine *La Cucina Italiana* began in Milan in 1929 as a monthly periodical. By design, it was cutting edge, promoting gastronomic culture and geared toward a readership of a certain sophistication. In 1932, it was sold to a Roman newspaper and transferred there. With the move to Rome the magazine steadily underwent changes. The content, aimed at the average middle-class housewife, was increasingly political, instructing women on what to shop for and how to prepare foods that were in keeping with the fascist party line, in particular rice, rabbit, chicken, fish, grapes; how to substitute foods for the dwindling variety in an ever more insular country. After 1938 when Mussolini had allied with Hitler, it became an out-and-out culinary propaganda magazine. The cover of the December 1939 issue, for example, is an illustration of a nicely dressed woman smiling as she holds up a white rabbit by the ears; the caption reads, "In the dietary realm, the rabbit is the autarkic animal *per eccellenza*." In order to conserve as much field space as possible for wheat, women were encouraged to raise rabbits and chickens and keep a small vegetable garden. Articles included, "Women in Mussolini's Time," with a photo of young women marching in military uniforms and rifles; a diatribe informing Italians that coffee is not a fascist beverage and that it should be eliminated; another warning women not to work, painting a hair-raising portrait of lonely suffering children; the joy of drinking in moderation; autarkic paps for children; sitting down properly so that your slip doesn't show; and "Citrus," which scoffs at the curious American and English enjoyment of the tasteless grapefruit, a fruit that would not take hold on the Italian market until the 1960s. The subscriber recipe section includes a contribution called "American-style tomatoes." Make a mince of celery, onion, parsley, basil, and tarragon, put in on tomato wedges and chill. Remove the mince and serve with mayonnaise. Tomatoes, being from the deadly nightshade family, took a long time to catch on, even in their cooked form; eating them raw would not become commonplace until after World War II.

Epilogue

With the fall of fascism in 1943, *La Cucina Italiana* folded. The movement toward culinary nationalism faded into the nebulous disorientation of aftermath of war. With reconstruction, appreciation of one's own region and community slowly came to the fore. After five years of travel and research, Anna Gosetti della Salda, who had revived *La Cucina Italiana* in 1952, published *Le ricette regionali italiane* (1967), a first-of-its-kind explicit exploration of the regional cooking of the entire nation expressed in over two thousand recipes. Little by little, regional gastronomic pride asserted itself and other volumes would come out celebrating the cuisine of individual regions. Most recently, it is foreigners who have made Rome their home who have become the messengers of Roman food and foodways, unveiling this little-known cuisine to an appreciative audience abroad. Notable among them are Rachel Roddy, author of the award winning *My Kitchen in Rome: Recipes and Notes on Italian Cooking*, and Katie Parla and Kristina Gill's *Tasting Rome: Fresh Flavors and Forgotten Recipes from an Ancient City*.

CHAPTER FOUR

Mobility

The Ins and Outs

Romani de fôra—Romans from Outside

Rome's ancient sewer system, the Cloaca Maxima, was the city's first major feat of urban engineering. The fact that construction began in the sixth century BCE speaks to the foresight the Romans had in laying the groundwork, or rather the underground work, for sustaining the future incoming throngs. And throng they did. From the time of its legendary inception, Rome has exemplified, arguably more than any city on earth, a social landscape characterized by migration and mobility, compelling us to rethink what is meant by the terms *local* and *global*. The forces fueling mobility derive from any number of motives from employment to art, from tourism to religion, from gastronomy to politics, and so on, perpetually testing the permeability of tolerance and modifying what it means to be Roman. The constant ebb and flow across the fluctuating borders guarantees, now as it has throughout history, endless combinations and novel reformulations of products and ideas, blending the local and the foreign, as well as their dissemination far beyond the confines of Rome's immediate sphere.

The influence of mobility on the culinary evolution of Rome is not limited to points of departure and arrival or lists of imports and exports. The intermingling of human agency as seen through the culinary lens must take into account the fluidity of passage in time and space as well as perceptions leading to refusal, disgust, appreciation, curiosity, and wariness, all of which impact the broader more generous definition of Roman gastronomy.

The area that would become Latium began with nomadic pastoralists, even before the arrival of the Latins. In the long term, the territory did not offer the wide-open spaces conducive to nomadism, but for stock raiser–agriculturalists it held untold promise.[1] Aeneas, part of the foundation legacy, came from foreign shores, and Romulus, or his more historical equivalents, could not have fortified Rome without a significant following of disparate peoples. Over the centuries, the urban fabric developed through myriad forms of mobility—the contributions of fortune seekers, traders, imported slaves, learned professionals, artisans, teachers, soldiers, aristocrats, priests, politicians, and colonists, none of whom operated in a culinary vacuum. Each contributed in some way, materially or ideologically, to the foodways that Rome offered in any given moment. Satisfying both the basic alimentary and the more discriminating gastronomic demands of the city had always required reaching much farther beyond the city limits than was necessary for the survival of other cities. The prevalence of importation was not merely owing to the limits of local supply, but because Rome was conceptually cosmopolitan and culturally voracious, traits that bode well for its prosperity. Fascination with the foreign often overrode the impulse toward tradition, but the moral dilemma therein was resolved by creating traditions out of novelty. The change was sufficiently slow that the assimilation of new foods and new perspectives, by the late Republican and early Imperial Age, gave the general appearance of timelessness, and a comforting illusion of continuity with the past.

La Santa Sede—Pilgrimage to the Holy See

If in ancient times mobility manifested through the travels of armies, traders, and others, a new phenomenon of travel to and from Rome emerged in the early medieval period, in the form of Christian pilgrimage. Rome was not the first or the only center where pilgrims went to pray and perform acts of piety in hope of healing or forgiveness, but the inaccessibility of Jerusalem for many centuries as well as the relics brought back from the Holy Land, added to Rome's own claims, centered on the martyr-shrines of Peter and Paul. Some pilgrims traced a web of routes across Europe, visiting Santiago de Compostella in Spain (from the ninth century on) or Canterbury in England (from the twelfth) before becoming *Romei*, pilgrims to Rome.

The extensive Roman road systems did not discriminate in the traffic they facilitated. Individuals and collectives traveled to the Eternal City under many guises and conditions, but all would at some point along the journey find themselves in need of nourishment. Thus, while the *Romei*, pilgrims en route to Rome, may have been seeking to fill an emptiness in their soul, the profane needs of the stomach could not be brushed off if they were to sustain the arduousness of their hallowed mission. The pilgrimage to the Holy City exemplifies a fluidity of exchange that was unique to Rome because of the volume of travelers, the diversity—men and women from all social strata and nationalities—and the brevity and purpose of their stay, most intending to leave soon after having satisfied their moral imperative. The pious Christian pilgrim may have aspired to sustain him/herself with bread, the symbolic food representing the body of the Lord, and water, the symbol of purity, but on a long trip such as that undertaken from Canterbury to Rome, bread and water alone would not suffice. Whereas prelates of a certain standing traveled by mule or horse, clerics, monks, servants, guards, and the faithful hordes were often on foot. Compounded with unpredictable weather conditions, health issues, and potential injuries, the four-month trip constituted a considerable burden of fatigue. As such, knowing where one could find succor was essential.

The first itinerary (990 CE) ever described along the Via Francigena was by Sigeric the Serious, Archbishop of Canterbury, who had gone to Rome to receive his pallium.[2] He indicates seventy-nine rest stops where the weary wayfarer could find basic creature comforts: a place to bed down under a roof, recover one's health, and eat. At the convents that received them there was no danger of falling into the clutches of gluttony, for in addition to the ubiquitous bread and water, the standard board may have included legumes, particularly peas and fava beans, a seasonal vegetable, and perhaps fruit. On fasting days, their meager fare was reduced to one meal a day while the march continued.

Pilgrims traversing along the Via Salaria from Picenum on the Adriatic coast might have encountered richer resources, though much depended on chance. On the coast, anchovies, squill fish, cuttlefish, and sardines could be obtained cheaply. Moving toward the hills, one might get lucky and find a peasant willing to serve up a country chicken. Further along toward the pastures were cheese, *salumi*, and an abundance of olives. If one were really fortunate, a townsperson might offer a bowl of hot soup and perchance even a convivial cup of wine. Information about the hospitable hotspots on the way to the Holy City was passed on from pilgrim to pilgrim, encouraging the accommodation business to develop.[3] Jubilee years saw a boom in taverns, inns, and refreshment stops of all sorts that would generally die a natural death with the end of the religious trade. In Sutri, the obligatory final stop before entering Rome, locals made quite a living from the travelers. They became renowned in particular as cobblers, given the need to repair and replace the well-worn shoes of the pilgrims with something more respectable for the blessed event and more comfortable for their weary feet.

In the sixth century, from his monastery in Monte Cassino, southeast of Rome, Saint Benedict wrote his *Regula monachorum*, chapter 53 of which dictates the rules of hospitality for pilgrims, travelers, or the indigent seeking respite in the monastery. Although they are to be well taken care of, guests must adhere to the diet of the monks, a diet conceived to restore serenity to the soul while supplying sufficient energy for intellectual and manual pursuits. The main meal included two cooked dishes (in case one of the dishes was not to a brother's liking) with additional fruit and vegetables if available. The Benedictine diet at Monte Cassino in the Early Middle Ages reflected the standard diet of local peasants. The daily bread allotment was one pound per day and was generally a mix of barley, millet, wheat, and legume flours. Soups were various combinations of vegetables, cereals, and legumes, or gruels that ranged from liquidy to the more compact *puls*. Meat from four-legged animals was not allowed, unless one was ill, but parsimonious amounts of fowl and fish were. Fish was cooked simply over hot coals or boiled. And to finish, fruit, cheese, or eggs. The meal was accompanied by a modest one-quarter liter of wine, with the understanding that those who abstained would be looked upon favorably. If the heat of summer and labor in the fields was such that individuals required more, that would be allowed so long as it did not result in disorderly conduct. Attempts to convince the monks that wine was unsuited to the monastic lifestyle met with protests, and so the kindly Benedict yielded to the will of his brethren. Pilgrims will have been grateful for the same indulgence.

Other pilgrims traveled under less humble conditions: well stocked, on horseback, and with one eye on the medieval wine itinerary. The German bishop and wine enthusiast Johannes Defuk sent his manservant ahead of him during his 1111 pilgrimage to signal the establishments with the best wines by writing *est* on the door, their code for *vinum est bonum*. When his attendant happened upon the exceptional wine of Montefiascone, in the area surrounding lake Bolsena, just north of Rome, he purportedly wrote *Est! Est! Est!*, which later became the name of this DOC wine.

The town of Bolsena is renowned for the miracle of the Eucharist of 1263. Another German priest on his way to Rome to atone for his sins stopped to perform mass, and just as he broke the bread, it began to drip blood, forming the face of Jesus then and there on the altar linen. Scientific experiments carried out in 1994 showed that *serratia marcenscens*, a bacterium that feeds on starch, produced the same effect and may account for the appearance of dripping blood.[4]

Pope Martin IV, though generally not known for extravagance, was also partial to the wine of that area and had a weakness for the Lake Bolsena eel (now on the official list of traditional local foods). According to a chronicler of the day, Friar Pipino, His Holiness kept a bevy of eels in his room in tubs of milk, upon which they fed. Prior to roasting, they were submerged in a tub of wine until they drowned. On March 28, 1285, Martin overindulged in both eels and wine exclaiming "*O Sancte Deus, quanta mala patimur pro Ecclesia Dei!*" "Holy God, how we have suffered for the Church of God!" and breathed his last. His demise is immortalized in the epithet "*Gaudeant anguillae quod mortuus hic iacet ille qui quasi more reas excoriabat eas.*" (Let the eels rejoice that this one lies dead, who tortured them as though capital offenders.)[5]

Religious traffic in Rome accelerated with the incentive of indulgences, formal remissions of sin granted to pilgrims among others. In 1300, Pope Boniface VIII inducted the very first jubilee, or holy year during which Rome hosted a daily average of two hundred thousand pilgrims. The city was hopelessly ill equipped to accommodate such numbers. Many were left to camp out wherever they could, building fires to keep warm. Not long thereafter linguistic groups of pilgrims began to arrange for their needs on their own. In 1350, the Spanish set up quarters in Santa Maria di Monserrato; Germanic speakers founded the hostel Santa Maria dell'Anima consecrated by the pope in 1399; resident Flemish established a confraternity for compatriot Belgians near the Sant'Angelo Bridge. Poles, Swedes, English, Portuguese, Slavs, Armenians, and Ethiopians all offered free room and board for short stays.

The Romans followed suit, setting up confraternities to provide assistance and comfort to the pilgrims during their sojourn. The most important of these would be the Santissima Trinità dei Pellegrini, the Most Holy Trinity of the Pilgrims Confraternity. Such was their dedication that entire buildings were donated for their use as hostels. Founded in 1548, Pope Pius IV raised their status to Archconfraternity in 1560, which further influenced the noble families of Rome and generous guests to donate goods, mostly in the form of food and wine. Contrary to the fare at the convents and monasteries, the meals at the Santissima Trinità were healthy and hearty. After a ritual foot washing, guests sat down to a meal consisting of a large salad, a decent portion of cold beef or lamb (tuna or herring on fasting days), soup (generally rice, farro, or vermicelli—legumes on fast days), a glass of wine, and bread.[6] Clerics were given an extra plate of figs and nuts. The women's table was set with napkins, whereas the men's was not. Wealthy families used the hostel as a forum to publicly display their largess by sponsoring one-off dinners wherein the resident pilgrims were treated to double portions.

Incoming pilgrims who were members of analogous Italian confraternities situated elsewhere in Italy found themselves in another situation altogether. For example, in 1650, when the Confraternità di San Giovanni Decollate received the Compagna di San Benedetto of Florence, the group was honored with a candlelit dinner with silver and gold candelabras: "myriad mixed salads lettuces, lemons served with gallantries like pine nuts, capers, olives . . . plates of Bolognese mortadella, plates of sweetbreads and testicles for the antipasto." The next course was boiled veal, roasted veal, various soups, savory and sweet pastries, apples, pears, ices, and *provatura* with red and white wine. Three nights later, a fasting day, the company were served

> beautiful salads with candied fruit, tuna belly decorated with fragrant greens, plates of sugared strawberries, white asparagus soup with truffles, peas and mushrooms, plates of dressed, poached sturgeon, fried mackerel with pastries, large grilled mullet in sauce, mullet in broth with dressing, roasted sturgeon with *salsa reale*, sturgeon pastries with candied fruit, sour cherry and other sorts of pies, plates of white asparagus with pine nuts, capers adorned with borage flowers, fried artichokes with preserved lemons, sweet cherries, pink apples, peas and pea pods, green and dark fennel, and then plates of candied citron, and lots of white confectionaries, different sorts of white and red wine, and also several ices.[7]

In the *San Giovanni* culinary archive from that same jubilee year there is also evidence of traditional Roman dishes like the coratella, a stew made with sheep offal, soup with greens and egg, roast quail, kid and lamb fricassee, fried sweetbreads, provatura and *marzolino* cheese, roast pigeon, macaroni with oil, *tagliolini* soup, *misticanza* salad, marinated veal shanks, and a dish that has fallen from vogue called *moscimmano*. This was a cured fish product made with tuna that had been pressed, smoked, and blackened on the out-side with squid ink. After scraping the outside, it was immersed in wine to soften. Then it was sliced thin, drizzled with olive oil and lemon juice and eaten raw.[8]

In 1650, an estimated seven hundred thousand pilgrims passed through, all of them needing to be fed and sheltered. It was an open invitation for merchants to profit as they might. The Papal State had to issue a decree fixing prices to prevent pilgrims from being taken advantage of during their stay. After all, there were indulgences to be paid, and fleecing them would have been bad for business. Wine was to be measured in officially sized decanters, unadulterated and undiluted; bakers, butchers, and salumi shops were to keep their establishments well stocked and not charge beyond the imposed tariff. The punishment for offenders was severe: a public flogging (three whacks) and twenty-five *scudi*. Unhygienic quarters and trafficking food that had gone off had become rampant, so anyone renting accommodations or providing meals had to obtain a license from the Hotel and Hosting Guild. A potentially ruinous murder mystery may have influenced the need to tighten governmental controls: in the piazza of the Pantheon, known as Piazza Rotonda, two *norcini*,[9] a husband and wife, became both celebrated and prosperous for their exquisite sausages. All over Rome people raved about them. It turned out, however, that the secret ingredient was human flesh. Ingenuous victims were lured into their shop where the couple carried out the deed à la *Sweeney Todd*. As suspicions arose, a trap was set. The couple were executed on February 3, 1638.[10]

Rites of Passage: The Grand Tour

If pilgrimage suffered somewhat as the Reformation took hold in much of northern Europe, a new thread appeared in the intricate weave of the Roman mobility network, namely, the Grand Tour. In the mid-seventeenth century it became the custom of the upper classes to send their sons abroad around the age of twenty-one. While generally associated with the English aristocracy, families from all over Europe sent their sons away to round out their upbringing. It was intended neither as a religious pilgrimage nor merely as a period of study abroad, but a horizon-expanding cultural experience and a sign of good breeding. The apex of the Italian leg was, of course, the Eternal City. In 1660, Richard Lassels wrote a lengthy preface in his travel book about Italy to encourage the practice, offering this poetic reasoning: "Traveling makes us acquainted with a world of our kindred we never saw before. For, seeing we are all come from one man at first, and consequently all akin to one another, it's but a reasonable thing, that a man should once at least in his lifetime, make a journey into foreign countries, to see his *Relations*, and visit this *kindred*, having always this saying of young Joseph in his mouth, *quaero fratres meos*"[11] (I seek my brothers). Indeed, it was Lassels himself who coined the term Grand Tour.

Having been received into a fine home (unlike many of the soul-seeking pilgrims, the tourists were by no means indigent) on his own journey, Lassels takes note of the Italian customs at table and in particular marvels at the *trinciante*:

> At great feasts, no man cuts for himself, but several *Carvers* cut up all the meat at a side table, and give it to the waiters, to be carry-ed to the Guests; and every one hath the very same part of meat carried unto him, to wit, a *wing*

and a *legg*, of wild fowl, &c. lest anyone take exceptions that the others were better fed then he. The Carvers never touch the meat with their hands, but only with their knife and fork, and a great silver spoon for the sauce. Every man here eats with his fork and knife, and never toucheth anything with his fingers, but his bread.[12]

For many, the trip abroad had the desired effect, stirring introspection and stimulating personal growth. One of the more poignant accounts is from young William Beckford, writing in 1780. Upon his return from the Coliseum, he lurks in the shadows and is moved by the scene before him:

Returning leisurely home, I traversed the Campo Vaccino, and leaned a moment against one of the columns which supported the temple of Jupiter Stator. Some women were fetching water from the fountain hard by, whilst another group had kindled a fire under the shrubs and twisted fig-trees, which cover the Palatine Hill. Innumerable vaults and arches peep out of the vegetation. It was upon these, in all probability, the splendid palace of the Caesars was raised. Confused fragments of marble, and walls of lofty terraces, are the sole traces of its ancient magnificence. A wretched rabble were roasting their chestnuts, on the very spot, perhaps, where Domitian convened a senate, to harangue upon the delicacies of his entertainment. The light of the flame cast upon the figures around it, and the mixture of tottering wall with foliage impending above their heads, formed a striking picture, which I stayed contemplating from my pillar, till the fire went out, the assembly dispersed, and none remained but a withered hag, raking the embers, and muttering to herself.[13]

Other traveler's reports were less eloquent. The high expectations of the English for the Rome they had studied in books, a lack of familiarity with the language, and what were often truly deplorable travel conditions may have weighed heavily on the criticism tourists had of their stay in the Eternal City. The routes to Rome were well traveled, but even for ready money, accommodation was reportedly wretched, and the food decidedly not to their taste. Along his travels between Rome and Naples, Scotsman Gilbert Burnet, Bishop of Salisbury, reports: "The wine is intolerable, the bread ill-baked, no victuals, except pigeons, and the oil is rotten. In short except one carries his provision from Rome or Naples, he must resolve to endure a good deal of misery."[14] His countryman Tobias Smollett, writing eighty years later, had much the same impression: "The houses are abominably nasty, and generally destitute of provision; when eatables were found we were almost poisoned by their cookery."[15] The British were unpleasantly surprised at the lack of roast beef and mutton and the abundance of salads and pasta. Their disgruntled air

Figure 4.1. A view of the Forum Romanum as Campo Vaccino, or the Cow Field, c. 1775. Etching

is said to have contributed significantly to the increase in butter production in Rome. Indeed, to keep up with demand, it was imported from Lombardy. Potatoes were another item that was sorely missed, as they had not yet become common Italian fare.

Grand Tourists, who had done their cultural duty, were admired as elite men of distinction. But by the late 1770s, that image was tarnishing. Despite their money and advantages, they often lacked the sensitivity and intellectual prowess with which to appreciate the sights and sensations around them, trudging from one obligatory cultural high point to another driven by a sense of moral duty rather than interest. Snap judgments were made, and the time gaps between cultural stimuli were filled with idleness and card playing. A satirical character emerged based on the young men who returned from Rome, called "macaroni," after the pasta they had brought back from their travels. It was a derogatory term for the ever-increasing group of fops donning, "fine sprigged fabric, tight clothes, oversized swords, tasseled walking sticks, delicate shoes, and, most recognizably, an enormous wig,"[16] on top of which perched a tiny, ever-so-fashionable hat. It was a fashion that

To dreſs Macaroni *with* Permaſent Cheeſe.

Boil four Ounces of Macaroni 'till it be quite tender, and lay it on a Sieve to drain, then put it in a Toſſing Pan, with about a Gill of good Cream, a Lump of Butter rolled in Flour, boil it five Minutes, pour it on a Plate, lay all over it Permaſent Cheeſe toaſted; ſend it to the Table on a Water Plate, for it ſoon goes cold.

Figure 4.2. Pasta recipe by Elizabeth Raffald from *The Experienced English House-Keeper* (1769)

the middle classes were eager to imitate as an identification marker of one who had been to Rome. But in the clumsy hands of the uninitiated, the new fashion became an object of grotesque parody. The familiar song "Yankee Doodle Dandy," whose punch line is "stuck a feather in his hat and called it macaroni" speaks of this social phenomenon of superficiality, but "The Macaroni; A New Song," a 1772 hit, may have said it best: "His taper waist, so strait and long, / His spindle shanks, like pitchfork prong, / To what sex does the thing belong? / 'Tis call'd a Macaroni."[17]

Macaroni in the more familiar form, as a culinary curiosity, traveled back to England with tourists and was revived in cookery books. "Revived" because the recipe that appears in *The Experienced English House-Keeper* in 1769[18] is nearly identical to the 1390 recipe for "Makerouns" in *Forme of Cury*, the latter predating even Maestro Martino.

Movement and the Middle Class

The French Revolution and Napoleonic Wars brought European travel to a near halt until the mid-nineteenth century. Once conditions permitted, wanderlust reasserted itself. At this point, travel had become more comfortable and reliable, and the growing bourgeoisie took an interest in what for the fortunate few would be a once-in-a-lifetime getaway, assisted by agencies in tune with their financial limitations. Thomas Cook & Son was the first to set up budget group tours to Rome, in 1864. A Baptist minister and temperance advocate, Cook had established his business on the belief that cultural enrichment would distract men from drink. Travel books catering to those with more disposable income, and not seeking moral reform, also emerged, such as *Murray's Hand-Book: Rome & Its Environs* (1858), part of a series of rigorously prepared travel guidebooks. These are prescriptive in travel advice and tend somewhat to chauvinism. Most English tourists stayed in private lodgings, particularly around the Piazza di Spagna, referred to since the Grand Tour as the "English Ghetto."[19] Meals were delivered by trattorias, which charged at a fixed rate per person. The food arrived hot, even if it had to travel a considerable distance because the porters used wire baskets fitted with a brazier underneath. Bachelors were advised to eat at restaurants with a *table d'hôte* or fixed menu, although, as our guide tells us, a decent restaurant in Rome was a "desideratum." He does concede by the 1864 edition that restaurant quality was making strides in the right direction. Hotels serving French cuisine were the most highly recommended, but on the list of acceptable local restaurants he does include, last but not least, a celebrated restaurant called Ristoratore del Falcone situated behind the Pantheon, which specialized in Roman cuisine.

Murray's told those who had cooking facilities that butchers, bakers, *pizzicaruoli* (who dealt in cured meats and fish, butter, eggs, and oil), being a privileged class above other food vendors, did not sell their wares in centralized markets. Their shops were located all over the city, but more concentrated here than there, depending on the clientele. The main market for game and fowl was at the Pantheon and offered a wide variety: "Every flying creature being eaten by the Romans, may be seen here, from an eagle to a tom-tit. The principal species, which vary with the season, are tame and wild pigeons, partridges, woodcocks, and three or four species of snipe, waterfowl, thrushes, quails, and an immense variety of small birds. . . . Of the larger game, wild boar, roebuck, hares, rabbits, and porcupines, and at certain seasons land tortoises, which are considered as game."[20] For fish, he recommends La Pescheria in the Jewish quarter, of particular interest to the naturalist, given the wide variety of species. The best of the local catch is the sea bass, grey mullet, cod, and sole, but he steers marketers away from the "inferior" cuttlefish and calamari.

At *Murray's* writing in 1864, white bread was still sold at a price fixed by the Papal State. Brown bread, what our guide calls "fancy bread," had no tariff controls and sold at twice the price. Could that be because only the foreigners were interested in it? Satirist Louis Delatre said the Romans laughed at the hordes of Englishmen and women who buzzed about the streets of the city with a copy of *Murray's* tucked under their arm, calling them the "people of the red book," as essential an accessory as hat, gloves, and boots; it was, he said, their advisor, their teacher, their custodian angel. They loved everything Murray loved and hated everything he abhorred. Wheresoever they found themselves, they would flip through the pages of their red book to see what they were supposed to think.[21]

Such was the glut of tourism that the visiting aristocratic classes found themselves in all too close proximity with their countrymen of lower status, conceptually tarnishing the luster of the Grand Tour. The late nineteenth century saw a rise in economy class tourists, who Delatre says came not for the art, culture or history but because "Italy is cheap," seeking their lodgings in dingy rooms at the end of wretched alleyways. "For this sort of tourist, Michelangelo and Raphael would have been great men had they invented some sort of cheap broth, but they made statues and paintings!"[22] In order to find respite from their inferiors, the wealthy were forced to seek out other more exclusive enclaves. Indeed, their sense of superiority had grown so lofty that Rome itself seemed provincial.

Figure 4.3. In this scene at the fish market, the man on the right is an American tourist and has a copy of *Murray's* under his arm. Detail of *Roman Fish Market* by Albert Bierstadt, 1858

"L'Italia ha bisogno di Roma!"—Italy Needs Rome![23]

Changes in the status of Rome gave rise to a different kind of influx in the late nineteenth century. In 1871, when Rome was made capital of what had by then become the "Kingdom of Italy" it was "an economic, cultural and political backwater, suffering from introversion and stagnation."[24] Despite this lack of appeal, the House of Savoy made the appropriate political gesture and took up residence at the Quirinal Palace, amid complaints from the king that the streets stunk like a barn and, with the hot winds of the scirocco, also of cheese.[25] The royal Savoys made the physical move south, but they came with their French/Piedmontese culinary culture fully intact. For years only chefs from such origin were deemed qualified to command the royal kitchen.

A significant change had been taking place at the tables of the nobility, from French-style service to Russian-style service. The originator of the latter was Borrisovic Kourakin, the Russian ambassador under Napoleon Bonaparte. Contrary to the old custom, wherein diners would be led to an intricately set table with all of the first-course dishes set out amid myriad sauces and gravy boats, Kourakin's guests were seated at a table of empty plates around a sumptuous centerpiece. At each place setting was a card listing the dishes that would be brought out, each one individually in due course at the pace set by the diners. Thus, the menu was born. It would become a standard feature of all prestigious meals and, in aristocratic homes, even of some simpler private meals. Important menus were valuable keepsakes, possibly even signed by the illustrious host.

Table setting and choreographed serving had hitherto been a fine art requiring a knowledgeable *scalco*, steward, an agile *trinciante* or carver, and a skillful *credenziere*, who was in charge of the sideboard and beverages. Guests were led to a richly set table with a delightful profusion of viands, but despite the stunning impact, accessing the wide variety of dishes was no small task, and one usually settled for what was closest at hand. As the meal progressed, the trinciante assumed his position at the end of the table with his charge on a large platter, heated from underneath by a brazier. He performed his act of daring-do while understudies dutifully served the artfully carved foods. At the end of the first service, the large plates and platters were removed and the second service, all of it at once, was brought to the table. The dessert course followed in the same fashion. Considering that the minimum for a service of twenty people consisted of four *potages*, four *relevés*, twenty-four *entrèes*, four large *entremets*, eight roast platters, followed by another sixteen *entremets*, and finally dessert: an assortment of candied fruit, biscuits, puddings, gelatins, cakes, ices, and fresh fruit,

Russian-style service offered the advantage of allowing each person to partake in or refuse each new dish as it appeared.

Vincenzo Agnoletti was one of the privileged serving on the staff of an aristocratic kitchen when the phenomenon arose, and he opposed it vehemently. Agnoletti had been brought up serving next to his father, who had for thirty years been head credenziere under the princely Roman family Doria-Pamphilj-Landi. Vincenzo spent his young adulthood working in prestigious kitchens throughout Europe, finally landing a permanent position as credenziere and *liquorista* under the Duchess of Parma, later returning to Rome to work for Cardinal Arezzo. In his book *The Cook and Pastry Chef's Manual of Refined Modern Taste* (1834), Agnoletti declares: "Russian-style service, that is, with just one course of sideboard dishes on the table and the rest of the meal served one dish at a time from the kitchen, and having it carved and plated away from the table, is highly inconvenient, most indecorous, and hardly allows the cook to fulfill his role. Not only do I not approve, but in France and Germany it is not the preferred system, so there is no point in speaking of it further." How wrong he was. It was one of the many imports that would firmly establish itself in Italian households, a trickle down from the aristocracy.

In the royal household of Victor Emanuel II, the first king of Italy, the ingredients, dishes and procession of courses for formal banquets were strictly French. Even the pasta arrived via French cuisine called *macaroni: à la napolitaine, à la royale, à la purée de lièvre*, and so on, with the exception of the two Piedmontese classics *agnolotti* and *tajarin*. Just to give a nod to the actual location, the royal palate was cleaned with a sort of sorbet called *punch à la romaine*, made with citrus juice, tea, whipped egg whites, and a bit of rum, cognac, and maraschino, before the arrival of the roasted meat course. The Savoys were passionate about the hunt, and game featured frequently at their table, particularly partridge, pheasant, lark, hare, and venison. As for vegetables, the royal favorites were asparagus, artichokes, watercress, peas, and cardoons. Cardoons were a Piedmontese specialty, and the French ranked them above all other vegetables. For a chef, mastering the potential of the cardoon was a non plus ultra.

The paired wines were almost exclusively French, sometimes Piedmontese (the latter preferred at private meals), but never Roman. The Pranzo di Gala to honor Victor Emanuel II's entrance into Rome opened with Potage à la Londonderry, a pheasant consommé with julienned pheasant breast, onion, peas, and cubes of flan made with pureed pheasant. The cascade of dishes that followed spoke volumes about the international image the Savoys wished to portray, as well as their loyalties:

Petites Croustades à la Normande Aiguillettes Villeroy
Poisson de Mer à l'Américaine Sauce Homard
Filet Boeuf à la Westphalienne
Canard à la Jardinière
Poulardes à la Piémontaisse et Truffes blanches
Filet de Soles à la Montpellier
Flan de Chicorée et Asperges sauce Hollandaise
HORS D'OEVRES: Pâté de Strasbourg et Salé à la Russe

Oddly, the ubiquitous Roman punch, which would have been more than appropriate for the occasion, was substituted with Punch au Kirschwasser. The intermezzo palate-wash was followed by a single roast dish of guinea fowl and four sweet entremets, with creamy chocolate and/or raspberry/citron ices to finish. Except for one German wine, all of the others were French.

Rome's emergence as capital of Italy was a costly venture that reverberated into food prices. The austerity measures necessary to bolster the new nation and keep it afloat during the first international economic depression, referred to as the Panic of 1873, coincided with the end of food subsidies formerly maintained by the Church. Both unification and the Panic stepped up emigration. Between 1876 and 1913 eleven million Italians emigrated, mostly motivated by hunger. Meanwhile, many of those who stayed in Italy migrated to the new capital, where the population rose from 213,633 in 1871 to 275,637 in 1881. The new political machine necessitated numerous bureaucratic positions to run the centralized administration, the prospect of which brought social climbers in from all over the nation. Most of the population, however, consisted of agricultural workers, craftsmen, unskilled laborers, domestic servants employed by the clergy or upper-class families, and the unemployed. The rapid influx spurred on a housing crisis that lowered the standard of living, reducing the quality, variety, and quantity of food one could afford on a budget.

The food market was worsened by the large estate owners, the latifondisti, who maintained a stranglehold on the over two thousand square kilometers of land surrounding Rome that might have otherwise fed the population: in 1870, 58 percent was in the hands of the nobility, 33 percent the ecclesiastics, and 9 percent the bourgeoisie.[26] After defaults following Rome's restoration as the capital city, 31 percent of the land of the campagna romana went up for auction, and was mostly purchased by an agricultural monopoly called the *mercanti di campagna*, a vehicle of the bourgeoisie that was gaining social and political power, thereby radically changing the face of social mobility. The mercante di campagna was "an experienced farmer who excels in his capacity for work; he hates easy enthusiasm; he resists innovation. . . . Even if his wife wants and gets jewelry and clothes, if his daughters have been well placed, and the sons are in the latest fashions, he will remain for the rest of his days the spirit of parsimony, dedicated to the herd and longing for *pezzata*, mutton stew."[27] With centuries of agricultural know-how at their backs, and a knack for turning a low-risk profit from the land, the *mercanti* often accrued wealth that rivaled aristocrats.[28]

The mercanti cleverly moved in on financially strapped nobles, leasing and then subletting large tracts of their land. Rather than producing for the population's needs, however, they speculated on cereal crops, forcing the city to import necessary foodstuffs from considerable distances and at ever increasing costs. In some cases they sharecropped the land. In *Roba di Roma* (1887), William Wetmore Story observes:

> This old system is destructive of all agricultural progress. The tenant lives from hand to mouth and from season to season. And having no capital, and being dependent for his living on the season's crops, he cannot afford to make experiments which look to the future, or to expend money upon betterments; each season must pay for itself. He distrusts new courses, and becomes stolidly fixed in the old way; and his method of cultivation is precisely what his ancestor's was a thousand years ago.[29]

The ecclesiastical landowners, many of whom were not Roman, were also easy prey for the mercanti, "The strong, able-bodied, fat and healthy friars, numbering in the Roman State 21,415, are an army of idlers, not of laborers: they do not spade and dig the earth, and plant and reap; but they carry round a begging basket to the farm-houses, or lounge through the vineyards and fill it at the expense of the owner."[30] The Church ended up in the clutches of the mercanti di campagna, but in accordance with canon law, leases could only last three years, for which neither side was willing to invest in improvements. The laws of God were a further impediment: "If the tenant desires to open canals for irrigation during a dry season, the priests cry out that this is flying in the face of Providence, who sends all the rain that is needful; and if the harvest be ruined in consequence of their obstinacy, they look upon it as a penance which it would have been irreligious to attempt to avoid."[31] But by and large the mercanti sublet to transhumant shepherds, keeping the seasonal passage along drove roads a constant feature of the Roman countryside. Transhumance was not a simple question of climatic determinism; the transference allowed herdsmen to bring the by-products of their flock to market, and in turn take away local goods. This use of the land lined the pockets of the mercanti, but left the city without sustainable means to provide the citizens with adequate nutrition at a reasonable price.

The later descendants of the House of Savoy were not as partial to formal banqueting. Humbert I (1878–1900) was said to be a bit of a curmudgeon and rather insignificant both physically and intellectually. In their ascent to the throne of Italy, the Savoys alienated many of the other royal families, so that Humbert, hard pressed to find a suitable wife, ended up marrying his first cousin Margherita, legendary namesake of the Neapolitan cheese pizza. The new queen was vivacious and sociable and frequently entertained with dinners, music, and dancing, despite her husband's lack of interest. He was not one to indulge himself at the table with the possible exception of gelato, for which he had an abiding passion.

Their son Victor Emmanuel III (1900–1946) was inclined toward simplicity and sobriety, his weakness being roast chicken, which he ate almost every evening. Breakfast was limited to one dish only and the main meal to two uncomplicated courses. Later in his reign, he tended toward the Fascist Party's

Figure 4.4. Two menus from the House of Savoy, the second exemplifying the move away from French culinary traditions under Fascism. Menus from *Pranzo al Quirinale*, courtesy of Mina Novello.

dietary platform, which encouraged rice instead of pasta and more vegetables and cheese. Italian wines won out over French wines, but most were still Piedmontese reds. Again, in line with fascist ideals, his menus ceased to be written in French and were written in Italian. Ada Boni applauded him for his effort and she encouraged her compatriots to follow suit:

> The matter of gastronomic terminology is an issue of prime importance. Our language is so rich in vocabulary that it can adapt to even the most complicated list of foods without having to rely on any other language. Our Sovereign has stepped forward to set an example for us. For years now he has insisted that his menus be written in Italian. And it would seem that his August lesson was not in vain.[32]

Austerity measures had dragged on into the twentieth century, but as Italy entered into World War I bread subsidies were eventually reinstated temporarily. At war's end, the subsidies weighed heavily on the new nation and had to be abandoned to avoid total collapse. As men returned from their tour of military duty expecting the jobs that had been promised them for serving their country, they were sorely disappointed. With no jobs and no bread, riots broke out with placards crying *"pane e lavoro!"* Bread had become an entitlement, and though some time had passed, many Romans romanticized about better days when bread was subsidized by the Church as a social pacifier. The ensuing violence and misrule would pave the way for the National Fascist Party and the strong dictatorial arm of Benito Mussolini.

Hollywood on the Tiber

The multi-complex movie studio Cinecittà was founded in Rome in 1937 by Mussolini, recognizing that cinema was a powerful weapon for achieving internal consensus and creating an image of Italy outside its borders. Cinecittà had been gutted during the war, but, afterward, reconstruction was a top priority. The Italian neorealism movement brought the Italian film industry international acclaim, drawing the attention of American producers to the quality of films that could be achieved in Italian studios. But there were other draws as well. The costs for big-budget Hollywood films could be significantly curtailed by moving the entire production to Cinecittà. Labor and materials were cheap and taxes were easily evaded. European production also facilitated European distribution, which accounted for 40 percent of the box office intake.

With the new chapter in the life of Cinecittà came a new kind of royalty. The laissez faire lifestyle in Rome, where divas could bar hop and dine their nights away between Via Veneto, Trastevere, and Appia Antica made for a pampered getaway that tempered the grueling work schedule of the Hollywood set. The original pioneers of Rome's gastronomic splendors were silent film actors Douglas Fairbanks and Mary Pickford, who happened upon the trattoria *Alfredo alla Scrofa* while on their honeymoon. So taken were they with the signature dish fettuccine Alfredo that they asked for the recipe, which they took back with them to the United States. In fact it was little more than a simple dish of buttered noodles with Parmesan that Alfredo di Lelio had concocted for his wife when she was pregnant and had trouble keeping anything down.[33] Anywhere else in Italy it would have been called *pasta al burro*, but Alfredo presented it on his menu as though it were his own secret recipe, and unwitting foreigners were duly wowed. In 1927, the Fairbanks-Pickfords gifted the restaurateur a gold fork and spoon set with the inscription: "To Alfredo the King of the noodles." Alfredo's became a VIP hotspot, but curiously fettuccine Alfredo is a dish only known by Americans and can only be found at the two Alfredo restaurants in Rome (both claiming to be the original and both with a set of inscribed gold silverware).

By 1950, Cinecittà was in business and already being referred to as "Hollywood on the Tiber."[34] Between 1949 and 1957, 314 Hollywood films were produced abroad, many of them in Rome. Romantic blockbusters like *Quo Vadis* (1951), *Roman Holiday* (1953), *Ben-Hur* (1959), and *Cleopatra* (1963), each featuring dashing men and mythic beauties, added a new dimension of star quality to the Eternal City. The privileged relationship between Rome and Hollywood did much to boost the image of Italy in general and made Rome one of the honeymoon capitals of Europe. The sub-genre "spaghetti western" was another cinematic export from the capital that came onto the scene in the 1960s. The name is a sort of metonymy derived from the fact that the production companies were mostly Italian, and more significantly that they tended to operate on shoestring budgets, but regardless, many went on to become colossal box office hits.

The most striking Italian cinematic export of the period was Fellini's *La Dolce Vita* (1960), which portrays postwar Rome through a cynical neo-modern lens. The film depicts the vice, glamour, self-indulgence, and excess of the cafe and nightclub society, made possible by the economic boom, and juxtaposes it with existential tension and the search for meaning. Dreamlike narratives like these of Rome promoted by both cinema and "the movies," alongside the growing fashion industry, made investment in Italian culinary imagery a highly profitable endeavor, the creation and fulfillment of a fantasy that would bring significant dividends. Catering to tourist expectations of "Italian cuisine" did much to conceptualize and reify the notion of a national cuisine as if it had always existed. It strongly influenced natural selection, dictating which dishes and ingredients would dominate over others and which would fall by the wayside—only to reappear with the advent of Slow Food and the revival of "traditions." In an economy emerging from twenty years of fascist rule and the aftermath of war, ready cash bought any number of illusions.

Rome: A Global City

Rome today has "global city" status.[35] Despite its role as capital of one country, its economic and demographic systems transcend national boundaries, and its various layers interact within the network of other globalized cities. In comparison to other such global cities, Rome's economy may not distinguish itself, but it has long been more than a sum of its parts; Rome is a metaphor or a brand for historical, aesthetic, religious, and political prowess in a way that is unmatched by any other city.

The spell of modern Rome also lies in its potent urban character, molded by the integral functionality of its services, resources, and institutions. Among these attributes, the Romans themselves—those who lay that claim—come into play: "Rome is a laboratory of intricate human relations and curious forms of sociability, of diffidence and civility, cynicism and humor, rudeness and kindness, a chaotic blend of distance and closeness, carelessness, apathy and engagement which defines what everyone knows as 'Roman-ness.'"[36] Given this larger-than-life reputation, Rome now seems a sanguine choice for immigrants seeking to better their lives. And the more of these modern pilgrims who successfully make the leap, the more others are persuaded to throw caution to the wind. At this writing, the Province of Rome has the highest immigrant population of any province in Italy.

Immigrants always bring food traditions with them. One's native foodways reflect not only the physical needs of the body, but cultural and spiritual needs. Yet the tastes and foodways that bind migrant communities together and to their culture of origin are inevitably juxtaposed with the local culinary tradition, foodways that loom large in their day-to-day context. Local foods are more accessible, expedient, and economical, and hence avoiding them requires a conscious choice. The issue of "belonging" tugs in many directions, as does loyalty, evolving as the generations of "hyphenated" Italians (Romanian-Italian, Filipino-Italian) reinvent themselves through consumption choices.

Retail sales of foreign foods and ingredients in Rome generally fall into one of two categories. First are the imported food shops aimed at an immigrant clientele, whose products tend toward the needs of one culinary orientation, for example, Eastern European or Indian/Pakistani or North African. The desire to maintain ties with the native country and to continue foodways from the home cuisine in the new country creates a market that fosters entrepreneurship: groceries, markets, butcher shops, restaurants, and eateries, all of which feed back into the local economy as well as providing opportunities for incoming co-nationals and trade for the native country. Customers are attracted to these shops for brand familiarity, price, and sometimes a shared language. Many of the items, particularly legumes and rice, can also be found in Italian supermarkets, although the packages tend to be smaller, more expensive, the selection less varied, and the brands are Italian. Migrants are reassured by familiarity, but also by knowing that certain products conform to religious dietary laws, halal meat being a specific case in point.

At the other end of the spectrum is the minuscule offering of token foreign foods sold in large supermarkets, items presented in non-threatening, ethnic-looking packages, foods that native Italians might have come across either in their travels, on television, or in local ethnic restaurants. These kits and semi-prepared foods are produced by Big Food companies of the El Paso and Suzi Wan ilk and would raise an eyebrow, to say the least, of a migrant consumer. Gentrification, evident in Roman neighborhoods like Testaccio, and the influx of non-Italian, gastronomically informed residents from elsewhere, has also created a demand for a wider variety of culinary choices. The significant number of discerning consumers influences quality and authenticity, and encourages the public at large to embrace culinary diversity.

In the last twenty years the number of immigrants in Italy has increased more than tenfold. Thirteen percent of Rome's population is immigrants.[37] Fears of unsustainability and loss of cultural intimacy through homogenization abet xenophobia, fragmentation, exploitation, and a knee-jerk reaction to perceived threats. For example, suggestions that the exposition of crucifixes and other Christian iconography in hospitals, businesses, and schools might be inappropriate in a multicultural context met with a staunch refusal that went all the way to the European court.[38] Amid the ambivalence, schools have made attempts to bridge the gaps by using food as a portal. Programs enacted in Roman schools explore the foodways of immigrant students, valorizing the culinary identity of each nation, and thus are designed to encourage integration and acceptance of others. Food sparks curiosity, and it is a realm that one can dip in and dip out of without having to speak the language or participate in other beliefs or customs that might be disconcerting. The experience and acceptance of other culinary practices also strengthens food security, making it imperative for the future.

A prime example is "Every month a country," which fortunately rhymes in Italian: *Ogni mese un paese*. Once a month for eight months, the Municipality of Rome, in conjunction with the University of Rome La Sapienza and the Istituto San Gallicano, organized an ethnic meal to be served as the school lunch at elementary schools, involving about one hundred sixty thousand students overall. The meal plans came from the countries whose immigrant members are most represented in the capital city. The objective was to educate the palate of the children by exposing them to different gustatory dimensions so that they might better conceive of the depth of other cultures by way of the foods they eat. Among the featured dishes were Polish beet soup, Bangladeshi curried rice, Peruvian potatoes, Romanian stuffed cabbage rolls, Filipino sweet and sour chicken, Albanian cheeses, Moroccan couscous, and Chinese baked pears.[39] The project did not stop at providing the meal; organizers set up a forum for the teachers, students, and parents to discuss the anthropological, geographical, economic, and nutritional implications of the cuisine of each country as well as the significance of specific recipes. Students were given brochures with a descriptive synthesis of the history, geography, dietary culture, and calendar of holidays of each of the participating countries.

Mobility and Labor
Food mobility research has been studied most frequently along the lines of ethnicity, gender, and class, but less frequently in accordance with labor. Rome's history as a political and administrative city echoes through to modernity. Rather than industrial, or even postindustrial, Rome is fundamentally a bureaucratically driven service city. The greatest demand for services in the Information Age is not computer scientists and technicians, but caregivers. An estimated two million Italian elderly need caregivers, as the social disgrace of placing one's parents in a care facility for the aging—not to mention the lack and expense thereof—is still palpable. This has ushered in a veritable army of immigrant women who leave children, family, and country behind to become *badanti* (the officially favored but rarely used term is *colf*, a compound of *collaboratrice familliare*). And with them, culinary change has also descended upon Italy's elderly. A 2015 estimate puts the number of women in Italy working as caregivers at eight hundred thirty thousand, 90 percent of whom have immigrated for that purpose.[40] Two out of three live and work in Italy illegally, and hence under abusive conditions unprotected by the law. But when the monthly stipend of a caregiver is eight times more than what her husband earns in Ukraine as an engineer, it is not difficult to see why one runs the risk.

Two of the drawbacks when hiring a foreign *badante* are language and cooking, the lack of the former compounding the difficulties of learning the latter. Badanti generally live with the elderly or disabled person and are relied upon to administer the household and cook as well. Sometimes the food may be Italian dishes picked up from experience, or following specific instructions of the employer. Often, however, the fare is a combination of the caregiver's and local foodways, or in some cases, the food of the caregiver's native country prepared with local ingredients. The Restaurant and Hotel management school in Rome, in association with the Catholic foundation ACLI Rome, began an initiative in 2017 called *Food, Integration, and Solidarity* to teach immigrant women who are interested in the "home care profession" how to cook "Mediterranean style." The stated objectives are to sensitize the students to volunteer work and to multicultural integration, to develop an "empowerment" path for the students, who will be the instructors for the course, and to give selected immigrants cooking skills that will increase their employment possibilities.

In Rome, despite the stigma of being a caregiver, more and more nonimmigrant Roman women are also finding that it is the last card they have to play. According to the Roman housewives association *Federcasalinghe*, which offers courses in domestic assistance, 20 percent of the 124,300 home care providers hired in 2011 were such Roman women. Most of them work eight-hour days, as opposed to the average twenty-hour days that foreign live-ins put in, but they make more money regardless—their asset being language, of course, and the fact that they can provide the client with home-style Roman food that will not shock the elderly person's dietary habits.[41] Despite the need for caregivers, culinary novelty can be met with prejudice and attempts to reform migrant foodways.[42]

Of greater Rome's 128,530 hectares, 51,729—that is, 40 percent, are dedicated to agriculture, for which opportunities also arise for seasonal work in the fields. Seasonal workers can get renewable permissions of stay lasting up to nine months and under certain conditions these can become permanent. Most agricultural migrants come from Eastern Europe and North Africa as well as South Asia. Food is provided for them in a number of ways, either directly from the employer, through a flat-rate agreement with a trattoria or food service, or they are given vouchers that can be used like cash at participating eateries or grocery stores. In this way, they are exposed to local foods (albeit within a limited budget) and the customs and habits that surround the repast. Yet international outrage about the slave-like treatment of migrant field hands has led to accountability laws designed to safeguard their fundamental human rights. Employers who offer workers accommodations must comply with housing norms, and if there is a charge for lodging, it cannot exceed one-third of the laborer's wage.

While vigilance over the rights of these workers has recently come under close and critical scrutiny, historically speaking, Rome has come a long way, as evidenced in this observation made in a governmental study carried out in 1883 on the conditions of migrant workers:

> As they are in open countryside there is no way for the laborers to freely procure food during their stay, and so they have to buy their food in what are called company stores . . . which more often than not take advantage by raising the prices or selling spoiled goods, from which the laborers take ill. This state of things reduces workers to choosing only those food items that are sold at company shops and at company prices. As such, every green that is not outright nauseating, every animal that has died who-knows-how, and not infrequently of contagious diseases, becomes a viable food for adding to the so-called pizza or focaccia cooked under the coals, or perhaps some simple cornmeal polenta, usually without salt, which is the most common meal for these poor folks.[43]

The description clearly recalls *The Grapes of Wrath*, with the exception that this is not a fictionalized account.

Migrants seeking refugee status in Rome come from many different religious backgrounds but frequently claim the presence of the Holy City as the reason for choosing Rome as their asylum destination, perceiving it thereby as a compassionate, tolerant, charitable place to take refuge. Indeed with nine hundred operative churches in Rome, the highest concentration in the world, one would hope that the milk of human kindness is plenteous. The Joel Nafuma Refugee Center of the St. Paul's within the Walls Episcopal Church is exemplary in its kind, providing asylum seekers and refugees with a simple breakfast of tea with either boiled eggs and apples or with rice and beans.[44] The center holds Christmas and Eid al-fitr dinners yearly, where they serve three hundred refugees a meal of rice with a meat curry, bread and fruit. Those staying in the camps (reputedly run by organized crime) are grateful for the break from the fodder that is supplied there, most saying they dislike pasta.[45] The center is attempting to use the common language of food as a way of encouraging public interaction and has begun offering dinners and cooking classes based on the cuisines of the countries of the displaced people who frequent the center. The aim is to raise funds, stimulate awareness, and create employment, albeit temporary, for the refugees themselves. Thus far the initiative has introduced the public to the cuisines of Mali, Afghanistan, Nigeria, and Ethiopia.

Studying Roman Foodways—Cultural Immersion

More than ever, Rome is attracting visitors just for the food. The deliberate exchange of culinary culture via ethnogastrotourism—cooking classes and vacation packages catering directly to those interested in learning and exchanging ideas about culinary practices, lore, and traditions. Interest in these endeavors is, however, a double-edged sword in that traditions easily become commodities of romanticism, modeled and packaged for ready sale to a public eager for an "authentic" experience. The line between folklore and fakelore is willfully blurred, particularly when the economy is sluggish and foreign customers are clamoring for the goods.

One center a cut above and beyond many offerings for gastronomic cultural exchange in Rome is Gustolab International Institute for Food Studies. Gustolab aims specifically at structuring an educational environment that combines local community engagement and a broad range of cross-disciplinary courses within the ambit of culinary studies. From their base in Rome, students and researchers explore issues of agribusiness, consumption trends, the sociology and history of foodways, sustainability, waste, mobility, and nutrition, in addition to language courses specifically designed for those pursuing interests in Italian Food Studies. Rome in its ever-expanding role as a global megacity is an ideal laboratory from which to examine how these issues play out locally, and, in turn, how the same scenario is expressed globally. Part of the mission of the institute is to provide a scholarly and experiential foundation derived from both urban and rural Roman contexts, whose end is not intended as a means of comparison between "home and Rome," but as an expedient to nurture and encourage a broad spectrum, critical vision of the interconnectedness of food studies issues in all of their manifestations.

CHAPTER FIVE

Al mercato—At the Marketplace

Camillus having pitched his camp before the gates, wishing to know whether the same appearance of peace, which was displayed in the country, prevailed also within the walls, entered the city, where he beheld the gates lying open, and everything exposed to sale in the open shops, and the workmen engaged each on their respective employments. . . .[1]

—Livy

Macellum

Markets were the lifeblood of urban living. The essence of Ancient Roman civic life gravitated around stands, shelves, baskets, and hooks offering desiderata from far and near, from the essential to the exquisitely frivolous. But the marketplace satisfied more than mere material needs and desires; it was an integral part of communal engagement, a backdrop for regular interpersonal exchange that nurtured social bonds, cultural development, and political schemes. Indeed the practice of entering into the daily fray was an extension of one's own home. The density of Rome's population and the layout of the city made urbanites dependent on markets and retailers for most of their material needs. As food was the most important commodity, venues dealing in foodstuffs abounded.

Markets evolved primarily in two forms in the middle period of the Republic. First, was the *macellum*, a permanent structure built expressly to house sellers and their wares. Previously, open markets and temporary structures

113

had set up in the *fora*.[2] As those areas were increasingly used for civic and political activities, the markets dispersed, leaving the public fora as stages upon which the Romans could publicly exercise their intricate social pecking order. The development of the macellum was an important step in the consolidation of the Roman identity, because the forum had been modeled on the Greek commercial concept called the *agora*. This new model of indoor market was propagated as the standard in many cities throughout the empire.[3] Macella had an inner courtyard with a basin or fountain, surrounded by *tabernae*, individual retail units. Although the word *macellum* evolved into the Italian word for butcher shop, there is evidence that these markets sold all manner of food items. Indeed, macella such as the Forum Esquilinum and the Macellum Magnum were strategically located in the southeast of the city making it convenient for conveying fruits and vegetables. However, the evidence indicates that meat and fish were the dominant products.

As the city grew and new buildings went up, the number of tabernae increased, becoming ever more specialized, and a decentralized system of specifically designated macella, proliferated: the earliest was the Forum Boarium, for livestock, identified as such by a gilded bronze statue of a bull. Animals were sold wholesale to butchers, although some were allocated for sacrifice and sold to priests.[4] Either way, they were driven from the market directly into the city to await their fate. Sacrificial victims were dispatched at the temples, and the meat that was not consumed or distributed directly entered into retail, fetching a higher price, as it had not only been ritually sanctified, but also selected for quality. The Forum Holitorium was where market gardeners sold their vegetables and fruits, mainly to retailers and middlemen, who either hawked them in the streets of town or sold them off to petty sellers. Other specialized markets were the Forum Vanadium for wine, the Forum Piscarium for fish, the Forum Cuppedinis for exotic foods and delicacies, the Forum Pistorium for bread and baked goods, the Forum Suarium for pork products, and the Forum Coquinum for cooked foods.

Sumptuary legislation designed to curb ostentatious spending on banquets and luxury went largely ignored.[5] In fact, many of the forbidden luxury items were supplied by wealthy estate owners who were instrumental in enacting those laws. Game such as boar, deer, and hares were hunted on their estates and channeled into the market. They also raised a variety of small birds in private aviaries, as well as the much sought-after chubby dormice, for profit. Honey from beekeeping was another delicacy that guaranteed good revenues. This, of course, was only a fraction of the fine foods that poured into Rome.

From its three ports (Portus, Ostia and Emporium under the Aventine) flowed in the legumes, fruit and wine of Italy, the grain of Egypt and Africa, oil from Spain, game, wood and wool from Gaul, cured meats from Baetica, dates from the oases. . . . There were storehouses and granaries in the Urbs and surroundings as far as the eye could see which filled the belly of the Urbs and in which enough was set aside to guarantee well being and luxury.[6]

One of the motives behind building market structures may have been to shield the upper classes from the vulgarity of making purchases in the open-air markets. Monumental markets like the Macellum Magnum, whose image was immortalized in coinage, indicated that these were exclusive and prestigious commercial outlets. Retailers of a certain status also paid house calls, again implying that public commerce was an uncouth business. In either case, the merchandise itself was intended for those with a high standard of living, the competitive members of the dinner circuit. The very fact that the food required cooking indicated that it was for the elite, as the majority of the population living in block housing did not have cooking facilities. Predictably, here too the voice clamoring for a return to traditions made itself heard. Despite their impressive purchasing power, those who had country villas were ridiculed if they could not satisfy their needs with products from their own estates.[7] Juvenal makes this point when he entices Persicus to come for a good old-fashioned country-style dinner:

> Listen to what I'll serve, without recourse to the market.
> From my Tiburtine farm comes a little kid, the most tender,
> The plumpest, of the herd, that's as yet unacquainted with
> Grazing, that hasn't yet dared to nibble the hanging willow
> Shoots, there's more milk than blood in its veins; then wild
> Asparagus, picked by my steward's wife when she's finished
> Her weaving; large eggs, still warm, wrapped in wisps of hay,
> Accompanying the hens themselves; and grapes kept for half
> A year, still as good as they were when they hung on the vine;
> Syrian and Signian pears; and in the same baskets of fruit
> Fresh-smelling apples equalling those from Picenum; don't
> Fret, their autumnal juice has been tempered by frost,
> And they've shed that dangerous lack of ripeness.[8]

The complex called Trajan's Market has often been assumed to be one of the milestones in the evolution in marketing in Imperial times. A broad, concave multistory building, spanning a vast area and embedded into the hillside between the Esquiline and Capitoline Hills, the edifice is an extraordinary architectural achievement with what appear to be one-hundred and fifty discreet tabernae dispersed over four stories, and thought to have made up the administrative and commercial center of the Forum and Basilica of Trajan. The structure itself was a marvel, a multifunctional compound that scholars neatly declared to be the world's first shopping mall. This seemingly logical assumption would have been in keeping with Rome's intense commercial orientation, but owing to the lack of archeological and literary evidence, the theory remains subject to heated debate. More recently, scholars have tended to the view that the "Market" was an administrative center, its "shops" actually offices for imperial bureaucrats. In some capacity, however, markets and cook shops most likely occupied the street level floor evidenced by the Via Biberatica, a road paved in volcanic stone that runs through the complex, worn smooth by the centuries. It connects the two grand staircases at either end, which lead to the upper floors allowing for a continuous flow of activity. *Bibere* means "to drink," indicating that this was perhaps a meeting ground that provided refreshment from the tabernae, the commercial units, whose wide doorways trimmed in white travertine face the road on either side. The scene would have been that of massive brick walls refinished with white stucco, the hustle and bustle of merchants and bureaucrats, citizens filing through, attending to the business at hand. There is also speculation that state distribution of wine, oil, and wheat may have taken place here.[9]

Emperor Trajan reigned between 98–117 CE, ambitious years in which the Roman Empire would reach its greatest territorial extent. He was loved by both the people and the patrician class, who even during his lifetime had him acclaimed *optimum princeps* (best ruler) due to his extraordinary abilities as a military commander, administrator, and politician. His achievements in the civil realm were equally exceptional and included bridges, aqueducts, gateways, canals, roadways, reclamation works, and thermal bath spas. Among the notable accomplishments of his reign is an artificial inland harbor of a perfectly hexagonal shape measuring 715 meters in diameter, and 5 meters deep,[10] with a capacity to hold well over one hundred mercantile vessels. This ancient harbor of Trajan, situated just outside of present-day Fiumicino, was built to manage the incoming provisions for Rome. It was a frenetic port, bustling with the comings and goings of maritime vessels and wagons, as well as enterprising merchants and the thousands of workers and slaves in their employ. The harbor was a major conduit, equipped with storehouses designed to accommodate large quantities of commodities and vendibles, including foodstuffs and amphorae imported from the vast expanse of the empire, destined for transfer to the urban markets. The goods were loaded onto barges and dragged up the Tiber by oxen walking along a towpath. But rivers were unpredictably susceptible to flooding, freezing, and drought, making transport perilous or at times impossible. Alternatively, imports were piled high on wagons traveling the long artery called Via Portuensis, snaking along the right bank and ending in the heart of Rome at the southern gateway, Porta Portuensis. The intense traffic led to the construction of the first-ever dual carriageway, an ingenious yet simple invention that facilitated continuous flow of incoming and outgoing goods.

Once the wares had reached their destination, items that did not require immediate resale, such as amphorae of wine, olive oil and garum were stored in state and privately owned warehouses, or *horrea*. Keeping the population fed required a constant turnover of foodstuffs, necessitating a vast network of horrea, most of which were manned by slaves. Goods brought in by road up to one of the city gates were often sold outside the confines to avoid customs taxes. These were auctioned off wholesale, turned over to middlemen for redistribution, or channeled directly into retail. Due to the amount of traffic, goods had to be unloaded from boats, barges, and wagons and then distributed on foot and/or with the use of a pack animal, as carts had been banned during the day since the late Republic. Oil was one of Rome's primary imports, as it was used not only for cooking, but also for lighting, as an emollient in the baths and for medicinal purposes.

Because opened amphorae could not be reused, a plan was devised for their disposal. The accumulated shards from the broken amphorae were systematically collected and piled into a clay vessel dumpsite now called Monte Testaccio. *Testa* originally meant vase or shell; hence *Mon Testaceus* is a mountain of vase waste.[11] The mound of detritus, a modern day tourist attraction, stands thirty-five meters high and is twenty thousand square meters at the base. Layer after layer was alternated with powdered lime to stabilize the structure and keep the oily residue from becoming rancid and releasing a stench. The very existence of a centralized dump for oil amphorae indicates that incoming oil was decanted and distributed in other containers.

Nundinae, Tabernae, Street Vendors

Not every day was a banquet day, nor was everyone a member of the elite with disposable income. In this void, the *nundinae*, which could be equated with a farmers' market, found their niche. Nundinae literally means the ninth day, and thus roughly indicates the frequency of the market. These mobile marketers maintained a connection between the rural and the urban, allowing peasants to participate to a degree in urban life while bringing diversified products into the city. The trade circuit included not only Rome, but also other towns throughout Latium and Campania. The nundinae were daylong markets, for which only a limited amount of produce could be brought in, and so the distance had to reasonably allow the peasant farmer to arrive in the morning and leave in time to get home while it was still sufficiently light.[12]

The system had been set up so as to bring highly perishable goods from the closest belts of cultivation around the city. As the food source moved progressively farther from the destination, the goods would logically also have to be more durable. Produce that would keep for longer periods could be traded along networks covering a considerable distance—again, allowing for more diversity in fresh foods. As Rome grew into a metropolis, however, these markets became somewhat obsolete, unable, as they were, to meet the goal of feeding a population of one million people. The practice slowed as other forms of marketing evolved, and nundinae simply took on the meaning of "market day."[13] But as a system, it transformed largely into a trickle-down organization involving market gardeners, itinerant traders, middlemen, and wholesale collection and drop-off management.

As could be expected of the most populated city in the world with a high concentration of magnificently wealthy citizens, purveyors of every conceivable sort could be found to cater to the desires of the contemporary consumer. The main streets were chockablock with stallholders and tabernae, well-stocked commercial units, the most ubiquitous being those in the food trade, carrying everything from the most basic staples to the latest exotic imports from the far reaches of the empire and beyond. Craftspeople requiring stable spaces set up in tabernae where the actual workshop was fronted with a space for dealing with the public. The characteristic wide doorway lent itself to showcasing merchandise, as well as keeping shoppers from blocking the streets while browsing. The tabernae also accommodated pop-up shops. The unreliability of shipping, seasonality, and the intermittent increase in demand, for example, during holidays, left retailers to deal with stock that arrived in spurts and short-term need.

Given the centrality of bread to the Roman diet, bakeries must have used a significant number of the tabernae, at least for their sales. In the city, only wealthy households could afford an oven and fuel for home-baked bread.[14] The complex processes of manufacture and commerce in bread, from milling to proofing to baking to selling, required considerable space. The evidence for bakeries in Rome is limited, but includes recently discovered remains of the tomb at Porta Maggiore commemorating the baker Eurysaces. Better-preserved facilities in Ostia and Pompeii, where a taberna was often attached directly to the space where milling and baking took place, offer an indication of how these complexes may have worked.

Ambulant street selling was one step up from begging, for which literary references to this line of work tend to be expressed in pejorative terms, in spite of the fundamental role it played in the economy of urban Rome. It behooved hawkers and peddlers to cluster near popular public venues to profit from, for example, the appetites of those emerging from bathhouses, the leisurely social atmosphere of the fora, the throngs of spectators at circuses and theaters, and the devout requiring cakes and decorative appurtenances to leave as votive offerings in the temples. Many of these ambulant peddlers sold prepared foods like bread for take away, or snack foods, such as fruit, sausage, pastries, or chickpeas, to be eaten then and there, serving both the casual passerby as well as the numerous residents who relied on these vendors to procure cheap, cooked food. Some positioned themselves regularly in neighborhoods where they could build up a clientele. Their "shops" had to be mobile, so as not to hinder the flow of traffic, but also because most were not licensed, some having begged, borrowed, stolen, or scavenged to obtain their goods.[15] With no overhead, minimal initial investment, and negligible language requirements, street peddling was the only hope of survival for the masses of unemployed men, women, and children. Fierce competition compelled hawkers to outshout each other, much to the chagrin of residents. Authors such as Seneca, who lived near a bathhouse, recorded their annoyance: "pastry cooks with their varied cries, the sausage dealer and the confectioner and all the vendors of food from the cookshops selling their wares, each with his or her own distinctive intonation."[16] Street traders were disdained as deceitful hucksters who stopped short of nothing to make a little money. Galen went so far as to accuse them of passing off human flesh for pork. He also attacked improvised sellers who turned to fish mongering, having obtained their product from the Tiber:

> The worst fish are nurtured at the mouths of every river that flushes toilets, kitchens, baths, the dirt of clothes and linen, and everything else that is to do with the city that they run through which must be washed away, especially when the city is densely populated . . . which is why this fish is the cheapest of all.

Juvenal too suggests that fish were sourced from the *cloaca maxima*, the city sewer:

> But what awaits you is an eel, the stringy snake's relative,
> Or a fish from the Tiber, covered with grey-green blotches,
> Slave of its shores like you, fed from the flowing sewer.

Though not without their reasons, the few literary sources that even bothered with such a lowly topic assumed a condescending tone that unsympathetically voiced the views of the elite. The Graeco-Roman contempt for retailers would later settle into the Christian mindset through the re-telling of Jesus's outburst in the Temple of Jerusalem, but in this case as righteousness rather than superiority.

The Aftermath

After the barbarian invasions and the Gothic wars, Rome went into a slow, steady decay. The frenzy and commotion in the marketplace faded to a whimper. The Forum was pilfered for spare construction parts, and layer upon layer of soil and detritus built up until it was all but buried under piles of earth. In the ninth century, the flooring slabs of the Roman Forum were removed in order to use the area for cultivation. Some of the materials of the ruins were broken down and recycled into building components to reinforce the rudimentary clay brick houses that were assembled to house the cultivators. Swamping made habitation nearly impossible, and by the eleventh century, neglect and the simple absence of people set in motion a rapid decline. It was not long before wild vegetation overtook the streets, and buildings and statues and the glorious Forum of Rome became pastures for sheep and cows. From the fourteenth to the eighteenth centuries it was the location of the livestock market called Campo Vaccino ("cow field"). Little if anything remained of the great Roman markets, and the flowing current of goods arriving from the far reaches of the empire slowed to a bare trickle.

With the restoration of the papacy to Rome and the rise of the Papal State in the sixteenth century, various aspects of the cityscape would be razed, rebuilt, restructured, and encrusted with facades. Bits were recycled, melted down, or simply abandoned, all in the name of accommodating the esthetics and function of the authority. Alongside the transformation, Roman merchants formed powerful guilds, the representative motto of the times being *Ars, Labor, et Fides*. Among the food guilds were the Millers, Bakers, Pasta Makers, Pasta Workers, Fishermen, Fish Mongers, detailed divisions of the meat trade, Cooks and Pastry Makers, Spice Traders, and endless others.

The number of ambulant traders increased with the resuscitation of the city and they too became ever more specialized with the backing of the guilds. An engraving by Nicolaus van Aelst from around 1600 meticulously catalogs 240 food items that he saw hawked on the streets of Rome, each vignette featuring a seller in characteristic garb. Typical goods included garlic, capers, onions, herbs; watermelon, imported dates, strawberries, fresh and dried figs; cardoons, artichokes, mushrooms; clams, crab, shrimp, snails, frogs; oil, lard, bread, cheese, salumi, vermicelli; geese, pigeons, starlings, and warblers, as well as a number of prepared foods: savory pies with meat or vegetables and egg; fire roasted, baked and boiled chestnuts, cheap and filling; *gialdoni fresche*, deep fried waffles; *mostaccioli fini*, biscotti made with honey, must, almond granules, dried figs, and raisins cut into diamond shapes; and *ravioli grassi*, pasta filled with ricotta.

The quaintness of sheep and cows grazing in the grassy areas among the ruins of ancient Rome also attracted artists of note from all over Europe, who left a poignant and colorful record of the pastoralized urban areas and the desolate countryside in numerous works. French intellectual Hippolyte Taine (1828–1893) describes the collage of sights and sensations he observed on his visit in the mid 1860s:

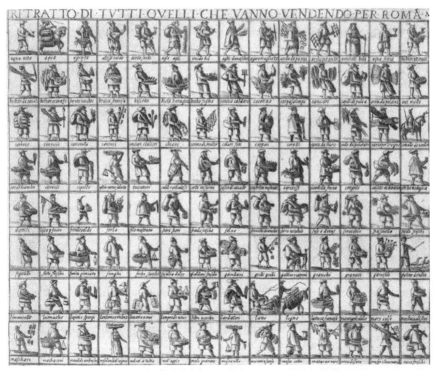

Figure 5.1.   Detail of *Portrait of All Those Going around Rome Selling*, portraying 260 sketches of ambulant vendors who filled the streets of Rome. Engraving by Nicolaus van Aeist, c. 1600. Furnished by Roma, Istituto centrale per la grafica and reprinted with the courteous permission of the Ministero dei Beni e delle Attivit. . . . Culturali e del Turismo

Through the arcades you might see green slopes, lofty ruins decked with shrubbery, shafts of columns, trees, heaps of rubbish, a field of tall white reeds [. . .]
all forming a singular combination of cultivation and neglect. One encounters
this everywhere in traversing Rome—remains of monuments, pieces of gardens, messes of potatoes frying at the bases of antique columns, . . . the odour
of old codfish, and on the flanks of a palace, . . . perhaps a bed of artichokes.[17]

Toward a Modern Market

Affixed to the wall of Portico d'Ottavia in the Roman Ghetto is a marble
plaque engraved with the following words: *Capita piscium hoc marmoreo sche-
mate longitudine majorum usque ad primas pinnas inclusive conservatoribus danto*
("The head, up to and including the first fins, of any fish longer than this
plaque must be given to the *conservatori*"). Under the inscription is a depiction
of a stocky sturgeon, harking back to a time when these fish teamed in the waters of the Tiber, some of considerable dimensions. Given that the plaque itself
is nearly four feet long, the head up to the first fins was a sizable piece of fish.

Not only was it a fair-sized chunk, the head of a fish was the most prized
part, sought out for the flavorful soups and sauces it rendered; hence the
ecclesiastics saw to it that they never reached the marketplace and were
kept as the exclusive reserve of the table of the high clergy. But why was this
plaque hung on this wall? For centuries this arch was the access point to the
city's main fish market. Here, upon the ancient ruins of a structure erected by
Emperor Augustus c. 27 BCE, the church Sant'Angelo in Pescheria, or Holy
Angel in the Fish market, was built (eighth century). In 1571, the Confraternity of Fishmongers, one of Rome's oldest and most powerful guilds, under-
took its upkeep and it was repaired, and restored many times over. In front
of Sant'Angelo, numerous inclined slabs of marble were lined up where the
day's catch was displayed. The prelate Paolo Giovio (1483–1552), a frequent
presence at the papal table and enthusiastic ichthyologist, wrote a volume
about the fish of Rome claiming there were ninety-six varieties in the Tiber
alone.[18] All incoming fish came to Portico d'Ottavia, but, our author tells
us, lowbrow fish, like tench, were hauled off for sale in Piazza della Rotonda,
at the Pantheon, which he thereby dubbed: Piazza Ignobile. As was true of
many foods, there was a hierarchy of fish delineated in accordance with the
constitutions of the social ladder. An aristocrat could not be expected to digest carp; sturgeon and eel were in more in keeping with their refined digestion. Attesting perhaps to the sway the Fishmonger's Guild held, they were
also authorized to sell pigs, stags, goats, hares, pheasants, partridges, pigeons,
doves, thrushes, starlings, and other woodland birds.

Portico d'Ottavia was a vibrant market that inspired many artists to immortalize the scene in engravings, watercolors, and paintings. In 1885, after Rome had become the capital, the market was transferred to San Teodoro near Circus Maximus. After having been abandoned for many years, the structure once again houses one of the liveliest markets in the city.

The Portico marked the beginning of the Roman Ghetto, the second in the world after Venice. From the time they had made their home in Rome in the second century BCE, the conditions for Jews had always wavered between tolerant cohabitation to embittered discrimination. A milestone of the latter came in 1555 when Pope Paul IV issued the papal bull *Cum nimis absurdum*, revoking all of the rights the Roman Jews had been conceded and ordering the institution of the ghetto, called the Enclosure of the Jews, *serraglio degli hebrei*. They were obliged to stay within the confines of the ghetto from dawn to dusk, forbidden any form of trade except for the purchase of rags and old clothes, forced to wear symbols on their clothes identifying them as Jews, and prohibited from owning property. Given the proximity to the fish market, once the fishmongers had closed for the day, Jewish women would collect the remains of the fish that had been piled up near Sant'Angelo in Pescheria. They were the dregs of the day's catch, heads, bones, and odd bits, which only lent themselves to soup, a soup that would become one of the prized dishes of the *cucina romanesca*.

Another famous fish recipe born of constraint was the result of the 1661 sumptuary laws. The laws themselves were self-imposed, but nonetheless in conformity with papal orders, stating that the appropriate fish for the Jews were bluefish, specifically sardines and anchovies. This, together with endive, inspired *aliciotti con l'indivia*, a simple dish made from equal weights of fresh anchovies and curly endive, the latter placed at the bottom of a baking dish with the cleaned fish arranged open-booked on top. Salt, pepper, drizzle with olive oil and bake.[19]

One of the lost traditions of the Portico d'Ottavia is the Christmas Eve fish auction called the *cottìo*. It is said to have started in the Middle Ages, but large fish had also been auction items at the macellum, the ancient Roman marketplace. Some fetched such high prices that money lenders found it behooved them to attend the auction in case anyone required financial assistance. The cottìo carried the tradition on through the first decades of the twentieth century.[20] As the meal of the vigil was rigorously meatless, enormous baskets of fish were brought to market and sold mostly in bulk to retailers, restaurant and trattoria owners, and cooks of the Roman nobility. It was a raucous holiday atmosphere of feverish bidding that began in the early morning hours of December 23. Part of the attraction was the jargon that was used between the fishmongers and the buyers, creating a spectacle that drew crowds of people from all social classes. Many may have gravitated there for the free fried fish. It was cooked on the spot in enormous vats of oil, wrapped in brown paper, and distributed to passersby, a reminder of the generosity of the Savior.

Today the Ghetto is one of the few places in Rome where the spirit of what Rome once was is still palpable, in spite of the fact that these old streets are becoming a tourist attraction. The walk down from the Portico is lined with groceries, restaurants, bakeries, and bread shops where kosher foods are made and served. Once past the limits of the ancient ghetto, one traverses via Arenula toward Monte di Pietà into the tangle of streets with artisan trade names: locksmiths, comb and brush makers, suitcases and trunks, and so on. Most of these side streets run into the main thoroughfares and commercial areas leading to the piazza where Giordano Bruno (1548–1600), the philosopher and Dominican friar, was burned alive for openly opposing such fundamental articles of Christian faith as the virginity of Mary, eternal damnation, and, not least, the divinity of Christ. This same piazza is also the location of the oldest neighborhood market in the city, Campo de' Fiori, literally, the field of flowers. Although the space had been used as an improvised market for centuries, it became an official daily fish and vegetable market in 1869 when the Piazza Navona market moved there. Joseph Collins notes the incongruence of the imposing and ominous statue of Bruno in the marketplace atmosphere in an essay from his yearlong stay in Italy (1917–1918):

> I not infrequently stand in a corner of this square, crowded by vendors of fish in every state and condition—dried, pickled, raw, cooked, fresh, stale—and of vegetables of every possible shape, size, and description, and watch the frugal housewife barter with the wily peasant vendor, and listen to the shriek of the modern billingsgate as she extols the virtues of her piscatorial wares or of her *piselli* and *fagioli*, and wonder if any one of this motley crowd has the meagrest idea of who Bruno was or what he accomplished for Italy and for the world in the shape of freedom of speech and of thought.[21]

The central markets like this that are closest to the major touristic thoroughfares have undergone significant changes in recent years in catering to tourists. Campo de' Fiori is perhaps the most evident example, where they sell fiery red spaghetti flavored with chili pepper or multicolored souvenir pasta striped a patriotic red, white, and green, jarred sauces hawking themselves as "genuine traditional Italian," along with an assortment of cheap fridge magnets and other such paraphernalia. Fruit vendors have refashioned themselves as centrifuge juicers with take-away cups. Rare is the Roman who comes here to shop.

In Rome there are now one-hundred thirty five daily food markets divided into three categories according to location type: *coperti*, covered markets that are ad hoc, or in spaces once occupied by other activities; *plateatici*, in areas earmarked and specially outfitted by the city, either uncovered or partially covered; and *stradali*, street markets without any sort of municipal assistance.[22] Most vendors deal in foodstuffs, whereas other stands cover a wide range including household items, clothes and shoes, various craft items, services such as knife-sharpeners, and the occasional used bookseller. Roman markets open early in the morning and close around two in the afternoon, though some of them are experimenting with hours extended into the afternoon. Itinerant pop-up vendors are also part of the market portrait, often selling roasted chestnuts in the winter, roast pork sandwiches, or general refreshments. In recent years, improvised farmer's markets have been cropping up more often, particularly on the weekends, selling their own wares directly, quality local foodstuffs, now commonly referred to as *chilometro zero*, brought into the city from the Campagna Romana.

The association of the countryside with fruitfulness is making something of a comeback. In recent centuries, land surrounding the Urbs had become infamous for its desolation, a barrenness so shocking that, like the urban ruins, it captured the attention of artists and travel writers through the ages. Upon his departure from Rome to Florence, Hippolyte Taine wrote in his journal:

> I hadn't yet seen this part of the Roman countryside, and if it had been for me, I never would have. Everywhere the same impression: it is an abandoned cemetery. The long monotone mounds in interminable rows, like the ones you find on battlefields, when they covered over large trenches filled with the dead. Not a tree, not a stream, not a shack. In two hours I saw but one round hut with a pointed roof like the ones on savage dwellings.[23]

These were not the just the complaints of ingrate foreigners. Native son Giuseppe Gioachino Belli, famous for his sonnets in Roman dialect paints this stark portrait of venturing outside the city limits to get cheese:

> God help me, Christ and the Madonna
> I have to go once again to that barn for the *giuncata*.
> What can I say? . . . I say that I'd rather
> be castrated by a norcino[24] at the Rotonda.[25]

You could run ten miles without seeing a tree!
Encountering only a ruin now and again!
Everywhere there is a silence like oil,
if you cry out, there is no one to answer!

Wherever you turn the land is flat
as if a planer had passed through,
without the least hint of a house!

The only single thing I found
on the whole journey was a cart
in which the cart driver fallen over, slain.

March 26, 1836

In town, observations are more spirited. Henry Noel Humphreys, in his travel book *Rome and Its Surrounding Scenery* (1840) remarks on the peasants coming into the city for the morning market:

The farmers on the confines of the campagna, which begirds Rome as the Lagune does Venice, are as industrious as the boatmen of St Marco; and have acquired as great skill in the construction of the light carriages which bear their produce to the Roman markets as the former in their unrivaled gondolas. It is a picturesque sight, every morning about seven, at the Porta del Popolo, or San Giovanni, to watch the string of vehicles that I can scarcely call carts, arriving in quick succession at the gate; and their drivers in their peculiar dress, settling their various *gabelle* (town dues) with the *doganieri* (customs officers). These vehicles, loaded with oil, wine, olives, cheeses, butter, gourds of every description, grapes, pomegranates and various species of vegetables, are most admirably constructed, each for its particular purpose. An English cart, while still empty, is already a load for a horse; but an Englishman's ideas of solidity and durability in all things, however unnecessary, must be satisfied.[26]

From his favorite perch in Piazza Navona, where he ogled at the "fresh-coloured faces of the picturesquely grouped peasant girls, who are generally congregated in such situations, and are always worth looking at," Humphreys offers his very British perspective on the cheese market:

Rome is not the most celebrated, and certainly not the best district for cheese—for what can equal that *strachino di Milano?*—yet the variety and singularity of the species of home produce to be met with, merit the particular attention of a connoisseur. *La ricotta! La ricotta!* is the next cry. In appearance and texture it is something like the new cream cheese sold in London as York cheese. It is turned out of a little wicker basket, like a lump of blanc-mange from its mould. It has a delightfully sweet creamy flavour and is made from *sheep's milk*; and when spread upon a good thick crust of genuine brown bread, I know nothing I could enjoy more after a ramble among the ruined aqueducts of the campagna. . . . A Roman farmer possesses no resource that he does not turn to account: for he likewise brings to market his *formaggio cavallo*, and his *formaggio di buffala*. This would make a British dairymaid open her eyes: mare's milk! and buffalo's milk! Both however are very good. The cheeses have a somewhat spongy texture, but remarkably fine flavour, and, as they are prepared and tied up in little skins, will keep for any length of time. Then there is the *provatura*, another preparation of the milk of the *buffalo*, which is very nice in any way, but, toasted upon bread like a Welsh rarebit, is excellent.[27]

The *mozzarella di bufala campana* he speaks of now has the coveted DOP or *denominazione di origine protetta* status awarded by the European Union to products whose characteristics depend essentially or exclusively on the territory in which they originate. The milk for this creamy mozzarella comes from water buffalo, whose large splayed hoofs are well suited to the waterlogged land of the Pontine Fields.[28] They feed on the fibrous semi-aquatic vegetation that other species cannot digest, but are not prized for their meat. Their virtue lies in the superbly rich milk that rendered exquisite cheese. Paul the Deacon (CE 720–799) tells us that the domesticated Asian buffalo was introduced into Rome in the late sixth century CE:

> In the following month of January, a comet appeared morning and evening through the whole of the month. . . . And in these same days, while the Bavarians, to the number of thirty thousand men, attacked the Slavs, the Cagan fell upon them and all were killed. Then for the first time, wild horses and [water] buffaloes were brought into Italy, and were objects of wonder to that country.[29]

By the twelfth century they were in full commercial use for cheese.

The *fiordilatte di appennino meridionale* is another fresh mozzarella-like string cheese. Unlike most Roman cheeses that are made with sheep's milk, *fiordilatte* is made with whole raw cow's milk derived from one or two milkings no more than sixteen hours apart, which lends a uniquely satisfying mouth feel to the final product. This cheese also bears the DOP seal of quality.

Rome's most famous cheese is Pecorino Romano. It was one of two cheeses (the other being Roquefort) to receive DOP status in 1953 from the newly formed international certification board, at which time the process and ingredients were codified. It differs from other pecorino cheeses in the processing and percentage of salt added. The higher percentage of salt results in a hard cheese that is more often used for grating and as an ingredient rather than as a table cheese. Its pungency makes it less suited than Parmesan to delicate dishes. Pecorino pre-dates Rome and may even have been first made by the Latins who occupied the southeastern left bank of the Tiber, opposite the Etruscan city of Veii. Today, the two main areas for Roman production are just outside the city in the Comino Valley and the Monti della laga range, but most of the Pecorino Romano is actually made in Sardinia due to an 1884 law that prohibited the salting phase of Pecorino Romano within the walls of the city, perhaps due to the state salt monopoly. While 80 percent of the Italian production is earmarked for North American markets, Pecorino Romano should not be confused with the powder sold abroad in canisters called "Romano" cheese, which is made with cow's milk.

Other noteworthy Roman sheep's milk cheeses include *Cacio fiore*, *Marzolino*, *ricotta*, *Caciotta* and *caciocavallo*, *provola*, and the *giuncata* mentioned in the Belli sonnet. Giuncata is a fresh sheep's milk cheese traditionally associated with the Feast of the Ascension, the day signaling the beginning of the milking season for sheep and goats. It was frequently made at home and gets its name from the simple baskets made of *giunco* reeds that left a characteristic mark on the curd as it drained and settled. Cacio fiore, which was described as early as 50 CE by Columella in *De re rustica*, is a cheese that is making a comeback. What makes this cheese unique is that the coagulants are derived from Rome's indigenous flora. At the turn of the new millennium, production of this historic cheese had nearly disappeared. Thanks to the willingness on the part of a few independent producers and the backing of Slow Food, today the production of Cacio fiore is expanding and it can once again be found on the retail market, made faithfully as it once was with raw sheep's milk coagulated with cardoon flowers or occasionally artichoke flowers. The final product presents a yellowish crust enclosing a creamy, almost liquid cheese that is intensely flavored, slightly bitter and not too salty. This cheese is one of the many products of the territory that binds Rome's culinary past to the present.

Today's open markets in Rome deal mostly in fruits and vegetables, rarely in fish or meat, and only sporadically in cheese and cured meats. Most of the produce comes from local farms and occasionally even from inner-city plots—the so-called *vignaroli*. A list of the streets in the historic center of Rome will reveal a number of street names with the word *vigna*: Via di Vigna Murata, Largo di Vigna Stelluti, Vicolo di Vigna Rosati, Viale di Vigna Pia, Via delle Vigne Nuove and many more. When in September of 1870, the soldiers of the Kingdom of Italy brought down the city walls with cannon fire near Porta Pia and stormed into the city, bringing a definitive end to more than a millennium of Church rule over the Papal State, they found themselves surrounded by vineyards and rows of grapevines that circled around along the inside of the city wall. One soldier recounts their entry into Rome:

> Those who tended the vines greeted us with the utmost courtesy. . . . We took advantage of the commotion to beg them for something to eat, and they very thoughtfully offered us some excellent bread, eggs, pecorino cheese and local wine; but one young man didn't find the refreshment up to snuff for persons of our ilk so he took off down the lane through the grapevines. We saw him reappear a little while later on via Nomentana looking quite proud of himself. He had gone to the Magnani osteria about a kilometer away and had come back with a tray full of a delicious "chicken cacciatore." That was our introduction to Roman osteria food, and I don't believe that from Bracciano onwards I had ever eaten so well.[30]

Up to the first decades of the twentieth century, before the broad-scale reconstruction that brought about the creation of the *umbertini* neighborhoods—so named for King Humbert of Savoy—wine was still produced in the immediate vicinity of Rome. Positioned as it was on the seven hills, the city enjoyed optimal conditions for cultivating grapevines. Elevated areas such as the Aventine, Janiculum, Monte Mario—the highest hill in Rome—and many others, have long been subsumed into the urban fabric of streets and buildings.

In the Roman dialect, *romanesco*, the *vignarolo*, whose generosity toward his enemies was captured in the excerpt above, was the person who looked after the grapevines, while the fruit and vegetable sellers were called *ortolani*, from the Latin *hortus*. In Trastevere, the historic church Santa Maria dell'Orto, literally St. Mary of the Garden, stands as a testimony to the importance of the ortolani. The church, constructed between 1489–1567, was financed by the Santa Maria dell'Orto confraternity, a conglomerate of thirteen *università* or guilds among which were both the ortolani and the vignaroli. The farmers who brought vegetables into town from their own gardens were actually called vignaroli because the grapevines were *maritate*, or married, to the gardens, meaning that alongside the rows of vines grew vegetables and legumes, above all fava beans and peas, planted in close proximity as they enriched the soil. Whereas the ortolani purchased goods wholesale and sold retail, the vignaroli, brought in their own produce to sell directly.

Globalization and greenhouses have altered agricultural methods and seasonality. But the vignaroli stands now offer produce picked and marketed the same day, and those who frequent them often can observe the colorful flow of the seasons. Artichokes, fresh fava beans, and peas, the lettuces, asparagus, and fresh garlic and scallions give way in the heat of summer to the green ribbed Roman zucchini with their ephemeral golden flowers, bright yellow peppers, apricots, and fragrant loquats, and brown and crimson streaked peaches. Around *ferragosto*, midsummer's day, a national holiday that takes its name from the *Feriae Augusti*, the festival period established by Emperor Augustus, come the red tomatoes and peppers, watermelon and cantaloupe, whose pastel orange foreshadows the thick orange-fleshed squash and sticky sweet persimmons; as the weather sobers these are contrasted with chestnuts and table grapes, the Roman heritage variety being the elongated *uva pizzutello da tavola di Tivoli*, also called *uva cornetta* because of its unusual shape.

With the cold, which can sometimes be biting in Rome, comes the romanesco broccoli, whose unique pointy swirling florets are a mesmerizing chartreuse, and *puntarelle*, whose crispy pale spears are julienned into a salad of curly shreds and dressed with the classic Roman flavors of anchovy and garlic. Several varieties of oranges flood the market after Christmas. Oranges are said to have been brought to Europe in the fourteenth century by way of Portuguese mariners, but ancient Roman sources mention them as early as the first century CE. St. Dominic purportedly brought a sapling to Rome around 1220 from Spain, his land of origin, and planted it at the Convent of Saint Sabina on the Aventine with his own hands. The original tree, old and dry after all of these centuries, continues to bear fruit from the other trees that miraculously grew out of the parent, symbol of perpetual goodwill toward humankind. Legend has it that Saint Catherine of Siena offered five candied oranges to Pope Urban VI from this very tree in the hopes of sweetening him up (his papacy having been soured by the Western Schism). The gift bore the desired fruit and prompted the return of the Holy See to Rome.

The return of spring is heralded by the all-too-brief window of succulent strawberries and cherries, the traditional Roman heritage varieties being, respectively, the *fragolina di Nemi*, which must certainly have been the inspiration for sweet tart candies, and *ciliegia Ravenna della Sabina*.

Not far from the Vatican City on Via Cola di Renzo is the beautiful Mercato dell'Unità, built in 1928. Up through World War II the market was laid out on two floors: an underground one where the fishmongers and spice vendors had their stands, which is now used for parking, and the ground floor, where the fruit and vegetable stands stood. On the rooftop there was a skating rink, the first of its kind in Europe. Today, many of the market stalls are empty; the outdoor fountains are dry and the indoor ones, whose spouts were shaped like the head of the she-wolf, were dismantled during the 1970s restoration. The market survives, such as it is, thanks to sentimental clientele and restaurant and trattoria buyers who come there for supplies.

In the immediate vicinity of the Vatican itself, just a few meters from the entrance to the Sistine Chapel, is the Mercato Trionfale. The market gets its name, as does the entire quarter, from the Via Trionfale, one of the oldest streets leading into city that joined Rome to the Etruscan city of Veii. The name *Triumphalis* stands for the festive welcome that the citizens gave to the general Camillus when he returned victorious from a campaign against the Etruscans (c. 396 BCE), thus making Rome the greatest power over the Italic peoples. The consular road became the showcase for other commanders to receive accolades when they returned to the city triumphant. During the Middle Ages, pilgrims came down this same road, having arrived on their journey from the Via Romea Francigena, the route from France to the Eternal City.

The market, with over two hundred seventy stands, is the largest in Rome and among the largest in Italy. It opened at the end of the 1800s to serve the needs of the new neighborhoods that were overflowing into the countryside. In addition to serving the local neighborhoods, it was also a convenient rest stop for hunters and travelers on horseback or with carts, who needed to stock up for the journey ahead. In the 1930s, the market transferred to Via Andrea Doria in what was then a working and lower-middle-class area. It gradually transformed into a more stylish residential area, but without losing any of its former familiar allure. These two orientations coexist side by side in the stalls of the marketplace and in the patrons: heaps of vegetables, still encrusted with dirt, are flanked by displays of upscale items; old ladies towing their well-worn shopping trolleys navigate the isles alongside the fastidious gourmands in search of truffles or oysters. Until 2009, the marketers utilized aluminum cage-style stands on the wide sidewalks, and then in March of that year, the new structure in glass and concrete was opened, with an underground parking lot, toilet facilities, and elevators. It is divided into corridors with color-coded stands depending on the category of merchandise sold: green for fruit and vegetables, blue for fish, red for meat. Everything imaginable can be found here. Fresh and dried fruit and nuts, every sort of rice and grain, fresh and preserved fish, salumi, cheeses, eggs, fresh pasta, mushrooms, vegetables, oil, wine, bread, pizza, baked goods, honey, and jam, in addition to home supplies, clothes, bags, shoes, toys, exotic products and ingredients for ethnic cuisines.

With some exceptions, the vignaroli are positioned at the back of the market, and somewhere on the stand is usually a sign letting the public know where his/her farmstead is located. Now and again the odd tourist ventures into the market, but it is essentially frequented by Romans and residents, even some who come relatively long distances given the high-quality products and low prices. There are a number of cooks and restaurateurs on hand selling prepared food, particularly fish, a great help to those in a bind to get something decent on the table at the last minute. Wait staff of the market's cafes navigate stalls and customers to bring coffee to the vendors, coffee that is often "corrected" with a drop or two of sambuca, particularly on cold winter mornings. Some stalls display photographs of their parents or grandparents from long ago, tables piled high with artichokes or grapes, or perhaps views of the countryside with stretches of farmland or orchards. Many of these businesses have obviously been proudly passed down through the generations, but there are plenty of new faces as well, often immigrants.

Among the vegetable stands there is always someone putting on a demonstration of how to properly prepare their wares. One of the most interesting is certainly the preparation of *puntarelle*, Catalonia chicory sprouts. The outer leaves are peeled off revealing an inner cluster of light green spears. These can either be pushed one by one through a specially made metal mesh, or carefully julienned with a knife and quickly dropped into ice-cold water so that they achieve the characteristic curl. Half a lemon is squeezed into the water to prevent oxidation. Once they have chilled and curled, they are dressed with a sauce made of olive oil, anchovies, and garlic—a quintessential Roman salad found in every trattoria with traditional fare. Catalonia chicory can be grown successfully in a greenhouse, but the best time to get them is between December and April.

The market merchants trim, or *capano* (from the Roman dialect verb *capare*, meaning to clean vegetables), not only *puntarelle*, but artichokes as well, which also need to be plunged immediately into a lemon juice and water solution, as they are rich in iron and blacken as soon as they are cut. The artisan takes a small knife and makes a few deft slices in the involucre, opening the round bud and removing the outer leaves or bracts, the protective foliage around the floret, exposing the inner delicate artichoke, whose heart is a green-gold tinged with violet. They are tossed into a bucket under a whiteboard with the market price for the day and the types in stock.

The artichoke arose from the domestication of the wild cardoon, a plant that is native to Lazio and was widespread in the Mediterranean long before Rome was founded. Not only was it a favorite foodstuff, but among the Phoenicians, Greeks, Carthaginians, Etruscans, and Romans it was also coveted for its phytotherapeutic properties. The many ways in which the wild plant was domesticated rendered over ninety varieties of artichokes classified as being either with or without thorns. The Roman variety is a thornless one, a fleshy, rotund artichoke called *mammola* or *cimarolo*. The ancient Latins called artichokes *cynara*, but its modern Italian name *carciofo* derives from the Arabic karshūf. In Tarquinia, seventy kilometers north of Rome, there is a renowned Etruscan necropolis of the ancient city *Tàrchuna*. In the center of what is dubbed the "Baron's Tomb" there are painstakingly painted artichoke leaves. This is the most northerly border of what can be called the home of the *carciofo romanesco*; it then carries on toward Montalto di Castro and Canino, and descends around Allumiere and Tolfa, picking up the coast of Civitavecchia, Santa Marinella, Cerveteri, Ladispoli, Fiumicino, branching out toward Rome and Campagnano and again descending toward the Pontine Fields in Sezze, Priverno, and Sermoneta, finding its southern most limits toward Campagna. Cimaroli have long been grown here, and cultivation has picked up exponentially since the post–World War II era. Ladispoli, Sezze, and Velletri pay homage with country festivals and markets specifically dedicated to the artichoke.

The *carciofo romanesco* was the first product in Italy to receive IGP status—*Indicazione Geografica Protetta*—a seal of quality similar to DOP that does not require that each step of a procedure be executed in the region of origin, only that it be traced back to the area. It does, however, have to be cultivated without the use of artificial fertilizers so as to maintain its genuine quality. Once purchased, artichokes should be used quickly because they do not fare well under refrigeration; freshness is of the essence if one is to enjoy it at its best. Their prime season runs from January to May.

Artichokes are flowers that are harvested as buds, long before they bloom, and are available at different times. Those on top, called *mamme*, or mammas (hence: *mammole*) are ready first (note that the word *cimarolo* comes from *cima*, meaning "top"). This is followed by the *figli*, the children, on the sides, and the *nipoti*, or grandchildren, which grow closer to the base. In all, about ten artichokes can usually be harvested from a single plant. Quality is defined in descending order, thus the best are those that are higher up. Sometimes the children and grandchildren don't even make it to market; generally they are sent to factories for pickling and canning in oil. A true *cimarolo* that has been well *capato* and sliced into a salad of thin shavings, needs only be sprinkled lightly with fresh lemon juice, with a hint of salt and a grind of fragrant black pepper to fulfill its potential.

There are two types of broccoli that are officially designated as traditional to Rome. Both are planted in September and arrive in the marketplace through the winter until April. The lesser known is *broccoli di Anguillara*, primarily a leafy green vegetable with the occasional thin stalk of loose florets. It is grown in many other areas, but the microclimate around Lake

Figure 5.2. Roman globe artichokes called *le mamme*. Photo by Karima Moyer-Nocchi, c. 2018

Bracciano, where it has grown since the Middle Ages, confers a unique flavor that is regarded as superior to those cultivated in other places. Legend has it that a local farmer was hunting and captured a pigeon with strange seeds in its craw. The man removed them and tossed them on the ground and not long after in that precise spot, a most flavorful broccoli appeared. The more famous of the two varieties is the previously mentioned broccoli romanesco whose geometric perfection may cause the uninitiated to wonder if they are real or the result of a bizarre genetic experiment. If a vignarolo catches you eyeing them, s/he'll start the slow pitch: "If you want I've got them already *capati* (trimmed). Speaking just for myself, I like them done *semplice semplice*, boiled until they are just done and then sautéed ever so lightly in *ajio, ojo, e peperoncino*. Why don't you give it a try and let me know what you think?"

When the warmth of late spring descends on Rome, the prices drop on *zucchine romanesche* and their flowers. These too are available year round from greenhouses, but it is in the summer months that they are at their height. These zucchini are distinguished by the deep ribbing running the length of the fruit and their unique, variegated lawn-green and pale yellow, an almost washed-out coloring. A brief sauté will exalt the texture and flavor that sets them apart from other zucchini. The flower attached to the end is the indicator of how fresh they are. These delicacies come in two forms, the female, attached to the end of the zucchini itself, or the male, flowers that grows on a stem and are cut to be sold in bunches like a bouquet. The latter are the basis for the recipes for *fiori fritti*, stuffed fried flowers, the most famous of which is stuffed with mozzarella and anchovy, dipped in a batter, and fried crisp. Although this is a "typical" or characteristic Roman vegetable, they are a rather recent addition to the agricultural offerings of the agro romano and surrounding area. They were cultivated widely only after the reclamation work carried out in the 1800s, which rendered swamplands viable for farming. Other vegetables that are essential to modern Roman cuisine had a similar history; vegetables such as carrots, eggplant, and bell peppers were planted intensively once sufficient land had been drained and leveled. Other players on the Roman table from the Campagna Romana, like fennel, Roman broccoli, and the majestic artichoke, have a considerably longer history.

There is an Italian expression that goes, *ha detto di cotto e di crudo!* Meaning that someone unloaded on you without holding anything back—literally "s/he said both cooked and raw!" The raw vegetable dish known in other parts of Italy as *pinzimonio* is called *cazzimperio* in Rome. Central to the dish are artichokes, celery, and fennel, cut lengthwise into chunky strips to be dunked, bite by bite, into a small dish of olive oil, salt, and pepper. In Roman dialect celery is called *séllero*. Its introduction into Rome is recounted by a certain Dottor Cavalier Andrea Belli in his book *On Houses Inhabited by Several Illustrious Men*, an eclectic collection of Roman curiosities:

> Speaking of the homes inhabited by distinguished men of science, letters, and the arts, I will permit myself now to point out one where the first man to introduce celery cultivation into Rome lived. On the street that is on one of the most beautiful blocks in Rome that leads straight to the Liberian Basilica at number 118 lived a Greek named Atanasio Kirgiu. . . . This Kirgiu was the first to sow celery seeds. And, seeing as how any novelty attracts envy and suspicion, he was accused of having planted poisonous herbs. But he managed to convince his slanderers by eating a bunch of it before the Holy Father Clement VIII who, having observed him over the course of a year in a state of optimal health, encouraged widespread cultivation, he even gave the man a silver medal. Everyone who then wanted to enjoy the new plant would say, "Let's go get some of that herb from the Greek's garden." . . . Returning to celery, I must warn, as do the other Professors of the health arts, that users of this aromatic mustn't abuse it, as it has been entered into the class of aphrodisiacs.[31]

Fennel is a common companion on the *cazzimperio* plate, and in good company with celery being of the same botanical family, the *apiacea*. There are two types of fennel bulbs, the male and female: the former is longer and stringier, while the latter has a round, fleshy belly. The verb *infinocchiare* means to hoodwink or bamboozle, which is attributed to the way it distorts the taste of wine. Dishonest innkeepers are said to have offered a bit of fennel before a meal to mask mediocre wine, blaming it on the fennel. The chemical makeup of both raw fennel and artichokes act upon the palate in a way that alters the taste of wine in an unpleasant way. In the distant past in Rome the cazzimperio was eaten at the end of the meal to aid digestion and refresh the breath. Its presentation as a starter comes from a more modern dietary concept, as well as the influence of cultures that consume salads at the beginning of the meal.

Among the salad items on offer, the long-leafed Romaine lettuce is ubiquitous and retains its name denoting Roman origin throughout Italy. *Misticanza*, has a more poignant biography. *Misto* means "mixed," therefore, the misticanza is a combination of tender field greens, edible plants of whatever variety that can be found and foraged along roads, even highways, in the woods, in fields, anywhere. Historically, it was an answer to necessity; it was free, tasty, life-sustaining food that filled in dietary gaps afflicting the poor. Today, these are a sought-after rarity, found only on occasion at the Trionfale vignaroli stand, due to the time-consuming way they are harvested and the unpredictability of even finding them, not to mention legal questions about food safety. It is all thrown together and varies depending on the season and the location. Some typical greens from the area include borage, wild chicory, fennel, radish and anise, dandelion, sow thistle, salsola soda, chervil, field scabious, endives, poppy, purslane, rampion bellflower, rucola, bladder campion, and many more. Unlike cultivated lettuces, these greens impart a decisive, often bitter, flavor and robust texture that was associated with indigence until they were reassessed in the age of rural revivalism. Up through the 1980s when the mass exodus from the countryside to the city was complete, it was not uncommon to see men and women bent over in the open country, or barren fields, or along consular roads, or even in the city foraging greens for their supper. The *cicoriari/e* were professional foragers who carried on this practice that linked the ancient sylvan world to the modern metropolitan one, leaving those who still remember with the image of gigantic bundles of misticanza balanced on their heads, bound for market, the fruit of hours of labor. Today, some amateurs have picked it up as a weekend hobby, a back-to-nature pastime. Although it romanticizes a life of fatigue, at least the tradition is being kept alive. Misticanza, being a true food of the so-called *cucina povera*, is best prepared simply as a salad with a dash of salt and a drizzle of oil. They can also be cooked and dressed in the same way, which is how they are served on the rare occasion that they are found in restaurants due to their ephemeral nature. More often than not, however, what is called misticanza in restaurants is actually a mix of some sort of domesticated greens like chicory, turnip greens, and/or spinach. One can only be certain that it is the genuine article by purchasing it raw at the market, or foraging with someone in the know.

Meat and Fish

Of all the vendors at the market, butchers are probably the category most steeped in tradition. Photos abound showing generations of burly men, grinning in their white shop coats, surrounded by rows of dangling carcasses or fowl strung up by their necks, fully feathered or plucked smooth, tantalizing buyers with visual testimonies of freshness and abundance, signs of a time when the reality of where meat came from was not a source of shock or surprise. The butcher once served as the mediator between the life and death of the animal, saving the public from the theater of the abattoir, but today's public needs to be even further shielded from the actual origins of the meatballs they are serving up for dinner. And butchers everywhere have acquiesced. Behind that glass barrier are ready-to-cook meats, breaded cutlets, roasts stuffed, rolled, seasoned, and tightly bound in string, and hamburgers called *svizzeri*,[32] stamped into perfect disks and individually wrapped in cellophane. The heads of sheep, pigs, and cows that used to pique the shopper's appetite are displayed more discreetly, with respect for the deceased.

Another tradition that has all but vanished is the specialization in specific kinds of meat. It used to be that each butcher shop had its specialization: pork and salumi was separate from fowl, which was separate from beef. Equine vendors have almost disappeared entirely. The old signs declaring "Lamb and chicken" are still found now and again, but these vendors carry other meats as well, or they would not survive. If butchery is to endure as a specialized craft, butchers need to distinguish their wares from those in the supermarket meat section, to exalt and guarantee the origin of their meat as coming from this or that farm, known for their experience and the humane treatment of the animals—and consequently for the quality of the meat. Very few do that, but perhaps that is because in reality, even at the market, most of them purchase from the same wholesaler. Consequently, it makes little difference if you buy from Sig. Proietti or Sig. Mammucari. But there are still some butchers for whom the butcher shop is not just a day job, dedicated artisans who put an effort into sourcing meats locally, and dealing directly with the farmer as well as offering interesting new products like the costly Japanese Kobe beef. The success of these novel ventures depends on the public's ability to discern quality and their willingness to pay the higher price tag, not to mention doing justice to their purchase once they get it home—and that is *un altro paio di maniche*, another matter altogether.[33]

As is true most everywhere today, fish for the Roman markets comes in from fisheries the world over. Atlantic shrimp fight for space on the ice with Indo-Pacific calamari, while the omnipresent tuna asserts itself as an alternative to steak. Fishmongers worthy of their name try to source as locally as possible, but if weather conditions are working against them, they will push you to accept what there is. Customers trawling for upmarket "wild" products migrate from place to place, as stocks are exhausted quickly. Trionfale now caters to the oyster cult, whose converts are offered stools and a glass of white wine or *spumante* to wash down their fresh mollusk. But Rome's best bivalve is the *tellina del littoral laziale*: small and flavorful, harvested along the sandy shores of Ostia, Anzio, Fegene, Ladispoli, and Santa Severa. These are not for the raw seafood crowd, though. They are best prepared in a hot skillet with oil, garlic, parsley, with a dash of white wine to mingle with the briny juices. As they are similar to clams, they are generally used to dress spaghetti, but the distinct flavor of the *telline* is more coveted and representative of the Roman seaboard.

Another distinctly Roman fish recipe is *pasta e broccoli col brodo d'arzilla*, part of the Roman-Jewish culinary tradition. *Arzilla*, the dialect name for the studded skate, is not a kosher fish, but is one of many representative foods that crossed, or rather joined, cultural contexts.[34] The appeal of this dish is the flavorful, velvety broth from the fine cartilaginous bones of the broad wing-like branchial fins. They soften and melt, creating a base for broccoli florets, broken spaghetti, and aromatics.

Minestra di broccoli e arzilla

Serves 4–6
1½ pounds of skate, cleaned, skinned, and cut into large pieces
1 carrot, sliced
1 onion, halved
1 celery rib, sliced
3 sprigs parsley
2 tablespoons olive oil
1 clove garlic, smashed
1 peperoncino or ½ teaspoon chili flakes
1 large broccoli romanesco, chopped
Sea salt
2 tablespoons tomato sauce
4 ounces spaghetti broken into 2-inch pieces

Put the skate, carrot, onion, celery, and parsley in a large pot and add cold water to cover. Bring to a simmer over low heat and skim. Simmer for 20 to 30 minutes, or until the fish falls away from the bone easily, and skim again. Remove from heat, filter the broth through a cheesecloth-lined strainer, and set aside. Pick the skate meat from the bones and set aside, discarding bones and solids.

Heat 2 tablespoons olive oil in a large pot over low heat. When the oil begins to shimmer, add the garlic and cook just until it begins to turn golden, then add the peperoncino and cook until fragrant, about 30 seconds. Add the broccoli, season with salt, and increase the heat to medium. Cook until soft and creamy, adding water a tablespoon or 2 at a time to keep the pot from drying out. Add the tomato and simmer for a few minutes, then add the fish broth. The consistency should be loose and soupy but not watery. Bring to a boil, season to taste, then add the spaghetti and cook until done, thinning with additional broth if needed. Add the skate, stir to warm, then serve.[35]

Some of what were once Rome's traditional fish, like eel and its relative the *ciriole* (now only remembered by way of a fish-shaped bread roll and a long thick pasta), have silently disappeared. When river fishing was still possible, they were one of the crowning glories of Roman restaurants; today they are a rare find.

The Whole Roasted Pig
One of the main attractions of the Roman market is the whole roasted pig, gutted, deboned, generously seasoned with herbs and spices and slow roasted. In 1957, author Carlo Emilio Gadda captured the cry of the *porchetta* hawker, the *porchettaro*, in Piazza Vittorio:

> La porca! La porca! We have *porchetta* here ladies and gentlemen! The good pork of Ariccia with a whole forest of rosemary in that there belly! With potatoes of the season! [. . .] a fine and delicate meat it is for good folks like yourselves! Taste it and try it, I say my fine ladies: here's some fine and tasty meat! . . . *Porchetta* with rosemary! And with potatoes of the season![36]

Porchetta attracts two schools of thought: one seasoned with wild fennel, and the other with rosemary, harking back to Etruscan and Latin times. Ariccia, an ancient town in Roman wine country, the Castelli Romani, was famous for its free-range swine raised on acorns and chestnuts. *Porchetta di Ariccia* was conferred the IGP seal of quality, although pigs, being one of the domestic animals most subject to globalization, are not necessarily free-range anymore—even in Ariccia. However, the difference is palatable; the diet and living conditions contribute significantly to the taste and texture of the meat.

Esoteric, Exotic, and Gentrified

At the other end of the spectrum from everyday market foods are stalls dedicated to aficionados, the *buongustai*. They hunt down the stands where the finest cheeses are displayed in the company of ten varieties of baccalà, a plethora of truffle products, caviar, and the most renowned salumi in Italy. Scattered here and there are mushrooms, exotic fruit, duck eggs, suckling pigs, buffalo meat, fresh pasta of every kind, and, oddly enough, pre-soaked

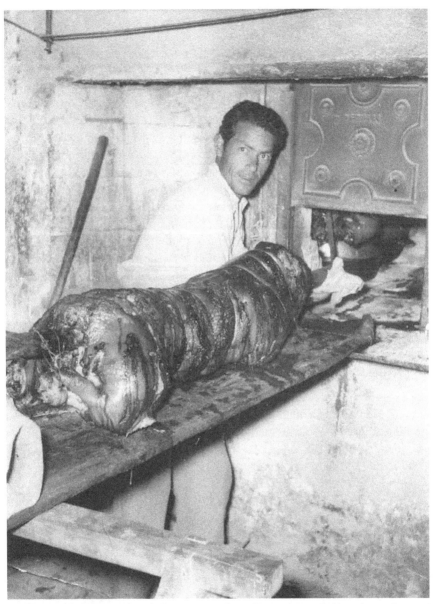

Figure 5.3. Empedocle Leopardi, founder of Porchetta Leopardi, historic producer of Porchetta di Ariccia IGP in the Castelli Romani. Photo courtesy of Salumificio Porchetta Leopardi Srl

chickpeas, a throwback to religious fast days when the common dish was *baccalà con ceci*.

The ever increasing sales of exotic foods, above all from the Far East, underscores the fact that a true wave of change is overtaking Italian society, owing both to the influx of immigrants and to Italians' recent curiosity about the gastronomy of other cultures. This offers a clear view of how tastes are actively oscillating between millennia of peasant-dominated culture and the frenzied drive of global consumption that is part and parcel of the era of superabundance, the overcompensation and reparation for centuries of hunger—a hunger that is still part of living memory.

Among the major marketplaces in Rome, there is a decisively different atmosphere at the frenetic Nuovo Mercato Esquilino opened in 2001. It is a large, indoor Asian market run by people of various origins who have made Rome their home. The fruit and vegetable stalls are heaving with just-picked produce, some of which is only recognizable to those whose traditions make use of those foods. And the fish is so fresh that holdouts are still twitching or panting in protest on the ice. Meats are scrupulously separated in accordance with religious dictates. This is not a market for the merely curious, but for people who love and are well acquainted with Asian foodways. The heady aroma as you enter immediately says that you have entered into a truly unique Roman space. Because the patrons are mainly people in-the-know looking to continue their home culinary traditions on a daily basis, the prices are exceptionally low and the quality high.

The Mercato Trionfale can be seen as a paradigm for the organization and operation of all of the markets in Rome; there are some variations, but the fundamental proposal is the same. At the same time, each one has its own unique characteristics and statement to make about the state of Roman food today. Worthy of mention in this regard is the market in Testaccio. It is a beautiful structure inaugurated in 2012 with over one hundred stalls; its hybrid soul unites tradition and the new gastronomic voices. Here you can shop for groceries, buy books or clothes, or eat street food made by top chefs. Of all the Roman markets it is the one that most has its eye on the future, undoubtedly due to the social trends in the area, moving ever more toward a bohemian atmosphere.

Another recently restructured building is the beautiful Mercato Nomentano with its wide windows, wrought-iron doors, and pediments adorned with the she-wolf nursing Romulus and Remus and Sabine women with fruit and vegetable regalia crowning their heads. It is a notable example of

Figure 5.4.   Stands heaving with fresh produce at the New Esqualino Market. Photo by Karima Moyer-Nocchi, c. 2017

industrial architecture of the mid 1920s, brought up to date with Wi-Fi and a food court. While it attracts the occasional interested tourist, most of the clientele is locals—housewives, immigrant caregivers, retirees, and the like.

Shopping at markets has become a luxury or even a hobby, convenient for those with time to spare or who are fortunate enough to live nearby, but unrealistic for those bound by the standard workaday schedule. Most of the Roman custom goes to supermarkets, hypermarkets, and deep-discount stores that offer convenience and predictability at a decent price, conditions that make it easier to turn a blind eye to quality. It gets the shopping, grocery and otherwise, out of the way in one fell swoop.

At the other end of the spectrum are the gourmet food boutiques and up-market groceries. Eataly is the prime example of the latter, where eager patrons can shop, eat, meet, and learn what to buy in the softly lit corridors of its pseudo-artisan food departments, whose shelves are brimming with pricy must-have curiosities. It allows the urban consumer to enter into a blissful, metaphysical shopping experience—and still be assured of a real parking place out front.

CHAPTER SIX

Er da magna'

Eats: La cucina romanesca

A Tradition in the Making

In his massive tome *Il ghiottone* (*The Gormandizer*) (1965), Livio Jannattoni, repository of Roman culture, elaborates a romantic vision of *la cucina romanesca* as having remained more or less fixed in time. The stove in a genuine Roman osteria, he says, is under the command of a woman,

> the wife or mother of the owner who has merely transferred her home cooking, simple and immutable, to a commercial sphere without changing anything else. Hence we can declare without a doubt that the strength and goodness of the *cucina romana*, as can be said of any institution taking its name from this city, lie in this immutability. Immutability in time and space (with the inevitable extraneous infiltrations brought about by social changes, "encounters" with other cuisines, and perhaps in part to a change in tastes), from the 1500s to Belli and from Belli to today, from the serenity of our domestic walls to the warm vitality of those crowded osterias.[1]

Gender politics aside, arguably the most significant part of this bold statement is what is tucked into the parentheses: inevitable influences, from outside and in, pressing upon the available resources and status quo as part of an ongoing culinary evolution. The evolutionary process only stops when it becomes codified, when enough time has passed for us to look back and realize that what was going on was "tradition making." That which had been right under our noses all along suddenly catches our attention precisely because foodways are not immutable in time and space, and it is only by taking that step back and comparing now with then that objects and practices can be sifted out, setting off a compulsion to cling to and save whatever might remain. We experience the mutation as loss; we feel as if we are watching "our" traditions slip through the cracks of time. It is then that cookbooks, essays, and articles are written picking apart and recording the hairsplitting details for posterity, creating terroir tales that prove, sustain, and validate the singularity and value of our culinary traditions. But the futility, even absurdity, of stopping a cuisine in its tracks and declaring its "arrival" negates the very evolutionary process that brought it to fruition. Perhaps the journey lies in observing how the multifaceted dynamics play out along their trajectory through time and space rather than establishing their timelessness and immutability. The story of the cucina romanesca is enmeshed in just such a dynamic weave. It oscillates between what may seem like two parallel universes, the *cardinalizia*, that of the aristocracy,[2] and *del popolo*, that of the people. A sound starting point to trace how these poles came together would be the return of the papal court to Rome.

Papal Preamble

> Rome no longer even looks like a city. . . . There is not a trace, a hint of an urban reality there!
>
> —*Platina*

Once the papacy had been restored to Rome after the Avignon captivity, a succession of popes were feverish to reconstruct and transform the Vatican into an aristocratic court and a center of art and letters. Papal cuisine was not only an instrument of ostentatious display, but also an expression of culture, piety, and power. German chef Johannes Bockenheim, who served under the first pope of the new era, Martin V (1417–1431), as his *cocus communis* (the cook for his guests), kept a culinary register of the dishes intended to satisfy a variety of gustatory needs.[3] It stands not only as a fascinating document of early fifteenth-century tastes and fashions (a profusion of spices, decisive contrasts of sweet, savory, and sour—the latter represented by the omnipresent verjuice), but also offers a unique sociological window onto the sort of foods that were deemed appropriate for a wide range of people in Rome. Each recipe is conceived of as being specifically suited to a particular category of persons, indicated in a notation to that effect. These categories include various strata of the nobility, the ranks of the clergy, commoners from "citizens" to rural types to the military to prostitutes, the infirm and sickly, as well as a variety of nationalities. Some of the recipe recommendations may reflect the personages who actually frequented the Holy See, but curiously, it also includes "types" unlikely really to have dined on the hallowed premises, thereby rendering select entries a sort of culinary caricature, or socio-gastronomic commentary. In his culinary typecasting, he distinguishes Romans from (other) Italians with recipe sketches that evoke old traditions, the tastes of the Middle Ages, while at the same time foreshadowing the *cucina romanesca del popolo*. Recipe suggestions for the Romans include chicken, boiled, stuffed with a saffron and egg mixture, and baked (18); grilled pork offal in broth with sweet spices (22); and Homestyle Soup (52):

> Take breadcrumbs and put them in a bowl and put a layer of hard grated cheese on top with sweet spices. Add another layer of bread and then cheese with spices until the bowl is full. Then pour a fatty broth on top. Finish with more bread, cheese and spices. And this is what the Romans call macaroni.[4]

Bockenheim's *Registrum coquine* bridges the culinary continuum, linking the bookends of Roman cuisine from *cardinalizia* to *popolare*. While aristocratic excess lay at one end of the continuum, not everyone in the high clergy subscribed to that lifestyle. The papal table, like that of the emperors, was not a continual banquet; some popes tended toward extravagance while others were parsimonious, with birdlike appetites. Alexander VI (1492–1503), the Borgia pope, nurtured a reputation for sparse, devout fare. It was belied by the outlay of costly spices, as well as the notorious after-dinner entertainments for which the meal seemed a pretense. His table was laden with favorites reminiscent of his homeland: anchovies, sardines, sausage, and every sort of salumi, all washed back with a fine array of wines from Italy, Spain, and France. He suspiciously took ill and died after a meal of shrimp, eggs, heavily peppered "curcubite," plums, sweets, and cakes wrapped in gilt paper. Whether it was poison, food poisoning, or his doctor's ministrations that killed him was never discovered.

His successor, Julius II (1503–1513), was so thoroughly disgusted with the Borgia reign that he had their apartments sealed, and they would remain so until the nineteenth century. Julius, however, was not exactly the picture of humility. He favored an open display of refinement at the table as a reflection of his superiority and taste, and was excessive even in times of famine, favoring chicken, kid, suckling pig, hare, and pheasant. He was also partial to caviar, harvested from the sturgeon, which were once abundant in local waters. At his banquets he ate alone at a table on a raised platform, and when the pontiff took his first sip of wine, all of the invitees except the cardinals were obliged to kneel.

At the opposite end of the spectrum was the Dutch Pope Adrian VI (1522–1523) who occupied the papal throne for a fleeting moment. His version of excess was expressed in frugality and an austere appetite. Most days he supped on a simple dish of beef, and on fast days, took only fish. Often times he would limit himself to just an apple. A diarist of the time said that each day, the pope would personally hand his steward a ducat that had to suffice for the day's victuals. Adrian would be the last non-Italian pope for 456 years.

Alessandro Farnese, Pope Paul III (1534–1549), came to the bishopric of Rome as it was reeling in the aftermath of the 1527 sack of Rome and shaken by the fervor of the Protestant Reformation. Not necessarily as a direct consequence, he was a renowned wine connoisseur and an avid enthusiast of viticulture. Among his first acts as pope was to ban French wines and privilege Italian ones. Paul's personal *bottigliere*, or sommelier, wrote a long letter scrupulously detailing his holiness's preferences as well as his own recommendations.[5] Regarding the wines of Rome he is rather halfhearted: "Although Roman wine is not very good, due to the heavy soil, there are some exceptions. And it is a pleasure to drink them, particularly during Lent. . . . At their best, they should be full-bodied, not smoky, nor sour. It is their [Roman] custom to add sulfur and long pepper, cinnamon, cloves, sambuca flowers, things that are a detriment to the body. Some people add cooked wine to conserve it. His Holiness did not willingly drink that wine and said that it was unpalatable and hard on the stomach."[6] Other Latin wines, such as those from Arricia, Bracciano, and particularly Albano, were duly lauded.

The pendulum swung back once again toward austerity with the ultra-conservative Pope Pius V (1566–1572), who purportedly adopted a daily diet that today would be called vegan. He shunned both elaborate and tasty foods, favoring a simple meal of cooked slices of stale bread with garlic, oil, salt, and pepper—bruschetta.

With the rise of the Papal State, the *latifundia*, the large estates, continued to expand, as did the tendency to leave the land uncultivated. One pope after another issued threatening mandates designed to force large landowners to cultivate their holdings to quell the food crisis in the Urbs, but they were blatantly disregarded. Rural living had taken a decisive downturn. If the intermittent raids, plague, lack of fresh water, and rampant hunger were not enough to drive people from the insalubrious countryside, the particularly aggressive wave of malaria that swept though in the summer of 1581, taking over 30 percent of the population, might have been the last straw for survivors. Without the manpower to work the land, menacing edicts and bulls were acts of futility. Swamping, a perennial problem in the Campagna Romana, and consequent cycles of malaria were worsened by the utter disarray of the hydraulic system that had once been the pride of Rome. The wealthy fled to the highlands, predominantly the Castelli area, where viticulture flourished.

Gregory XIII (1572–1585) was conservative at the table, fasting every Wednesday, and taking only bread and water on Saturday. Indeed, his doctor complained that he did not consume nearly enough wine. But regardless of his personal habits, he was not an adept economist and left the papal purse empty for his successor, Sixtus V (1585–1590). Undaunted by the dire backdrop plaguing Rome coupled with the glaring lack of funds, the bulldozing Sixtus laid out elaborate plans to revamp Rome. He pulled in revenue by levying a tax on commonly used items, wine being a prime target. Alessandro Petronio's dietary of 1581, written as advice for Romans, may have provided the pope with the necessary scientific backing. Contrary to the generally held conviction that wine was nutritious, Petronio argued that wine hardens the gut, evidenced by the way that fish and meat toughen when cooked in wine. Food eaten with wine will react in the same way, thus slowing digestion.[7] Therefore, armed with the excuse that it was unhealthy, a tax could be justified as a deterrent. This was only part of an extensive taxation reform that crippled Rome but accrued the funds he was seeking.

If the people couldn't afford wine, let them drink water. In his treatise *Del Tevere*, Andrea Bacci, Sixtus's personal physician, encourages the use of the Tiber for drinking and cooking water, claiming that it had been wrongly maligned. In fact, it had once been called the Albula for its limpidity. Bacci explains away the installation of the many aqueducts as an attempt to bring even more water into the city, supplying baths and fountains, and not because the river water was undrinkable. Aqueduct waters had their adherents and achieved brand status then just as bottled waters do today. Gregory XIII had been a devotee of Aqua Vergine, a reconstruction of the ancient Roman aqueduct Aqua Virgo, and saw to it that it was distributed throughout Rome.[8] It enters the city through an underground aqueduct and diverges into several conduits, one being the Trevi fountain, which in Gregory's time was still utilitarian. Sixtus built the first modern aqueduct, Aqua Felice (1586), named for himself, Felice Peretti. By the time of its completion it fed twenty-seven fountains in Rome. The water that was perhaps most renowned for its curative quality was the iron rich Aqua Acetosa, first studied by Bacci. It quickly became the papal favorite. Paul V (1605–1621) had an elaborate fountain built at the source (1619) with the inscription: "Kidneys and stomach, spleen and liver are healed; that health-giving water comes forth for a thousand ills." Weather permitting, devotees would stroll up *lungotevere* and take the waters. For those who could not get out, ambulant vendors, called *acquacetosàri*, made the rounds of the city with bottles loaded onto a cart, pulled by a mule. Their hawk was: "Fresh *acquacetosa*! Come and get it, my ladies! It'll do you good!"[9]

Adrian's ambition set the stage for Clement VIII (1592–1605), who opened the century of true papal feasting, a spectacle of unrivaled pomp and magnificence. He is also credited with giving coffee, the "devil's drink," his official approval. As coffee was associated with Arab importers (read: infidels), it had been considered at odds with Christian values, the antithesis to communion wine. According to legend, Clement found the bitter black drink and consequent kick irresistible, and so went against his advisor's request to ban it.

As Rome progressed into the seventeenth century, the Barberini papacy, that of Urban VIII (1623–1644), brought the papal debt up from sixteen million *scudi* to twenty-eight million in just two years, and then again to thirty-five million after seventeen years. While Clement, had bestowed his blessing upon the "infidel" coffee, Urban issued a papal bull *Cum Ecclesiae* (1642), forbidding the use of tobacco in any way shape or form in the churches in Seville, which set a precedent that later spread to Rome. It would seem that both priests and followers were coughing, sneezing, smoking, and spitting on the ornaments, altars and floors that the church had spent good money on, and it had to be stopped. The penalty was high: excommunication. The law was finally revoked by Benedict XIII (1724–1730), a man who enjoyed his snuff, because he was annoyed that too many people were getting up and disrupting mass to go out for a smoke or a snort.[10]

Taking It to the Streets— Transhumance and Urban Meat

For Roman landowners seeking to make a return on their land *in absentia*, leasing it as pastureland for sheep was a low risk, reliable option.[11] In so doing, however, the *latifondisti* systematically sabotaged the papacy's efforts to stimulate cereal cultivation. A new class of pastoral entrepreneurs arose that controlled one of Rome's most important natural resources: sheep. They oversaw the transformation of pasture grasses into cheese, wool, meat, leather goods, parchment, and even strings for musical instruments. The *vergaro* was the figure who managed transhumant flocks for more than one herder. The move to the pastures began in autumn with the ewes due to bear young, while the others remained behind for a time. The team traveled with wagons loaded with netting, buckets, and cauldrons, traveling between 6 a.m. and 10 p.m., stopping as necessary to bring a lamb into the world, but otherwise trying to cover twenty kilometers per day along the *tratturi*, the customs roads. Most of the births took place between September and October and were registered so that the *abbacchi* could be dispatched when they were a minimum of twenty days old. Others were earmarked to live in order to replenish the herd. When the time came, the lambs destined for slaughter were hung by their hind legs on wooden hooks and their throats were cut. Once the blood had drained, a long reed was inserted between the skin and the muscle. By blowing into the reed, the skin stretched, making it easier to strip it from the body. A cut was made into the belly, the stomach removed, and set aside to dry. Lambs thus processed were packaged for market.

Pastures were then carefully selected for the ewes designated to produce milk for cheese. In December, the rams, grazing separately, would be reunited with the ewes so that coupling could recommence for the spring lambing. In the meantime, milking ewes were herded into stalls where they were milked at 4:30 a.m./p.m. in autumn and 5:00 am./pm. in spring. Workers collected wood for the fire that would heat the milk in a large cauldron. While the milk was heating, the cheesemaker prepared the coagulant. The lamb stomach that had been removed and hung in the rafters to dry was pulverized with a hatchet and placed in a bowl of water. Using a cloth, it was drained and the resulting liquid was the coagulant. Once the milk solids had been transferred into molds, the whey was brought to the boil again to make ricotta. The rising solids were skimmed off and put into characteristic reed baskets. The remaining whey would feed the dogs or pigs—it often happened that a few pigs were raised with the sheep. After April 15, the sheep would be shorn.

As for the team of shepherds, assistants, and cheesemakers, all bedded down in the barn, except for the leader, the *vergaro*, who lodged in the farmhouse. Their diet consisted almost exclusively of bread and ricotta, sometimes polenta and occasionally mutton stew from an old sheep. When edible field greens were available, they would make *acquacotta*, "cooked water," a simple herb soup that truly reflects the culinary resources of the indigent.[12]

At one end of the meat continuum was veal, specifically *vitella mongana*, from female[13] calves under one year of age, and at the other mutton and water buffalo. Prices and the names of the meats had to be clearly marked at the butcher shop lest mutton, for example, be passed off as beef. Goat was considered a meat for the poor, and, as a result, prices were strictly controlled by the state. The Caffè dei Caprettari in Piazza dei Caprettari (goat mongers square) was a hub where wholesale deals were brokered until the

Figure 6.1. Transhumant shepherds in the campagna romana. Photo courtesy of Professor Alberto Manodori Segredo

late eighteenth century when the state saw that taxes were being evaded. Thereafter, all meat availability had to go directly through customs. Meat was a seasonal product and its sale was regulated in accordance with the Christian calendar: lamb from Easter to St. John's, beef from St. John's until Lent, pork from November (traditionally the 30th, St. Andrew's) to St. Anthony the Abbot's feast day, January 17. Anthony the Great, as he is also known, was the patron saint of pets, livestock, farmers, and most any occupation having to do with food. His association with pork goes back at least as far as the Order of Hopitallers of St. Anthony, a group of monks known for a remedy based on pork fat that eased the symptoms of ergotism, a painful, convulsive affliction; as such, St. Anthony is sometimes depicted in paintings with a pig. The other date for closing the pig slaughter was *giovedi grasso*, "fat Thursday" or the Thursday before the quadragesimal period.

Pork, used almost exclusively for *salumi*, brought out the squeamishness in the Curia, who in 1787 passed an edict prohibiting any funny business in the sausage, specifying the addition of "rancid grease, old caul fat, heart, and other similar foul stuff. The Shankmongers and Tripemongers dare not carve out bits from pig heads, feet, and respectively tripe, as they are food for the poor."[14] Apparently, the problem was such that it merited legal intervention.

Figure 6.2. Goat herders in negotiation outside the city portals. Photo by G. Primoli, reproduced with permission from the Fondazione Primoli, Roma

Fowl also featured frequently in the Roman kitchen of the period. Vendors led their charges through the streets guiding them with long rods and dealing directly with housewives and cooks.

For longer journeys, mules or horses bore the burden and were loaded down with baskets packed with chickens, turkeys, capons, woodland birds, and sometimes wild boar, a much appreciated alternative meat. While domesticated meats were preferred, game meat was in abundance and supplemented the income of these itinerant sellers.[15] Cleaned fowl were sold at stands near the Pantheon; a law had to be passed stipulating that they had

Figure 6.3. Turkey herder walking into town with his charges. Photo by G. Primoli, reproduced with permission from the Fondazione Primoli, Roma

to be dry and not soaking in water, which made them weigh more. By the 1700s, turkey had become a standard product and the birds were commonly referred to as *gallinacci*—bad roosters.

Carnivale is derived from *carnem levare*—to eliminate meat—and is reminiscent of the pagan *Saturnalia*. Prior to Lent, rich and poor alike cut loose, as their means and manners permitted, carousing, banqueting, and dancing, pushing the bacchanal to its limits. The devil-may-care atmosphere screeched to a sobering halt on Ash Wednesday.

> Broccoli, dried figs and baccalà,
> This is what we dine on these days.

Two walnuts and half a herring
It is best that we stick to that in the evening.
And with my stomach growling
Having to endure that for forty days . . .
Tell me, Father, how can I do it?
I'll never make it to Thursday.
. . . But fortunately, through His mercy
The pain of fasting I feel no more,
As I am filled already with something unknown,
The sweet words spoken from on high
Have made me forget my hunger,
So that I wish Easter would never come.
      (Sonnet 376, Vincenzo Maria Conti, d. 1849)

Dietary laws for Lent dictated that no meat was to be butchered, sold, cooked, or eaten so as not to undermine the mortification of the flesh until Easter Sunday. With a doctor's prescription, however, castrated lamb, veal, and kid could be obtained for the sickly from one of five authorized butchers. Care had to be taken not to display the forbidden wares to the public eye. No other meats, eggs, dairy products, or other prohibited foods were allowed. This also held true for inns and hostels housing people from abroad.[16] In years of scarcity, papal decrees were issued allowing the residents of Rome to eat eggs and dairy except for Wednesday, Friday, and Saturday. In 1780, restrictions were relaxed further. The aforementioned quadragesimal meats for the sick were also permitted, and Wednesday taken off the list of fast days. A dizzying number of dietary edicts continued to be disseminated, revising and hairsplitting the details of fasting. It was the perennial problem of giving an inch and having a mile taken. In those cases where meat was permitted, fish could not be consumed in the same meal. When children, the old, and the sick were permitted to have milk, cafes in particular scandalously interpreted that to include mixed milk products with eggs, like gelato—and more than just the designated few were taking license. Noncompliance was not only a transgression, it was punishable by law, although policing these infractions was nearly impossible. Word of a scandal coursed through the peninsula in 1825 (a jubilee year no less) when a butcher went to a local inn and ordered some meat during Lent. The innkeeper refused. Incensed, the man bellowed to his wife to cook him up a dish at home and bring it to him. When she returned, he dug in, but before he had finished the police were taking him to jail.

Although alcohol is generally associated with transgression, wine, the opiate of the Romans, was exempt from fasting rules.[17] Wine was an integral

Figure 6.4.   A lively etching depicting the osteria scene in the early nineteenth century. *Drinkers and Mandolin Players in an Italian Inn with Landscape*, by B Pinelli, 1820. Wellcome Library London

part of Christian liturgy and the Church would have been hard pressed to justify it being both the vehicle for the blood of Christ and an occasion of sin. Thus, abstinence at the table was compensated for at the tavern. *Bére a crudo*, drinking on an empty stomach, made osterias theaters of public disorder. The orgiastic chaos prompted the unpopular conservative Pope Leo XII (1823–1829) to force drinking establishments to bar the bottom half of the door and only serve customers outside. No one was permitted to "loiter and carouse, damaging their families and their health, inciting fights and fomenting carnage."[18] What he did, in effect, was to deprive them of an important freedom, to collectively lose their inhibitions and become unruly in a sanctioned environment. Leo's successor, Pius VIII, abolished the law, thereby securing his popularity. The planks barring the entrances were duly burned in the public piazzas.

The Rise and Fall of the *Cucina Romanesca*

The *cucina romanesca* emerged in phases and in layers; some aspects have far reaching historical threads, while others are innovations that developed along a more recent timeline. While it is not always immediately evident, papal and aristocratic cuisine were part and parcel to the development of Roman cuisine; if the permeability between the *cucina cardinalizia* and that of the people seems doubtful, consideration must be given to the fact that popes were followed and surrounded by an entourage, a trail of compatriots and other hopefuls seeking appointments, commissions, and prebends—in short, a meal ticket. Therefore, by way of example from the *cardinalizia*, or elite stratum, three men from Emilia-Romagna, a region of great renown for its hearty cuisine, assumed the papal throne in the eighteenth century. In order to ingratiate themselves into high society, the compatriot followers came bearing food gifts of salumi and Parmesan cheese. It was through the hangers-on that Roman foodways had a more ample opportunity to intermingle with Bolognese and Romagnolo culinary traditions.

In the eighteenth century, the foodways of the kitchens of humbler homes and eating establishments, now referred to as the *cucina povera*, began to conceptually evolve into popular cuisine, a veritable culinary culture with a modest dignity of its own. "*Povera*," however, should not be mistaken for how indigent people were forced to survive. Poverty and hunger are not a cuisine; the plight of those who found themselves in such conditions, and in Rome they were numerous, should not be romanticized as "simple abundance." A bare-bones dish like *semmolella*, a watery gruel of fine cornmeal (one tablespoon per person) in broth, true fare from the tables of the poor does not feature on "rustic" menus today, even less so in its fasting-days version, made with salty water. It was common enough to have its own singsong ditty: "semmolella, semmolella, mucks up pots, plates and guts," and Ada Boni includes it as a standard of the *cucina romana*, so, it was clearly a dish about which people with few alternatives had mixed feelings.

Other genuinely poor dishes worked their way into the classics of the *cucina romana* after having undergone a transformation to pull them out of subsistence and into something more substantial or sophisticated. An example is the colorfully named *aquapazza* (crazy water), which originated in the southern Pontine area. The base was a very simple garlic, oil, parsley, and chili mince, lightly sautéed then boiled in seawater. This saline broth was poured over bread that had sat for a time in the same baskets where fish or algae had been, thus conferring a fishy taste.[19] The dish as it is sold today in "traditional" eateries, however, is sea bream poached in a shallow bath of water and white wine. The garlic base is the same, except for the addition of chopped tomatoes.

The frugal table had been advocated as an expression of piety through many Christian teachers, including Basil of Caesarea, Augustine of Hippo, Benedict of Norcia, and Francis of Assisi.[20] Their example cast a noble light on deprivation. But popular cooking of the day undeniably required resourcefulness, creativity, and the wherewithal to assess the cheap raw materials at hand and work them into something that was not merely palatable, but appetizing enough to enter the ranks of tradition. Notably, these included animal foods considered discards, unsuited to society's upper tiers—foods that would, in the twentieth century, become the sought-after centerpieces of Rome's trattorias and osterias of the emerging cucina romanesca.

Under such stringent conditions of dearth as those that characterized the eighteenth century, it is curious that wariness of the potato persisted. Father Occhialini's pamphlet of 1784 and other advocates after him had made little impact. Carlo Amoretti's publication *On the Cultivation of Potatoes and Their Use* (1802) repeated the plea.[21] He claims that some progress had been made in Rome because of the high number of foreigners who yearned for it during their sojourn abroad. As a hard-to-procure item, potatoes fetched a good price that outsiders were willing to pay; a few enterprising farmers were therefore encouraged to try their hand at it. Amoretti suggests that as a starch staple, the fear of cultivating it may not be due to its falsely reputed toxicity, but to the economic threat it posed to the wheat market.

The issue had yet another complication. From an affective viewpoint, the idea that another foodstuff might rival bread, the staff of life, enrolled in the process of transubstantiation, was distressing. Bread reinforced familial bonds as well as representing the government's most basic duty toward its citizens. It was also a cultural achievement of human ingenuity, whereas potatoes were indecorously harvested from underground and, as such, designated, according to socio-agriculturalists, for the lowly.

In the end, much of the fault for the food crisis that gripped Rome was blamed on the obstinacy of the *contadini*, who refused to innovate. Instability coupled with obvious alternatives would eventually force the populace to adopt other starches such as corn, rice, and above all, those potatoes. Fortunately, however, despite insufficient supply of various basic foodstuffs, wine was always in abundance.[22]

The unremitting fear of famine compelled the Curia to organize a rather complex *annona*, or food welfare system, and *Grascia*, a body that policed the food trade. The Governor of the *Annona* and *Grascia* was active from 1571–1848, until they changed to a ministerial system. This welfare office filled volumes detailing every crop and domestic animal on every farm around Rome, in an effort to ensure that no one was exporting or hoarding food.[23] In the eighteenth century, nearly a quarter of the population lived by begging and depended on public charity. To maintain public order, the Curia established fixed prices, or what were called "perpetual tariffs" on bread. Reassuringly, the price did not fluctuate, but the weight of the state loaf, the *pane a baiocco* (penny bread), did in accordance with wheat prices. Bumper crop years saw bigger loaves than drought years. Somehow, the prospect of putting less into one's stomach provoked less public strife than taking more out of one's pocket. Later laws cleverly allowed for flours other than wheat to be added to make up the difference in the *pane a baiocco*. When times were particularly desperate, Swiss guards with halberds were positioned outside the bakeries.[24] Into the nineteenth century, bread was distinguished by quality, fine white bread being the bread for *signori*, while large loaves of second- and third-quality flour were the outgrowth of *pane a baiocco*, what is now revered as traditional *pane casareccio*, Roman bread.[25]

Despite constant instability, welfare provisions and importation over the course of the eighteenth century left Rome in better shape than many other Italian cities as far as eating goes. Standards were changing along with the times, a shift that was inevitable and unstoppable as the concept of Europe consolidated socially, culturally, politically, and economically. How likely would it have been in centuries past that Pope Gregory XVI (1831–1846), another pontiff who was not impartial to good food and wine, would have become close friends with Camillo Abbina, chief rabbi of the Jewish community in Rome, so much so that the sardonic poet Gioachino Belli would write of the pair: "Here, either the Rabbi is going to become Christian, or the Holy Father is going to end up a Jew." Their friendship is said to have been "fed" by their common passion for *carciofi alla giudia*, one of most beloved foods of the *cucina ebraica*, Roman-Jewish cuisine.[26]

La cucina ebraica-romanesca—Roman-Jewish Cuisine

Many of today's popular dishes from the cucina romanesca are attributed to the Roman-Jewish culinary tradition.[27] Perhaps topping the list of ubiquitous menu items from Rome's "typical"[28] osterias and trattorias is Pope Gregory XVI's favorite, the *carciofo alla giudia*, a whole artichoke whose leaves have been trimmed and opened, then deep-fried until the outer leaves are brown and crisp and the heart is soft. A very close omnipresent second is *coratella*, mixed stewed sheep offal, in particular lung and windpipe, part of the *quinto quarto* tradition, discussed below. Historically speaking, it is difficult to tease out whether a dish originates from the Roman-Jewish tradition per se, or whether it belongs to a more generalized category of the *cucina popolare* as it manifested in Rome, both being part and parcel of the inventiveness of peoples, Jewish or gentile, faced with hunger and limited local resources. One indication used to determine such origin is coherence with *kashrut*, or Jewish dietary law, which identifies foods or combinations of foods as being edible and inedible. Even within the Jewish community, however, individual laws might manifest in different ways. For example, the prohibition against mixing meat and dairy (see Exodus 23:19) for some means combining them in the same recipe, for others on the same plate, or within a certain number of hours one from the other, with separate cutlery, and/or different pots and pans. Whatever the specifics might be, the centrality of these laws often deterred observant Jews from sitting at the tables of non-Jews, and as such led to a recognizable culinary culture.[29] However, the intersecting and overlapping of the triple matrix of the cucina romana—the Roman-Judaic tradition, the neighborhoods and the *quinto quarto*, and the practices of the outskirts and countryside—leaves us in most cases with myriad tendencies and influences, across as well as within communities, rather than strict delineations.

Jewish presence in Rome has been traced back to the Republican Age, so that we can speak of indigenous Italian Jews or *Italkim* who practice *minhag Benè Romi*, the traditions and customs specific to Roman Jewry, followed by groups that immigrated later as a result of persecution, notably from the Iberian expulsion of 1492. In later years, the Alhambra Decree rippled through Italy to include areas under Spanish rule, Calabria (1524), and then the whole of the Kingdom of Naples (1533). Emigrating peoples tend to go where tolerance and opportunity lie, and the popes from Alexander VI (1492–1503) to Paul III (1534–1549) allowed the Jews to prosper, which encouraged immigration during that crucial period, potentially fostering a multifaceted culinary exchange.[30]

Although Spanish food imports had long been part of the culinary landscape in Rome, incoming refugees brought both a distinctly Sephardic approach as well as sophisticated nuances from the refined Catalan cuisine into Rome's Jewish community.[31] While the newcomers had their own practices based on the foodways and local foods from their place of origin or most recent sojourn, and the native Roman-Jews saw themselves and these Sephardim as somewhat different groups, Jewish identity, and a mutual understanding of the pain of persecution, overrode their differences and forged a bond that facilitated new cultural borrowing.

Such a sense of connection and consequent interchange also occurred to a degree with Jewish foodways in northern Italy, influenced by the Ashkenazim; therefore, many of the dishes that are part of Italian-Jewish and/or Sephardic cuisine were adopted into the long-standing canon of Jewish foodways of the community in Rome, but are not specifically Roman. A dish like "Red mullet with onion, pine nuts, and raisins," is now traditionally eaten in Rome as part of the feasting that takes place both before and after the fast of Yom Kippur, the Day of Atonement. It has clear ties to Sephardi cuisine evidenced through the addition of abundant pine nuts and raisins, while the generous dash of vinegar is part of the escabeche culinary style. Notably the recipe does not call for spices, as they are not permitted before the solemn day. An hour before sundown and then again when the fast is broken, one is expected to eat and drink with abandon. The structure of the breakfast meal as it has been replicated in twentieth century cookbooks is decidedly Italian. For example, the feast in Rome might include a first course of egg noodles in broth, followed by the mullet, then boiled turkey or turkey meatloaf, *pizzette al marsala* (finely ground beef patties dipped in bread crumbs and deep-fried), with a side of pumpkin or pickled eggplant, and finally *dictinobis*, yeast-raised fried donuts.[32]

Eggplant was another vegetable that, like the potato and the tomato, took some time to catch on, despite the fact that it is now considered one of the mainstays of Italian cuisine. Ercole Salvi in *L'imperatore dei cuochi* (1894) gives this tepid introduction: "Eggplant is rather insipid and contains hardly any nutrients. They are either white or purple. The latter are said to be better."[33] But early on, before they were accepted elsewhere in Italy, they were being put to good use in the Jewish kitchen. An example is *melanzane alla giudia*, chunks of eggplant slow-cooked confit style in abundant olive oil, permeated with garlic and parsley until buttery soft, and then finished on a high heat until they turn slightly brown. Notably, in *La cucina romana*, Ada Boni does not include a single recipe with eggplant.

Religious festivities for Roman Jews are a mix of local and standardized traditions combining local foodways with those of the larger religious community. *Pesach* or Passover is a case in point. A member of the modern Roman-Jewish community described how the culinary practices of Roman Jewry at Passover reflect how the community has engaged in some creative elaboration on the historical record to explain its customs:

> The only community in which you can eat lamb is in Rome, because we were here before Christ, so we make artichokes and lamb. . . . In Rome, on the first two evenings of Passover we eat boiled eggs, because eggs are the continuation of life, and vegetables. We can't have anything leavened so no bread or pasta or legumes. We eat rice, matzo, and lamb. In all of the communities in the world a basket with a lamb shank is put on the table (the *korban pesach*) for the blessing, but you can't eat the lamb. Whereas in Rome, because we are Romans and have grumbled endlessly about the Talmud, we were given permission even before Titus razed the temple. We're talking sometime around 70 CE, there were Jews in Rome and this exception was made for the Jews because there were some problems with the food, and so, the Jews who are residents in Rome can eat lamb. So, that's what we have and we usually bake it, but there is a ritual to follow: there are different sized plates, the prayers are said, . . . we have to drink about seven or eight glasses of wine, and we eat a sort of jam

called charoset. . . . There are a lot of different recipes. . . . It's made with dates, figs, walnuts, olives, and bitter herbs. Anyway, the last dish is charoset, boiled egg, bitter greens, lettuce, a piece of celery and a prayer is said for everyone.[34]

A Roman Passover sweet is *pizzarelle*, made with matzo meal, sugar, cocoa powder, eggs, raisins, and pine nuts formed into walnut-sized balls and deep-fried. Deep-frying is a signature cooking method of the Roman-Jewish kitchen, as it is both economical and satisfying. Deep-frying in lard was commonly used across the board in the cucina romanesca, but as kashrut does not allow pork, the Jewish community relied on goose fat, or olive or seed oils, for frying. Salumi in the Jewish quarter were made with beef. Salumi made with goose, a holiday treat, was imported from the ghetto in Venice and from Emilia-Romagna. A simple homemade salumi called *la carne secca* ("dried meat"), was made with oxtail. The whole piece was salt-cured for three days, after which it was weighted down to drain as much liquid as possible. It was then salted and peppered and hung outside in the cold to age—a poor version of bresaola. To observe kosher rules, all meats must be slaughtered and drained of blood; then the organs are meticulously examined for anomalies. If anything suspicious is discovered the carcass is discarded. This attention to detail gave Jewish butchers a reputation for quality that brought in business from the general public throughout Rome.

Keeping kosher was not always clear-cut, however, given the financial constraints imposed upon the community and a mixed sense of belonging. Sometimes nonconformity arose from the allure of local foods—eel and sturgeon (fish without scales) and mozzarella from the countryside (set with rennet from non-kosher animals) might have disturbed some rabbinical authorities but became accepted features of the Roman-Jewish table.[35] Deep-fried zucchini flowers stuffed with mozzarella and anchovy, another trattoria favorite, brings together the delicacy of battered fried foods; anchovies, recalling both oppression and Sephardic influences; and, by way of the cheese, indulgence in non-kosher local foods. *Ovo e latte* is another such rags-to-riches delicacy made with fish roe, often from sturgeon, and fish liver, parts that would have otherwise been discarded by fancy hotel kitchens. The name suggests that there is also milk, but the liquid is white wine vinegar. The whole ovaries, packed with eggs, are lightly sautéed in oil and then vinegar, salt, and pepper are added to finish.

Romans who are unfamiliar with Jewish dietary law willfully attribute much of their cuisine to the foodways of the Roman Jews, although in error. In an oral history interview, Renata, born and raised during the fascist era in San Lorenzo, the poor quarter of Rome, expresses the view held by many:

All those centuries of isolation had made them a strong community. Food is a mighty force in their culture, but also because they are Italians. The *cucina romana* IS Jewish. Roman food doesn't exist without Roman-Jewish cooking traditions.

Everybody in the world knows about *pasta alla carbonara*, in America and China and everywhere, and it comes from Italian-Jewish cooking. Have you ever had pig's liver *alla Romana*? Pig's liver is a dish that has been passed down to us from the time of the Roman Empire! And it is Jewish. What about the *pajata*? The intestines of lambs that have only ever had their mother's milk? Jewish, all of it.[36]

Particularly after World War II, Jewishness did not always mean "kosher-ness." *Kashrut* became more of an affective term of nostalgia relating to Jew-ish folk culture that was celebrated through Italian-Jewish cuisine.[37]

Libyan Jews in Rome

Jews who resided in Libya, many of whom emigrated there during the height of the Ottoman Empire, had established a community that would go on to flourish in the eighteenth and nineteenth centuries. Some of those families had gone to escape Italian oppression. In 1911, Libya was colonized by Italy, but because many members of the Jewish community were of Italian descent and spoke Italian, they integrated easily with the new order and continued to do so under the fascist regime. In 1941, even after racial laws had been put into effect, 25 percent of the population in Tripoli was Jewish. After years of having lived together peaceably, the situation took a turn for the worse in 1942. The community was subjected to an onslaught of indignities: pogroms, riots, forced labor, property seizure, and other forms of persecution.

In 1951, when Libya achieved independence, thirty thousand Libyan Jews emigrated to Israel. For those who remained, the persecution continued and eventually six thousand Jews had to be evacuated to safety in Rome. Today the Jewish community in Rome has approximately fifteen thousand members, four thousand of whom are of Libyan descent. Although it may seem con-tradictory, an essential part of successful integration in a new context is the maintenance of ties not only with one's religion but also with the culture of their place of origin. This reinforces a sense of pride and self, allaying sensa-tions of isolation and disorientation associated with forced emigration. Many of those who took up residence in Rome were already of Italian descent, but their Libyan heritage was an indelible part of their identity, an integral part of which manifested through their foodways. With them, they brought spices whose use harked back to the scents of the Middle Ages—pepper, cinnamon and saffron—but they also introduced novel nuances: cumin, caraway, turmeric, and paprika. In contrast to the delicate cuisine that had come to define the Roman-Jewish kitchen, the Libyans decisive tastes, rife with spices, garlic, and onion, as well as the cloyingly sweet, buttery phyllo pastries laced with pistachios, almonds, and dried fruit and drenched in honey, were typical of North Africa and the Middle East. The recipe here for Hraimi is a typical dish reflecting Libyan-Jewish culinary identity.

Hraimi (Spicy Fish) *con couscous*

This is a classic Shabbat dish and a pillar of the *cucina tripolina*. It is best to cook the dish in advance and allow it to marinate overnight, in typical Shabbat fashion. For optimum flavor, salt the fish twenty minutes before cooking.

Heat ¼ cup olive oil in a medium saucepan over medium-low heat. When the oil begins to shimmer, add two diced onions. Season with salt and cook, stirring until translucent and very soft, about twenty minutes. Add the paprika, one tablespoon red pepper flakes, one teaspoon caraway, and one tablespoon ground cumin. Cook until fragrant, about one minute. Add ¼ cup of tomato paste and cook until it turns a deep brick red, about two minutes. Add one and a half tablespoons fresh lemon juice and one cup of water and stir to incorporate. Simmer over low heat, covered, for fifteen to twenty minutes, stirring occasionally.

Carefully lower the fish (two pounds amberjack steaks or sea bass fillets salted) into the sauce and cook over medium heat until opaque and cooked through, about fifteen minutes, or ten minutes per inch of thickness. Served with couscous immediately or the following day.[38]

The Lost and Found

Watermelon, *cocommero* in dialect, was celebrated as quintessentially Roman insofar as it was "rotund like the coliseum, like the breasts of our womenfolk, like our picturesque sayings in dialect, . . . it can truly call itself Roman. . . . You can hear the tastiness even in the name itself—the sound of the syllables fill your mouth and make you want to swallow."[39] Watermelon was central to the festival celebrated on the tiny Tiber Island, initially dedicated to Asclepius,[40] then later, in keeping with the times, to Bartholomew the Apostle. After church devotions on his feast day, August 24, the festivities began with copious amounts of cut and whole watermelon festooning the island's two bridges. As part of the tradition, hordes of young men and boys stripped to the waist, piled onto the balustrades of the bridges waiting eagerly for someone to throw a watermelon or even a piece of one into the Tiber. They dove headlong into the river amid screaming and fistfights as they made their way to the bobbing fruit.

Fatalities were not infrequent, not only from the brawling, but because the water in summer was not quite as deep as the young divers thought; others were drawn into the wheels of the numerous cereal mills on and along the river. Today the jocularity has died down to a mundane occasion to eat watermelon.

Writing in 1960 in the annual *Strenna dei Romanisti*, a publication by Romans for Romans about Rome, Misserville, cited above on watermelon, revisits the festival in order to reflect generally upon the downhill turn Roman food had taken:

> Let's not even talk about the "battery farm" chickens that make you cry for the "free range" ones of bygone days. Where can you find the *baccalà in guazzetto*— adorned with raisins and pine nuts that our old folks talk about? There is no point getting worked up about the so-called *gnocchi alla romana* made with semolina, or turning your nose up at a big plate of tripe doused with parmesan instead of pecorino romano. We have to go with the times and not grumble.
>
> But did watermelons have to change? No, this we were not expecting.
>
> Some time ago, the most monstrous oblong-shaped watermelons appeared in the market that leave you perplexed. . . . I insist: watermelons have to be round. Where did these oblong things come from? I don't like them. . . . It doesn't matter if they are not perfectly symmetrical—so long as they are Roman.[41]

Already in 1960, the "good old days" of genuine Roman cooking seemed to be a thing of the past. Ideas of traditional culinary correctness came to the fore with the rise of the post–World War II "economic miracle." The concept of a glorious, timeless, immutable, and uniquely Roman cuisine entered into the collective conscious as something worthy of protection and veneration— that is, once the situation of desperation from which it had arisen had been safely tucked into the past. Mutation in time and space, the keen sense that these rapid, and otherwise welcomed, changes taking place were overshadowing revered ways of the past set revival and protectionism in motion. That *and* the economic return.

Ada Boni had already felt the impetus to "save" Roman foodways when she wrote *La cucina romana* in 1930. She too, however, was enmeshed in a time of deep and perplexing social change in the age of Mussolini, who sought to create single-minded Italians who recognized the state first and foremost before their regional or local identity. Ada Boni was a fervent fascist advocate; *Talisman of Happiness* (1926) was her response to the nationalist call, as well as a rebuttal to the much-revered Pelegrino Artusi, whose work she considered inferior. But she also felt the call of Rome, of *campanilismo*, a need to record and codify the foodways of the era that had preceded hers, an era that was fading into the past.

The paradox of codifying recipes is that they are the products of culinary evolution. Codification leads us to culinary fundamentalism, to gastroarcheological digs to find the holy grail of "authenticity," the True Cross. It fixes in black and white what had previously been handed down, altered by changing tastes, improved methods, and sage revisions. This is perceived today as contamination. But fear of losing traditions seems to be part of the human condition. Consider that Pliny the Elder had voiced the same fears in the first century.[42]

Neighborhoods and the Quinto Quarto

Over the course of the nineteenth century, Europe underwent a wave of socioeconomic upheaval. *Modern*, and not *traditional*, was the byword of the century. In 1815, the Congress of Vienna convened to repartition Europe, and that moment is used as a convenient marker for the beginning of the Italian Risorgimento, five bellicose decades that would ultimately unite Italy into a single geopolitical concept under the House of Savoy. Divisions between the classes changed significantly as the Third Estate—the working class, *piccolo borghese*, and middle class—became a dominant force. Under severe austerity measures to keep the new nation buoyant, millions had expatriated, but many more moved to Rome, filling the petty white- and blue-collar jobs in the growing bureaucratic network. New shops and workshops opened, and improvements in education increased the number of professions, adding exponentially to the number of people who had a paltry but stable income. Although the framework was tenuous, the sense of social security provided fertile ground for a culinary culture to stabilize and for foodways to become a source of identity and pride, despite having evolved from origins of paucity.

Offal and other less desirable animal parts had long been used as affordable protein sources by the poor and working class, but what consolidated them as part of the cucina romanesca were the butchery facilities based in Testaccio. The project to build a modern centralized *ammazzatora*,[43] or slaughterhouse, in Testaccio, the poor and working-class quarter of Rome, came to fruition in 1888. The plan, begun in 1872 under the auspices of the Kingdom of Italy, was to replace the abattoir that Leo XII had had constructed in 1825 in the hemicycle of Piazza del Popolo. Prior to that, *butteri* rustled livestock into the city on Thursdays and Fridays, toward main urban slaughterhouses. It was a public spectacle that drew in would-be daredevil urbanites who beat on the animals, whooping and hollering. The spooked beasts bolted down the streets that led off from the piazza. The real fun was watching the panicked bystanders flee to safety.[44] Leo's centralized plan had included a detour to herd the animals around the city walls and into Porta del Popolo, rather than through the streets; it was experienced as the end of a great era: "It is not a lie that Rome is dead / even more so than the slaughtered beasts."[45]

The 1888 abattoir was more than just a display of power and a strategy to garner consensus by the incoming regime. The stockyard and butchery needed upgrading and enlarging to meet the needs of the increasing population, and the old site was close enough to the Tiber that run-off of blood and other refuse was polluting the river. The project included new housing in the vicinity for the working class, most of whom were employed at the slaughterhouse. This gave them access to meat, but given the limitations of their income, it consisted mainly of the discards called the *quinto quarto*, the "fifth quarter," the less appealing parts that did not fetch a high price on the market one hundred years ago. For the uninitiated, the quinto quarto was all the offal and "less noble" parts of the animal: pancreas, shanks, spleen, hanger steak, stomach, intestines, liver, lungs, heart, kidneys, thymus, tail, and testicles. It also included brain and tongue, but those were more marketable items, thus set aside for butchers whose clientele were more solvent. Each of the parts had its own very distinct texture and taste, some requiring more culinary manipulation than others to render a mouthfeel, appearance, and flavor that was not only edible, but also appetizing. "Manipulation" and "appetizing" should not be confused with refined, which was not the aim or intention of the cucina romanesca; on the contrary, while requiring skill, the calling card of this cuisine is its homey, hearty, chunky, decisive, down-to-earth quality—true grit, nothing capricious. It is artful without artifice, embodying the frank, unassuming people and environment from which it arose: a place where boys, being boys, unpack the old initialism SPQR as *Salame, Presciutto, Guanciale* [oops], *Ricotta*.[46]

In addition to the *coratella d'abbacchio*, associated with Jewish foodways, emblematic dishes coming from the slaughterhouse tradition include the *padellotto alla macellara*, a mixed fry-up chock-full of the range of offal: lung, sweetbreads, *pajata*, testicles, liver, and kidney, each bit cut in a determinate way and added to the pan in a prescribed order. The lot is finished with a good dousing of vinegar and served piping hot, the ten o'clock breakfast at the slaughterhouse.

Coda alla vaccinara is considered the "queen of the quinto quarto," and quintessentially Roman: chunks of bone-in oxtail browned in lard, slow braised for several hours in a tomato-based sauce with onion, garlic, celery, and red wine, then finished with pine nuts, raisins, and grated bitter chocolate. According to culinary folklorist Secondino Freda, the name *vaccinara* derives from the name of the workers who skinned the butchered bovine. They were called *vaccinari*, as the animals in Roman dialect were called *vaccina*. These laborers all resided in the same area, presumably with their families. In addition to their wage, they were paid in kind with the head and tail, which placed them in a sort of culinary think tank. The tail was used to make broth, but because the fibers held a notable amount of blood, the resulting broth was quite dark and the meat was not particularly appetizing. As time went on, a cooking method developed, but it remained a neighborhood dish. Then, when the *vaccinari* were moved to the housing at the new slaughterhouse, the number of tails increased with the growing demand for meat in Rome. New ingredients were added to the oxtail stew, and the recipe stabilized.[47]

Figure 6.5. Women in the Testaccio neighborhood with cowskins drying in the background. Photo by G. Primoli, reproduced with permission from the Fondazione Primoli, Roma

Others consider tripe the dish that best represents the urban cooking of the quinto quarto. *Trippa alla romana* also requires hours of preparation. Once the tripe has been precooked, it is cut into strips, and stewed in a sauce made with a *soffritto* of minced carrot, celery, prosciutto fat, and chili pepper, simmered in a tomato base with bay leaves. Plated up, it is topped with grated pecorino romano and a mince of the distinctly pungent Roman mint—neither are optional.

The cartilaginous pieces of the brisket were used for the dish *punta di petto alla fornara.* The thick-cut, fatty slices of beef were placed in a baking dish with garlic, rosemary, pepper, and olive oil, then taken to the neighborhood baker in the late morning when he had finished baking for the day. Most homes did not have a proper oven, and roasting was done with the residual heat from the local bread oven. In addition to the organ and discard meats, the frugal cucina romanesca includes recipes to reuse leftover meat scraps from making broth. One is the simple meat and potato balls—minced, mashed, breaded, and fried in lard. Another is *picchiapò*, a stew that gives boiled beef a second go-round in a tomato based sauce. One of the more subtle, though not strictly refined specialties is *rigatoni con la pagliata*, short tubular pasta with a chunky sauce of lamb intestines filled with their mother's milk. The partially digested milk tastes like a delicately pungent cheese.

Many recipes from this tradition did not clear the test of time, that is, given our present aversion to fat and timidity about organ meats, they simply do not make the modern mouth water. A prime example would be "Lung stew with peas and rice," recorded in Ada Boni's *La cucina romana.* Interestingly, it is reminiscent of one of Bockenheim's "recipes for Romans":

> This is the way to make soup for the Romans. Take a goat liver and lungs and boil them, then cut them in little cubes and soak them in almond milk diluted with some good broth enriched with spices. Keep the whole thing boiling for a while. And it will taste good (9).[48]

Despite the recipe's distinguished ancestry, lung stretches beyond the borders of curiosity into the realm of repulsion. In addition to lung, another organ meat fallen from grace is spleen. An intriguing dish associated with the Roman-Jewish quinto quarto tradition is *milza ripiena*, "stuffed spleen," minced spleen and beef fat mixed with egg, diced onion, and salt. The mixture is reinserted into the rubbery dermal covering of the spleen and sewn closed. Simmer for an hour and a half, allow to cool completely, slice thinly and serve. Today it would be difficult to find this on anything but an extremist gastronomic revivalist menu.

Countryside and Outskirts; or, *"Se non è vero, è ben trovato"* (If it isn't true, it oughta be)

In the Roman countryside, broth, soup, gruel and stale bread paps, foods assisted by water to fill the stomach and comfort the soul, were the basis of most meals, if not the meal itself. The combination that most typifies the food of the countryside is *pasta e ceci*, a thick soup made with any sort of pasta that could be eaten with a spoon, chickpeas, and whatever else might have been on hand, be it a simple flavoring with garlic and rosemary or a hint of fish or seafood—the classic being razor clams. Legume soups are, however, the common ground where all three matrices meet—poor food *per eccellenza*. Akin to the ancient tradition of *puls* was Roman *minestra di farro*, a soup made with farro, pork rind, onion, garlic, and herbs. With little extra effort, simple country soups took on another dimension with wild aromatic herbs, notably Roman mint, fennel, anise, and sage. Soups did not require recipes. They too were codified when country folk moved to the city and longed to re-create that taste of home.

There are several pasta dishes that are the very core of the cucina romanesca, whose origins are a remove from the Urbs itself. Nonetheless, they are an essential and inextricable facet of the Roman culinary identity. Each one is wrapped in a gastronomic history that may have no basis in truth whatsoever, but no matter. As culinary scholar Alberto Capatti said, "In Italy, every food has to have a story, and if it doesn't, one is made up."[49]

Spaghetti alla gricia: This simple dish is the keystone to the three main pasta recipes of the cucina romanesca. The elders from the Amatrice area recount that just above Lake Scandarello there was a beautiful woman, stunning even though she had gotten on in years and had gone gray. She was called *la gricia*, which in dialect made reference to her hair color, and it was she who had created and given her name to this recipe. This dish became the mainstay of the *carbonari*, or colliers, people who lived in the woods for the better part of the year and made charcoal. They always brought with them a supply of pasta, cured pork belly, pecorino, salt, and pepper to make the simple but warming and caloric *spaghetti alla gricia*.[50] Without any preface or explanation, Ada Boni refers to this recipe as *spaghetti alla marchigiana*, as the area where it originated is situated on a point where Lazio, Marche, Umbria, and Abruzzo meet. Notably, it was not until 1927 that Amatrice formally became a part of Lazio.

La grice is again the progenitor of the more recent *matriciana*. Amatrice was well known for talented cooks, many of whom transferred to Rome where they could find more secure employment. Indeed, the creator of the sauce for *spaghetti alla matriciana* was once such cook who had taken up residency in Rome. At the end of the nineteenth century, he worked at a restaurant called La Matriciana situated in front of Teatro dell'Opera. He used *guanciale* instead of pancetta, a more compact product that gives the sauce its characteristic texture. To that he added local tomatoes, *pomodoro casalino*, preferred for their sweet yet slightly acidic taste that held up to cooking. It is finished with pecorino romano. So the dish is called *alla matriciana*, not because it was ideated in Amatrice, but to pay homage to the cook's origins. It is sometimes made with *bucatini*, long hollow pasta, instead of the original spaghetti because it is heartier and provides a more substantial support to the robust sauce, or perhaps it is due to the appetizing whistling sound produced when air comes out the end as it is being sucked into the mouth.[51]

Of these three signature pastas, *spaghetti alla carbonara* is probably the one whose background is most unclear but at the same time, as a national favorite, the Romans are very proprietorial about it, and "authenticity" has become an issue of vociferous debate. One does not have to be an *intenditore* (in the know) to see that the path from *la gricia* to *la carbonara* is a simple addition of eggs beaten with cheese. It is the details of that journey that separate scholars and enthusiasts into various camps. First, is the case based on the *carbonari*, whose standard provisions would have had them eating *la gricia* quite regularly during their long stay in the woods from March through November. Upon their return from the grueling work, Roman cookbook author and food historian Secondino Freda tells us the men hankered for something more. He gives us this heartfelt account:

> Their complaints reached the ears of their housewives, who, downhearted from their husband's absence, tried with their unsurpassable culinary flair to come up with a new dish. Naturally, it should be tastier, why not? It should also be visually appetizing so as to appeal to the eye and at the same time lend an air of festivity. Hence, to the *gricia* ingredients they added some egg beaten with grated cheese in order to achieve a different taste and color. The dish was an overwhelming success, so much so that on Sundays and holidays this spaghetti that had taken its name from the carbonari, was sought after to the point that it became a tradition, particularly during Carnival. . . . Unfortunately, the recipe created by these skillful housewives while waiting for the return of their dear carbonari has undergone many variations, for example, pecorino romano has been substituted with butter and parmesan, and even heavy cream, which distort the simplicity and taste of the original recipe.[52]

This affective theory is heavily weighted with purposeful agency, and not surprisingly proposes no date of origin, falling under the amorphous aura of "timeless traditions." It reflects a collective romantic vision of the Romans, yearning to construct a dignified frame around what has become a fundamental culinary identity marker—that is, a source of pride.

The *Trattoria La Carbonara*, established in 1912, is entangled in this story. The restaurant, located in Campo de' Fiori, is said to have been opened by a family of wood colliers (*carbonai*) where naturally, this dish was a main feature. Their version was made with the short tubular pasta *penne*, and according to a 1974 rave review in the *Ludington Daily News*, it contained both cream and butter, ingredients that alarm purists.

The search for a documented progenitor would lead some researchers to the Neapolitan cookbook *Cucina teorico-pratica* (1839). Among the variations proposed for *maccarune de tutte manere* (macaroni all ways) the last is *caso e ova sbattute*, cheese and beaten eggs, thereby reflecting two key ingredients of the carbonara, as well as the basic method, but it leaves open the question of how the dish is related to the carbonari.[53] The addition of cured pork and pepper to the mix cannot have been a eureka moment, but a logical addition, utilizing available foods that would render a tasty dish.

Two other theories arise from the immediate aftermath of World War II. In 1944, American troops occupied Rome and brought provisions to quell the starvation in the war-torn city. Among those foods were bacon and eggs, the latter most likely powdered. Add this to existing resources, pasta and cheese, and not a little bit of hunger, and you have created a memorable dish. While this story may seem all too easy, its existence and, even more, its persistence is remarkable given that the heroic agent is foreign.

The second wartime story spotlights Roman agency, but the main thrust is bourgeois enterprise: during the German occupation, middle-class families fled to the safety of the hills in the Ciociaria and Abruzzo, where they picked up the foodways of lumberjacks and colliers working in the woods, who reportedly used egg, lardo, and pecorino to dress pasta. When the danger had subsided, the Roman families brought back with them the know-how they had learned from the woodsmen. After the postwar "economic miracle" took off, there was ample opportunity to put their knowledge to profitable use and the rest is history.[54]

The real origin of carbonara is most likely a mix of elements from all of these ideas. Ada Boni's *La cucina romana* does not include it in this otherwise comprehensive collection of the *cucina popolare romanesca*. It is also noteworthy that the charcoal trade declined rapidly after World War I as combustion, cooking, and heating methods modernized, setting in motion the nostalgia for days gone by. The name *alla carbonara* could have derived from a collective impression of the sorts of ingredients that might have been (or even were) stocked by colliers given their practical and economic circumstances, as is true with other dishes that present a trade name preceded by *alla*.[55]

Regardless of its origins, *carbonara* does not appear in writing until 1954 in *Tourismo gastronomico*. The following year the same guidebook cites four locations featuring the dish—notably three restaurants and only one osteria, *Alfredo* in Trastevere.[56] Over the next ten years *spaghetti alla carbonara* would slowly enter Italian cookbooks, but always with variations for modern tastes. Before the advent of the Mediterranean Diet, carbonara had grown into a national passion, but due to its saturated fats and absence of vegetables, it now has been demoted to a guilty pleasure by heart-healthy advocates. There is even a canned vegan version that replaces the meat, cheese, and egg with tofu and seitan. Everyone wants to get in on it.

Of all the fine foods in Italy, this dish, perhaps more than any other, is enveloped by an inexplicable aura of sacrality. Recently, a decalogue of commandments has been laid out governing its proper preparation. The original, written in Roman dialect with a distinct Roman attitude, went viral on Facebook:

1. Always use *guanciale*. Hey, if we wanted bacon we would have gone to America.
2. No parmesan, only pecorino romano. Those who say half and half are kidding themselves.
3. Don't cook the egg. Better you end up with an infection than a frittata.
4. No garlic or onion. You're not making *ragù*, you know.
5. No oil, butter, or lard. You've got enough to deal with with the *guanciale*.
6. No chilies. You can go to Calabria this summer.
7. Don't use any spices except pepper. If you've got a problem with that, go to eat at an Indian restaurant.
8. Anybody putting cream on it should get thrown behind bars.
9. Never say the word "carbonara" and "vegan" in the same sentence.
10. *Tonnarelli*, spaghetti, *bucatini*, *rigatoni*. Those are all fine, just so long as you don't overcook the stuff.

Another *primo piatto* whose origins are somewhat elusive is *gnocchi alla romana*. Pelegrino Artusi, considered in some respects to be the custodian of Italian cuisine, includes them in his cookbook *Science in the Kitchen and the Art of Eating Well* (1891) as one of his Roman entries. He has admittedly altered the recipe and, indeed, instead of being made with the principal and defining ingredient, semolina, he uses "flour" and adds gruyere cheese to the dough itself. Oddly, it is preceded by a recipe called *gnocchi di semolino*, which very neatly replicates what are now called *gnocchi alla romana*. Ada Boni also has a recipe called *gnocchi di semolino*, notably not *alla romana*, which in fact is a recipe for *gnocchi alla romana*. Boni's uncle, Adolfo Giaquinto, a well-known Roman author and poet specializing in home-style cookbooks, did not include it in his collection of family-style recipes (1899),[57] which is curious because nine years prior he had written an homage to the dish in rhyming Roman dialect:

> If you want to make gnocchi alla romana / you gotta take 200 grams of flour, / sixty grams of butter from Milan / and seven yolks from hen's eggs. / You put it all into a bowl / so that it melts little by little / with fresh milk from Serafini[58] / then cook it on the fire slowly. / When it has cooled on a towel / cut it like biscuits and then you add / butter, parmesan, and cinnamon. / Five minutes in the oven and they are done.[59]

Anna Gosetti, in her seminal work *Le ricette regionali italiane* (1967), has a recipe in the Lazio chapter called *gnocchi di "semmolella."* She uses Gruyere as a topping but does not include egg yolk, saying that historically they were made without egg, and that, significantly, "some experts" believe that the dish was originally Piedmontese. The ingredients would certainly lean in that direction. Given their elegance and delicacy, these semolina cakes may very well have been imported to Rome by way of the Quirinal Palace with the arrival of the House of Savoy. Artusi suggests them as a *tramesso* (the Italian replacement for "entremets"), a dish between courses that was more of a treat, or amuse bouche, than a proper course.

Roman Culinary scholar Luigi Volpicelli, although an admirer of Artusi, takes him to task for inaccuracies regarding his Roman recipes. Volpicelli prefaces his scathing critique saying, "No one eats by recipes; we eat by tradition, by influence, for which every dish is inadvertently transformed. That means that recipes are conditioned by taste and by the local cooking style." Before launching his attack, he quotes Artusi himself, "All dishes can be altered in various ways according to the whim of who is manipulating them, but modifying at will does not mean losing sight of simplicity, delicacy, and pleasant tastes."[60] In "Peas with prosciutto" Volpicelli finds Artusi brazenly haphazard with his ministrations:

> "Cut two spring onions lengthwise and cook them in oil with enough prosciutto fat and meat cut into small cubes. Fry them until dried out; then throw in the peas, with little or no salt and a grind of pepper; stir and finish

cooking them in broth adding a bit of butter." For a Roman cook [female], this borders on monstrous: to start with, no one would ever cook prosciutto until dried. It has to be added when the peas are almost cooked so as to maintain its flavor and remain tender. And no one would add broth. Given the excellence of Roman peas, something Artusi seems to treat as an after-thought, they will melt in your mouth after only a few minutes of cooking. They are tender and sweet, so of course, they only need "little or no salt." And then, the very idea of adding butter. Rome knows nothing of butter, or at least it didn't back then. But Artusi, for as much as he wants to associate himself with Tuscan cuisine and its oil, has never managed to rinse all of his rags in the Arno, that is, to free himself of the gastronomic culture of his birthplace,[61] so laden with butter.[62]

And yet, with so much ado about buttered peas, Volpicelli says nothing about Artusi's *gnocchi alla romana* and Swiss cheese. Finally, internationally renowned Roman chef, author, and gastronome Luigi Carnacina (1888–1981), took a forceful stance on the issue in a magazine interview: "I am going to unmask here and now a mystery. Those things that cooks present as *gnocchi* made with semolina *alla romana* have nothing to do with Rome or even with Italy. They were created in France and that is how they got here. Real Italian gnocchi are made with potatoes."[63] And so, as everyone knows in the Lazio, Umbria, Marche, Abruzzo regional quad, Thursday is gnocchi day, that is, real potato and flour gnocchi with meat sauce.

Roman Holidays

Ottobrate

Diversions, especially those whose theme included wine, were well integrated into the Roman cultural calendar. Until the beginning of the twentieth cen-tury, the Ottobrate romane, the Roman Octoberfest, was an important series of celebrations that followed the grape harvest. They were occasions to take advantage of the last warm days of the season, to picnic along the banks of the Tiber at Testaccio or some other picturesque setting. A main attrac-tion was an ornate horse-drawn coach filled with people, mostly from the middle class, all dressed to the nines, with a lineup of pretty young women, the prettiest positioned center stage. But people of all classes were involved, even the Borghese princes opened their gardens to the public and sponsored entertainments. Amid music and dancing, food was served, often tripe soup with pancetta, chicken stuffed with sausage, spiced beef, lamb kidneys and leg, and goat with garlic, pepper, and anchovies—a menu and ambiance designed to encourage drinking.

La festa di San Giovanni

"*Lumache, lumaconi, e lumachette. Si cavan con le spille se son strette*"[64] was the cry of the ambulant snail vendor. San Giovanni Battista, one of the most important holidays in Rome, was celebrated on June 24 with a great feast featuring snails. The best ones were found in among the grapevines, or in the grasses along the Tiber near the source of Acqua Acetosa, anywhere the gastropods might still find refuge in the cool and damp. Planning was crucial because they needed to settle and flush themselves out in a basket for two days before they could be scrubbed in a basin of water with salt and vinegar to remove the impurities. When immersed into boiling water, their cries are audible but brief. After ten minutes, they are ready to mingle with the spicy garlic, anchovy, tomato sauce, and the distinctly aromatic Roman mint. After twenty minutes on a low flame, they are ready for the celebrants, who sat on long benches at tables ornate with garlands of garlic.

The date corresponds to the summer solstice, around which there is an aura of magic. The biblical figures of Herodias and Salomé, John the Baptist's murderers, were summoned for dramatic condemnation as the assassins of San Giovanni. Well into the 1800s, the festivities began on the eve of the saint's day as crowds gathered in the piazza and streets near the Basilica of St. John Lateran. They walked around with strings of garlic, torches, brooms, and pitchforks, singing, shouting, and clanging cowbells on the pretense of keeping witches at bay. It was nothing less than a Christian remake of a Roman bacchanal, this one including a symbolic baptismal dip in the Tiber. At dawn, the pope brought the merrymaking to an end with a cannon blast calling the faithful to mass; he encouraged attendance by tossing a few gold and silver coins to the crowd from the loggia of the basilica. The daytime festivities on the 24th are meant for friends, family, and neighbors to come together, bury the hatchet and restore harmony. Snails, whose little tentacles were reminiscent of demonic horns, represented discord. By eating the snails, all traces of enmity were buried, and the slate cleared.[65]

La festa di San Giuseppe

The feast day of San Giuseppe, St. Joseph, is celebrated all over Italy but the Romans feel a particular affinity to it. It is close to the ancient Roman Liberalia, in honor of Bacchus, celebrated on March 17, just two days before, in correspondence with the equinox—hence occasion for another bacchanal, this one to propitiate fertility. Varro tells us that laurel-crowned priestesses, devotees of Bacchus, had gathered in front of a fire to sell flatbreads, *frittelle* (fritters), and honeyed wine to passersby.[66]

Eventually, the festivities proved too lively and had to be banned. But the tasty fritters would have been missed, so San Giuseppe was adopted as its new representative, thereby acquiring the more wholesome context of Father's Day.

The new story associated with the feast was that Giuseppe, in order to please his guests the three kings, and not wanting to treat them inhospitably as he had been treated at the inn, whipped up a batch of fritters. He lit a fire to heat the oil with the shavings that he apparently had in abundance, as he was a carpenter by trade. According to another popular legend, the saint, having had to abandon his true trade after the flight from Egypt, refashioned himself as a *frittelaio*—a food frier. Until the end of the nineteenth century, San Giuseppe was a holiday celebrated throughout Rome, closing down all shops and offices. The only people permitted to work were the *frittellai*, who fried up frittelle in their huge vats of boiling oil. Fried food was a much loved and important part of the culinary culture and skillful frittellai ran a brisk trade.

In 1871, when Rome became the capital of the Kingdom of Italy, the pyramids of fritters for sale on the stands, generally accompanied by depictions of Joseph and the baby Jesus, were joined by portraits of Garibaldi and Mazzini, heroes of Italian unification—and both named Giuseppe.[67]

Fascism: The Making of Italians and Italian Cuisine

Fortunately, the Italian people are not used to eating many times a day.

—Mussolini

The dream of the ambitious fascist leader Benito Mussolini was to create the New Roman Empire, to make Rome great again. It would require discipline summed up in the self-obliterating slogan *Credere, obbidire, combattere*. In order to achieve the goal, belts needed to be tightened and sacrifices had to be made. The white bread that had been a status marker through the ages was banned in favor of the official *pane unico*, more familiarly known as *pane nero*. So as to discourage hasty consumption, it was not sold fresh, although wariness alone of the dubious ingredients may have sufficed. Myriad experts concurred that hard bread was easier to digest than freshly baked, resuscitating a belief held by the ancients.

Water was a key ingredient, the basis of soups that were the mainstay of the daily meal, and so the expression *fare un piatto di maccaroni*, "make a plate of pasta," meant living it up, as it had become a special dish relegated to the main meal on Sunday. Hence the proliferation of expressions like "if his skin comes undone you can make a basket of bones." As for wine, propaganda proclaimed: "The best surrogate for wine is pure water, limpid and fresh, a source of energy, health, and morality." Meat consumption, which had never attained great heights, bottomed out. Once again specialists were on hand to discourage consumption:

> Nutritionists scrambled to defend the reduction in the availability of meat by deducing that it was not a physiological necessity. One expert declared that humans can only digest meat protein halfway, while the rest lingered to poison the body, boldly adding, "Animal protein is the worst kind of protein because it has died twice, once when slaughtered and then on the fire, which destroys the vitamins. Expecting to build a healthy organism with food that has died twice is a grave error."[68]

Miriam Mafai, through a series of interviews with women about their daily lives toward the end of World War II, vividly reconstructs their experience. A firsthand account from "Hunger in Rome" reads:

> In those months we ate anything. We lined up for hours to get onions, broccoli, squash. At the close of the market there were women picking through the garbage looking for leaves or cores that they could cook. The only sure food was the 100 grams of bread per person per day, one roll made of rye, chickpeas and sawdust. . . . Some days there was nothing in the house to eat. My mother was ashamed to go out. My father went to the soup kitchen and I went with him so that we could have two portions. When it was fava bean season, after eating the beans we boiled the pods and passed them through the sieve to make soup.[69]

> In the spring of 1944, the search for food had become women's primary activity in Rome. Mothers banded together spontaneously and went to riot in the bakeries. There was one bakery in Via dei Giubbonari that got emptied. There were sacks of flour everywhere. The women knocked down the door and before the police could get there, everyone had escaped with their apron or their handbag full of flour.[70]

In Rome, an intricate black market network was set up. They duplicated, counterfeited, and "lost" ration cards (that then needed to be replaced)—if it meant getting food, nothing was too illicit. After repeated bombing by Allied troops, Rome was declared an "open city," meaning that it had abandoned defense efforts. American troops moved in, bringing in tow large supplies of food, preempting the sharp drop in the lira that would follow. For a time, considerable stocks of incoming food aid was stolen and filtered onto the black market. Despite the defeat of the twenty-year totalitarian regime, hunger had made an indelible mark on the population, and it would take time before reality settled in. After the war the "economic miracle" was set in motion and gastronomy took off. Rome was on its way to becoming once again a world-class tourist destination, but the first objective was to get white bread back on the table.

Figure 6.6. Post–World War II painting titled *It's All There!* A man looks on at the bounty he cannot partake in while American soldiers strut by. C'è tutto! Pio Pullini, 1946. From Strenna dei Romanisti, p. 31, VII, Staderni Editore. Reprinted with permission from Presidenza Gruppo Romanisti

CHAPTER SEVEN

Eating and Drinking Out

Rome's unique urban history predisposed it more than any other city in Italy, and arguably in Europe, to a tradition of eating outside the home—both from necessity and for pleasure—that dates back thousands of years. While Paris may have its restaurants, London its pubs, Vienna its cafes, and Berlin its cabarets, Rome is the undisputed capital of the osteria.

Roman food, both ideologically and in reality is, or at least was, about tucking in, digging in heartily, even savagely into food that is unpretentious yet ostentatious, bold and satisfying. It is a rough and ready sort of cuisine, enticing but unrefined. Within the scheme of Roman life, osterias were not an occasion, but part of the daily ebb and flow, a badge of belonging, whose merriment, stupor, violence, and lusty advances have been left to posterity in innumerable paintings, memoirs, chronicles, songs, and poems.

The roots of the osteria tradition reach back into classical antiquity and naturally underwent changes with the passing of the centuries. But then slowly over the course of the nineteenth century, and more rapidly from post–World War II onward, the entire experience was covered over with a coating of bric-a-brac, clouding up and diluting the character and authenticity of the *cucina* and the Roman osteria. The genuine article was substituted with a facsimile, the purposeful fabrication of "quaint" that sullied not only the defining characteristics, but altered the connotations of the term itself from one of living expressivity to a static concept leaning inexorably toward kitsch. The process of transformation was almost inevitable in a city that

181

underwent a vertiginous urbanization after the fall of the Papal State. The population increased from 209,022 inhabitants in 1871 to 650,258 in 1921; and even more so after World War II with a total of 2,739,952 countable inhabitants by 1971.[1]

Osteria romana: The Foundation

One of the most debated historical questions about ancient Rome is its population when the city was at its height, between the first century BCE and the second century CE. Calculations have been proposed based on the quantity of water supplied by the aqueducts; on the amount of grain distributed through the *lex frumentaria*, in accordance with lists of eligible recipients; or on the city limits and the number of housing units within the city walls. The average estimate based on recent archeological research is between one million two hundred thousand and one million eight hundred thousand, but hypotheses vary from two hundred fifty thousand to four million inhabitants. Regardless, what can be said is that Rome was the most populated city in Europe. As most dwellings lacked cooking facilities, the question of how the people of Rome organized and conceptualized eating and meals reveals much about the economy and socialization of the densely populated and highly chaotic *intra muros* community.

The fire hazard presented from open flames used for cooking was one of the most feared perils of the ancient city. The *insulae*, the urban housing blocks, were packed far over capacity with plebs, and in some cases rose ten stories high. As such, the threat of a blaze growing out of control limited or excluded the possibility of cooking indoors. The *domus*, residential homes of wealthy families, were fully equipped with separate, well-constructed cooking facilities, significantly reducing potential fire hazards. Public food outlets also had isolated and/or separate facilities for food preparation. Consequently, for the greater part of the population eating out, that is, obtaining cooked food outside the home, was a habit born of necessity.

The ongoing stratification, destruction, and alterations in the city's architecture has made it difficult to formulate a clear idea of how these commercial food outlets operated. Fortunately, much reliable information can be gleaned from the ruins and remains of Pompeii, Herculaneum, Ostia Antica, and other centers that, for various reasons, crystalized in time. However, ancient literary sources and archeological evidence, despite the existence of the former and abundance of the latter, resist clear application one to the other. Regardless, eighteenth- and nineteenth-century archeologists eagerly and casually applied known names of food outlet types to archeological structures as they were being discovered, leaving a record rife with inconsistencies. Inaccurate records of the types of artifacts found and their locations further confounds attempts to discuss public food services in anything more than general terms.

> We know from the excavation diaries that, where necessary, Maiuri had no scruples about displaying artifacts actually found elsewhere. There is no reason to be confident that this grain was found here, not (as so often happened) in an upper storey. The amphorae may be reassembled from this and other houses. What we are looking at is a skillful composite, true to the spirit of the original, but not actual archaeological evidence of what was found.[2]

Tabernae were, broadly speaking, shops or taverns; *popinae*, the most diffused of the eateries, were restaurants and bars consisting of either a single room or an adjoining backroom for customers. In Pompeii, most of these bars were strategically positioned at intersections along the main thoroughfares, generally in the vicinity of a public fountain. The *cauponae*, restaurants and hotels, were more spacious, often including a *viridarium*, an internal garden with triclinia and fruit trees or vineyards used to produce wine for the clientele.[3] Referring again to Pompeii, these spaces were located close to the gates of the city walls, where, as *stabula* and *hospitia*, they were spread throughout the city center, all three fulfilling the same function of providing a relaxing meeting place with refreshments, as well as lodgings, gaming dens, and sexual services. Not infrequently, residents converted a room of the lower floor of their home into a food and drink outlet. Of the 158 food counters in Pompeii, 81 percent appear to have offered cooked food, some of the cooking facilities being shared between more than one outlet.

Despite the fact that eating out was a necessity, governments have always been wary of public assembly, whether of like-minded or disparate groups, particularly if conflict might be fomented by alcohol. Several emperors imposed bans on various foods sold at Roman bars, which may have been an attempt to make them less appealing as places to convene.[4] With public gatherings in food and drink establishments under state scrutiny, guilds, which required membership, assumed the role of restaurateur, to the point of it becoming one of their defining characteristics. It allowed the non-elite to establish their own exclusivity and internal hierarchies in a comfortable, companionable setting. In the end, the very power structures the emperors sought to curtail were nurtured even more by the membership-only conviviality of the guilds.[5]

Rome: City of Hospitality

In 1300, Pope Boniface VIII (1294–1303) proclaimed the first Jubilee a "year of forgiveness of all sins." A visit to the tombs of Peter and Paul were the highlights that brought pilgrims to Rome. While the Apostolic See was still in Avignon, Pope Clement VI (1342–1352) approved Rome's request to hold a Jubilee year every fifty years and added St. John Lateran to the Roman itinerary.[6] Despite the derelict condition of Rome and general unpreparedness, the city welcomed the unprecedented influx of wayfarers—which turned many a Roman into an improvised cook or innkeeper. The plague of 1348 did not deter the hordes from flocking to Rome in 1350. On the contrary, repentance for whatever sins might have angered God and the hope for salvation motivated many to undertake the arduous journey to Rome. Clement himself did not manage to make an appearance, but he may have brokered a cessation of the Hundred Years War to assure safe passage along the *Vie Romee*.

But it was the return of the papacy under the auspices of Martin V that revitalized Rome's pride and sense of purpose. With the papal seat firmly restored, hotels and osterias prospered, encouraging competition for quality service and products. From this time onward, there would be few interruptions to the flow of incoming travelers. The osteria, where one could also find lodgings, became a distinct reference point, the cradle of tourism. The word *osteria* itself denotes hospitality, the giving of food and succor. Its short form *oste*, means host, from the Latin *hospes*. In the Jubilee year 1450, there were 1,022 osterias with a name and countless others without. The pilgrim intake regenerated the Roman economy, albeit mostly through drink.

Roman osterias are mentioned by name in the works of notable Italian authors of the Renaissance, such as Ludovico Ariosto, remembered on a "here slept" plaque of the Albergo del Sole; Pietro Aretino, makes mention of four that he frequented, and Benvenuto Cellini, in *Vita* says: "There was a certain osteria, outside Porta di Castello, a place called Baccanello. This osteria had as a sign a sun painted between two red colored windows."[7] Cellini was an artilleryman in Castel Sant'Angelo, defending it during the 1527 sack of Rome against mutinous troops of Charles V, the Holy Roman emperor. The author describes the torturous streets, the noisy osterias, the princes, bishops, and prostitutes, pages of literary finery that display his quarrelsome character. During the siege, with one decisive blow, Cellini strikes the Prince of Orange, the high commander of the enemy troops. He was immediately taken to shelter: "This was the Prince of Orange, who was taken through the trenches to a certain osteria nearby, followed immediately by all of the nobles in the army."[8]

Nearly one hundred years later, on April 24, 1604, another impetuous artist is in the Osteria del Moro on Via della Maddalena near Piazza Navona. It is Michelangelo Marisi, known as Caravaggio. He has ordered a plate of artichokes, but an altercation with the waiter ensues and Caravaggio ends up throwing the vegetables in the waiter's face; he retreats to the police. In his deposition, the waiter says that he had brought a plate with eight artichokes, four with butter and four done in oil. Caravaggio asked which were which, and the waiter replied that all he had to do was smell them to see which ones had butter and which ones oil. Without another word the dish went flying and the waiter was injured. In his rage Caravaggio reached for his friend's sword lying on the table and the waiter fled. According to the testimony of a witness, the waiter missed an important detail:

> I was at lunch at the hostaria del Moro and Michelangelo da Caravaggio, the painter, was across the way. He asked the waiter if the artichokes were done with butter or oil as they were all on one plate. The waiter said: "I don't know," and he took one and put it up to his nose. This did not sit well with Michelangelo, who stood up angrily and said "You think you are dealing with some idiot, that you are serving a bumpkin."[9] And he took that plate of artichokes and threw it in the waiter's face. I didn't see Michelangelo reach for his sword against him.

Andrew Graham Dixon offers a culinary interpretation of the argument. He claims that the conflict had arisen between the Lombard tradition of butter and the Roman tradition of oil. Lombards were often made fun of as being cowpokes from the Padana plains, folks who would not eat anything that was not dripping with butter and cheese.[10] In Dixon's view, Caravaggio was still touchy about his social status, and the suggestion that he might be an undiscerning northern oaf set him off.

This interpretation runs slightly askew when one considers that both the waiter and Caravaggio were originally from Lombardy. Both would have heard in the other's accent that they were from the same area; as such, any show of prejudice would have been the pot calling the kettle black. Perhaps the artist's hair-trigger rage was sparked by the fact that a rude server had put his dirty hands in Caravaggio's food.

Figure 7.1. One of the most famous depictions of the Roman osteria. The attributes of the osteria are represented through the sensual open mouth, the brandishing of sharp instruments, the flash of anger, and the phallic wine carafe. *In a Roman Osteria*, by Carl Bloch, 1886

What we do know is that there was one matter about which there was no disagreement—the patria that united the disparate parties: wine. *Veni, vidi, bibi.*

Baccus amat colles—Bacchus Loves the Hills

Up until the years of urban expansion, the city of the seven hills produced copious amounts of wine. There were vineyards both inside the city walls and on the land surrounding them. The wines sold in Rome were divided into three categories:

- *Vino romanesco e dell'agro Romano*—from within the city or the immediate vicinity.
- *Vino dei castelli*—from the highlands situated southeast of Rome: Frascati, Albano, Grottaferrata, Velletri, Marino, and other municipalities in the area that produce high-quality grapes from the volcanic soil.

- *Vino ripale*—takes its name from the two active ports on the Tiber: Ripa and Ripetta. By extension, the term indicates that the wines have been brought in from areas that are not in the immediate vicinity. Small consignments came in by boat from Umbria, as well as the venerated *Est! Est! Est!*; in Ripa Grande, vessels sailed upriver from Fiumicino to the city, bringing various goods including wine. As Goethe records in a memoir from January 19, 1787: "Today was a day well spent, seeing a part of Campidoglio that I had overlooked up to now; then we boarded a boat on the Tiber and drank an excellent Spanish wine aboard a boat that had recently docked."[11]

The figure of sommelier advanced in the 1500s, evident from the letter that Paolo III's bottigliere, Sante Lancerio, addressed to Cardinal Guido Ascanio Sforza.[12] Although he does not bring new wines to light, his way of describing them denotes a modern approach, and his linguistic juggling foreshadows the dubious figure of the "wine expert." The letter itself is shrouded in mystery, as the whereabouts of the original copy are unknown. It came to light only in 1876, when it was printed in *La Rivista Europea*. The content reveals that it must have been written after the scourges of the pirate Redbeard on the island of Giglio in 1553,[13] and perhaps before the death of Pope Julius III in 1555, with whom Lancerio had pleaded in vain for the post of papal sommelier.[14] The desire to impress a potential employer may account for the expressivity of the language and display of sensitive insider information:

> Greco di Somma comes to the Ripa Romana from the Kingdom of Naples, from the mountain of Somma, XII miles from Naples. They are very cloudy and potent wines and can be drunk through the whole meal, but they do go to your head; some are smooth, not turbid and fragrant. At their best they are not cloudy but golden in color. . . . This wine needs to be clarified more than other wines. His Holiness drank one or two glasses at every meal . . . and wanted it when he travelled as well, because it did not provoke distress. He used it to wet his eyes in the morning, and to splash on his manly parts, but he preferred it when it was 6–8 years old when it was at perfection.[15]

Greco di Somma was one of the strongest wines and one of the most consumed in Rome in the sixteenth century.[16] Its usefulness as an ablution tonic for the papal brow and genitals may seem questionable, but highlights the fact that wine, besides being a pleasure, was considered both nutritive and medicinal. Andrea Bacci, physician to Sixtus V, who had extolled the waters of the Tiber, also authored a book on wines.[17] He meticulously details winemaking, the characteristics of wines, matching wine to food, as well as the ways in which the various wines available in Rome should be consumed at different ages and for a variety of infirmities to maintain or restore health. The wine of Albano and Velletri were praised from the physician's viewpoint because they were mediocre, and as such were suited to daily consumption. He too mentions Greco di Somma as one of Rome's favorite imports.

Not only was wine a sacred part of mass, essential to the performance of the Eucharist, it also brought in considerable revenue to the Papal State. There were an endless number of edicts, laws, and decrees detailing taxes and commercial regulations from wholesale to retail. Each phase of the wine trade from producer to pourer had its own guild. Due to the high traffic of pilgrims, the sale of wine was so intense around the Vatican that the retailers concentrated in that area had their own guild. The incoming monies to the papal account were allocated to public works, the university, and the restoration of the city for the glory of Rome and God. The protest to prioritize bread instead of buildings was railed at one pope after another; by the time it got to Benedict XIV (1740–1758), he quipped back, *non in pane solo vivit homo!*

To keep the wine flowing and revenues pouring in, it was only right that the state protect consumer interests as well. The dubious sincerity of *osti*, the barkeepers, left a trail of proverbs and anecdotes over the centuries, and prompted strict regulation of measurements and fixed prices in an effort to combat the many who watered down the wine or cheated on the serving size. In 1588, the state issued official glass carafes, whose transparency guaranteed quantity. Previously, liquids and dry goods were measured in containers made of terracotta, metal, or wood made by *vasellari*, artisans who made vases. The Venetian scientist, inventor, and glassworker Maggino di Gabriello Hebreo, came up with the idea of the glass carafe. He had presented the pope with a "curious and bizarre drinking vase" and obtained both the funding for and the monopoly on glass and crystal production, an exemption from import taxes on raw materials, and most importantly, permission to live outside the ghetto.[18] The move toward accountability was met with violent protests; some proprietors even attempted to pay their way out of adopting the new system. But the law went into effect followed by ever more severe punishments for transgressors. These carafes were the forerunners of those used in osterias today. The approximate measures were:

> *Sospiro* or *sottovoce*—100 ml, a small glass. The names "sigh" and "low voice" are thought to refer to the embarrassment of not being able to

afford a decent-sized glass of wine; hence, they were ordered hush-hush.

Chirichetto—200 ml, a dialectal distortion of the Italian *chierichetto*, altar boy, so named because the dimension is similar to the ampulla of wine used during mass.

Quartino, quartarolo, baggiarola, or *mezzo fojetta*—400 ml, the standard size for which it went by many nicknames.

Fojetta or *foglietta*—500 ml, a hearty slug of wine and the favorite size. The name may derive from the custom of hanging a leafy branch outside the drinking establishment to signal the presence or new arrival of wine. *Frasca* has the same meaning, for which taverns in Castelli are called *fraschette*. The proverb *il buon vino non ha bisogno di frasca*, good wine doesn't need to be signaled, extends broadly to mean—quality goods need no advertisement.

Er tubbo—1 liter

Er barzilai—2 liters, the largest size, named after Salvatore Barzilai, a Roman politician from the radical Left, who in the late 1800s made the rounds of the osterias during the campaign season, reputedly offering generous quantities of wine to garner votes.

Fire and Fury in the Osteria

In the wake of the French Revolution, the osteria changed from a place to unload and grumble to a conspiracy headquarters. For a brief time after a successful French invasion, the Papal State became the Roman Republic, a satellite state under Napoleon Bonaparte. After a reign spanning two decades, Pius VI was forcibly taken to France where he died. This set a precedence of fear that was not unjustified, as a similar fate awaited Pius VII in 1809. Upon his return to Rome in 1813, he reinstated the Inquisition and the Index of Condemned Books as well as Jewish confinement to the Ghetto, which had been terminated under French rule. Gatherings of clandestine groups like the Carbonari and the Freemasons posed a potential threat to the state, thus an edict was passed in 1814 that not only forbade the societies, but also threatened severe punishments for those who allowed them to meet on their premises. These threats made little impact, so the members were excommunicated in 1821, which again had little effect. Pope Leo XII passed an edict in 1824 prohibiting osteria barkeeps from serving wine unless it accompanied a meal, a significant move for the development of local cuisine. Those who were not eating could only be served outside, over a gate covering the lower half of the front doorway—the infamous *cancelletti*.

Upon the death of Leo XII the law was abolished but, regardless, it would seem to have had the desired effect. In 1832, the director general of the police reported:

> The government saw with true satisfaction that, just as it had been wise to impose such a measure to halt so much disorder, it was also not necessary to reinstate it as the good people of Rome behaved in moderation, without taking advantage of this Sovereign concession.[19]

They may not have reinstated the same laws, but they enacted others. Twenty-one strict regulations were passed for trattorias and osterias and other drinking establishments serving food, ordering them to hang signs,[20] remain within the definition of their category, use the proper measurements, and respect opening and closing hours. Any sort of card playing and gaming was forbidden, and if disorder of any kind arose, the person in charge of the establishment would be held responsible. The Romans were outraged.

Osteria or Trattoria?

Pilgrims and tourists brought in considerable profits through drinking establishments, but Rome was hardly dependent on outsiders and exceptional events to keep the numerous taverns afloat. Alessandro Rufini reports in 1854 that there were officially 573 osterias, 153 cafes, 31 inns, 22 hotels, and 20 trattorias serving wine and other spirits, in addition to an estimated 227 others without a name.[21] By matching those figures with church registers of parishioners from the same period, it works out that there was one osteria per 238 inhabitants, including children, the infirm, and the clergy.

Of note is the number of osterias and cafes in comparison to trattorias. The osteria was principally about wine consumption, whereas cafes had stronger alcoholic beverages. Trattorias aimed at being a cut above osterias, a middle road between the drinking hole and a proper restaurant, in hopes of attracting a more solvent and sophisticated clientele. The most famous trattoria was the Lepre (literally, "Hare") on Via Condotti. Together with Caffè Greco, they were the social fulcrums of the Piazza di Spagna area, the so-called English Ghetto owing to the high concentration of English (anglophones) who lodged and frequented the area. It is here that foreign sojourners gathered. Theirs was a close-knit community, particularly as many of them stayed in Rome for long periods of time, sometimes even making a life there. The list of VIPs was long, comprising centuries of artists, writers, activists, and thinkers: Montaigne, Montesquieu, de Sade, Goethe, Stendhal, Chateaubriand,

Keats, Browning, Shelley, Cooper, Ruskin, Dickens, Florence Nightingale, Corot, Gogol, Madame de Staël, Thackeray, Hawthorne, James, Wagner, Liszt, Thorvaldsen, Twain, and many more, who oscillated between being tourists and residents. There are, however, precious few travel memoirists who dedicated time and space to detailing their gastronomic experiences in Rome; therefore, William Mitchell Gillespie's ten-page account of dining at the Lepre and drinking at Caffè Greco during his two-year sojourn in Rome, is a treasure trove:

Some travelers are most interested in Antiquities; others in Painting and Statuary; others again in Palaces or Churches; but all agree in having one taste in common, and in appreciating the importance of one matter which comes home every day to the bosom of all, in the shape of DINNER. . . . If you take apartments at a hotel, you are not expected to breakfast or dine there, unless you announce your intention each day in advance; and you usually find it more pleasant to breakfast at a Café, and dine at a restaurant, at any hour that may best suit you, and on such viands as you may choose; instead of sitting down at a crowded table, at such time, and to such dishes as may please your landlord, not yourself. The Roman *trattorie*, or eating houses, are inferior to those of most continental cities, but still the experienced traveller will find them quite competent to satisfy his daily needs. . . . But before you enter on the discussion of the solids, the waiter will ask you—not whether you wish Wine, but *what* wine you wish. Though the Romans have the most abundant supply of good water in the world, they never drink it at dinner. Its place is supplied by some of the numerous varieties of wines, as Velletri, Marino, Grotto Ferrato, Orvieto, &c, which figure on the list. . . . Your selection being made—and I recommend *Grotto Ferrato*—you will then look at the list of *Soups*, which contains fifty names, including the many varieties of *Paste*, of which only two, *Macaroni* and *Vermicelli*, are usually found in America, though I have counted fifteen species in one shop-window, all based on the original flour and water. Among them are, *Capellini*, finer than *Vermicelli*; *Semolino*, looking like melon-seeds; *Capelletti*, twisted and spiced; *Amandoletti*, shaped like small almonds; *Agnellotti*, *Lasagni*, and a host beside.

You are now prepared to choose something substantial from the long and puzzling list before you. Besides the English names already given . . . the rest will be darkness to you, for even if you understood each separate word, what would you expect from a "Mosaic of Mutton" or from "Gilded Brains," or how could you guess that this poetic language called Tomatoes "Apples of Gold" and Cream "Flower of Milk," or that "English Soup" meant a piece of sponge-cake swimming in wine-sauce with a cherry at its top? You must, therefore, trust to chance, if you have no experienced companions, and you will at last learn that the favorite Roman dishes are *Cignale*, or Wild Boar—the hunting of which is a favorite sport—; *Porcospino*, or Hedgehog ; *Lepre*, or Hare; and *Testicciuola*, or Lamb's Brain. Of Birds, you have Quails, Larks, Plovers, Thrush, Woodcock, and the delicate Beccafica, or Figpecker; but of fish you will find a scarcity, excepting *Ranocchie*, which signifies frogs. . . . Lemons are used as a universal sauce to relieve the grossness of meat. *Funghi*, or mushrooms, are added to most dishes in spite of their dangerous character.

From the *Trattoria*, everybody adjourns to a *Café*; and directly opposite to the *Lepre* is the *Café Greco*, the general rendezvous of the artists of all nations.[22]

There is a menu that has survived from the Lepre dated 1847 with the heading: *Daily list of dishes and prices of every portion.* It is a fascinating document listing over six hundred dishes, more than one hundred of which were indicated as being available that day with prices handwritten into a side column. It is, in essence, an extensive overview of what was trending in trattorias in mid-nineteenth-century Rome. The menu is divided into sections starting with Soups, then cooking types: Boiled, Fried, and Stewed foods, Vegetables, Roasted (fowl, game, meats, and fish), Cold meat dishes, and closing courses: Desserts, *Credenza* (sideboard—salumi, salt cured fish, dried fruit, and cheeses), Fruit (including nuts and raw vegetables), and of course a list of wines and liquors.

Extensive as it is, the menu features almost none of the signature dishes of the cucina romanesca. The Lepre's niche was the trendy, new transatlantic/international, middle-class cuisine that tended toward French methods and tastes, held as an ideal in nineteenth century Italian cookbooks. Sauerkraut, potatoes, *maccaroni alla napolitana*, *sciantigliè* (chantilly), and *risotto alla milanese*, *gnocchi alla veneziano* were some of the standards of international cuisine included on their menu in an attempt to appeal to foreign tastes. The pasta dishes are listed in the soup section, as pasta had not yet come into its own as a dominant category. Fettuccine, capellini, cappelletti, lasagne, maccaroni, and so on, are all featured in the same three ways: in broth, with butter, or with meat sauce. The fried-foods section may have been the most Roman part of the menu. Anything that could be fried was. Heading the list was testicles, a range of lamb and bovine offal, goat or calf's head; contrary to Gillespie's report, the fried-food section included a wide range of salted and fresh fish, as well as artichokes, mushrooms, cardoons, and *soplis* (discussed below). The most expensive items were the sweetbreads (thymus)—fried or in tomato sauce—whole roasted pigeon, and a variety of cuts of *mongana*, veal. Among the stewed dishes, chicken was as costly as veal, the latter proposed fourteen different ways, mostly with legumes, another nod to Rome.

Ravioli was considered a stewed dish rather than a "soup." There are few surprises on the vegetable list—spinach, yellow and orange carrots, artichokes, cardoons, celery, peas, endive, cabbage, turnips, and a range of legumes—the exception was the extensive potato listings. In addition to being mashed (transliterated *mascè*), they were buttered, pan-fried, with meat sauce, prepared as a salad, or *alla methrodotel* (à la maitre d'hotel), again, tending more toward French traditions. Tomatoes were in the early stages as a stand-alone food and are listed here as "stuffed" and appear again in the roasted section. Notably, there were no zucchini or eggplant sides, while bell peppers were only served pickled under *Credenza*. As Gillespie pointed out, there was a vast array of domestic fowl and wild woodland birds, the latter now illegal, as over-hunting and urbanization had left them in small numbers. The wines were mostly local Roman wines, *Est! Est! Est!* being the most expensive. The imports are spelled phonetically despite the fact that most of the clientele were non-Italians: *sciampagne, bordò, coniac*.[23]

The Lepre traverses two culinary pathways, one tied to fashions and customer expectations, the other to local customs and basic, readily available ingredients. The Roman cuisine represented here is largely defined by dictates of the market—a market that had little interest in sampling the "traditional local fare" or having an "authentic culinary experience," quite the opposite of travelers today. One osteria tradition maintained on this menu—held sacred in Rome and still in use today—is the half portion. "Anything that doesn't have a price in the half portion column cannot be served in half," for those with little appetite or money. Hearty eaters, on the other hand, could order a dish *abbondante*, hoping to get a more fulsome serving. For regulars, there is a tacit agreement that the price will stay the same. The clever customer would put the two concepts together, "I'll have the half portion, but make it *abbondante!*"

Osteria from Reality to Fantasy
The nineteenth century witnessed the consolidation of the osteria and the development of the cucina romanesca, a golden age permeated with nostalgia that is revisited and recounted as being the heart of Rome and *Romanità*, Roman-ness. Fantasy blurs over the reality, the two folding over each other in time until it comes out as a single mythology, willfully perceived as immutable and timeless. An integral part of the mythmaking comes from the poetry of Giuseppe Gioachino Belli, who immortalized the spirit of the osteria and the cucina romanesco in verse. At one end of Viale Trastevere on the Fabricio Bridge, the city's oldest, a statue was erected in his honor for

the fiftieth anniversary of his death. Donning a long tailored coat and top hat, and sporting a fashionable walking stick, Belli leans casually onto the backdrop of the monument looking down pensively. The travertine plaque behind him reads: To G. G. Belli poet of the people of Rome.

Through 2,279 sonnets, written between 1830 and 1847, he creates a vivid portrait of the city, its people and language, but also, and perhaps most significantly, of its culinary customs. Through his poetry, he transmits his abiding devotion to Roman food and wine reconstructing not only recipes, but the emotions, attitudes, and inclinations of the Romans in relation to their food. In *Li connimenti*, for example, he sings the praises of lard: "Yes, food cooked in lard is good / actually, the barber told me that it is good for the heart/ like pepper and fresh air. / It goes well with prosciutto crostini. . . / with chicken, pork roast . . . / whether stewed . . . braised . . . in sauce . . ." Despite lard's admirable qualities, Belli stops short of recommending it for frying fish: "You want to fry fish in lard? Eh, no. / Fish needs to be fried in oil."[24]

Belli's sonnet, called "The Lady's Lunch," while a parody of the pretentious display of the middle classes out for an Ottobrate meal, sheds light on Roman trattoria food as it might have been at the Falcone near the Pantheon—recommended by *Murray's* for anyone with a bit of money to spend who was looking for Roman fare. In this sonnet, a wife responds to her husband who has just recounted his disastrous outing with the boys:

> Well, listen to my lunch. Rice with peas,
> boiled beef and turkey,
> clove spiked roast, tripe, stew,
> a skewer of sausage and pork liver.
> Then fried artichokes and testicles,
> some gnocchi that were as good as sin,
> an airy pizza from the vendor,
> sweet and sour wild boar and birds.
> There were pickled peppers
> salami, mortadella, *caciofiore*,
> a table wine and wine from Orvieto.
> And then *rosolio* and *Parfait Amour*,
> coffee and doughnuts, and then I left out
> certain radishes to die for.[25]

The authorities may have been right in keeping a watchful eye on congregations gathering in dark taverns, as rebellion came to the fore once again during the European Revolutions of 1848, which manifested in Rome in 1849 as the Second Roman Republic. Pope Pius IX fled and would not return for seventeen months, but when he did, he too reinstated forced enclosure for the Jews and took down the statue of the heretic Giordano Bruno that rebels had erected. Another would be inaugurated in the market square Campo de' Fiori in 1889. In the meantime, the Risorgimento spread with Giuseppe Garibaldi as the military commander in chief. His legendary persona is that of a man's man, rugged, opportunistic, anachronistic, provincial, an emblem of Italian virtues and at the same time embodying all of the vices of masonic Italy. As Garibaldi and his troops marched onward, despite his mythic status, the commander did need to eat, drink, and sleep, and thus left in his wake a trail of inns and osterias qualified to hang a "Garibaldi was/slept here" plaque. One of his favorites was the osteria Da Scarpone, which is still in existence today, as is the Locanda Filomarino, the latter now in the urban center, although in Garibaldi's day it was in the countryside outside Porta Salaria. General Rafaele Cadorna lodged there the night before he and his troops took Rome in 1870. One of the walls of the inn was covered in signatures and dedications, among which was: "Filomarino, your macaroni is the best in all of Europe—Giuseppe Garibaldi."

The city whose population had for "Ages of ages" delineated itself as nobility, commoners, and clerics became a haven for the Third Estate, the *borghesia*: middle-class businessmen, clerks, and professionals. The anticlerical House of Savoy did what they could to sow the seeds of discontent against the Church, their defeated rival. The Italian people would agonize over the division of church and state until 1929, when Mussolini and the pope signed the Lateran Treaty. With the *Unità d'Italia*, Romans could convene more freely in the osterias, but disapproving conservatives continued to see them as dens of sedition. The flames of this sentiment were fanned by the wave of socialist and communist politics aimed at stirring the lower classes, who were mostly made up of the throngs of *buzzurri*, northern riffraff, a group that the Roman Catholic establishment both feared and despised.

The expanding city was abuzz with renovations, like the razing of Villa Ludovisi, among the most beautiful palaces in the city, for the construction of a neighborhood by the same name, where Palazzo Margherita was built, which today houses the American Embassy. Naturally, new osterias went up as well, often frequented and run by *mangiapreti*, "priest eaters," like Checco Scrocca:

> When Checco Scrocca came to Rome around 1892, he worked initially as a carriage driver. . . . With his first savings he set up an osteria at the end of Viale Giulio Cesare, a humming construction site at the time. It was almost rural,

just outside the customs line of demarcation. During the papal reign, for the republican anticlerical Romans, contraband had an air of political rebellion and was a weapon against the established authority. Such sentiments were hard to dispel and the osteria was well placed. . . . Around the same time, a guy called Gigiotto had opened an osteria in Piazza della Rotonda, but things didn't go so well for him because he was one of his best customers.[26]

Scrocca's opened a new place called the Temple of Agrippa. His shopfront sign is one of the most remarkable from the Roman Belle Epoque. Business was good and he had a loyal clientele of Leftist politicians and parliamentarians, among whom were Salvatore Barzilai, the namesake of the two-liter carafe.

> The osteria was cleaned up and fixed up with new decor, the owner was both tough and affable, the wine good and serious. Fortune smiled immediately on his business. . . . At the beginning, you could only drink, a primitive and pure rite. Then some travelers started to ask if they could have something to eat, and thus the Signora Giulia, Checco's wife, came out and showed herself to be a formidable cook.[27]

The story of Scrocca is an iconoclastic example: a young man from a town outside Rome opens an osteria just outside the city wall; he later moves up in the world by opening a place inside the city; he successfully makes the passage from drink to food, and then leaves the business to his head waiter; the place continues on for a time out of notoriety and then folds. Numerous trattorias, osterias, and taverns succumbed to the same fate, having been passed down through the family or left to a trusted worker. Some did survive, but the success of many others was directly linked to the personality of the owner or manager who created a familiar atmosphere that kept customers coming back.

Construction in the late 1800s did away with many of the areas used for the Ottobrate, one in particular becoming the site of the new working-class neighborhood and the slaughterhouse in Testaccio. Osterias serving food also flourished in the area consolidating the quinto quarto as the centerpiece of the cucina romanesca. The advent of industrialization began to dismantle the way of life in preexisting communities. The lackadaisical flow that had been part of the workaday of manual laborers and craftworkers broke down, and a rigid system of factory timetables, and fixed salaries, markedly delineating work and leisure time, was imposed in its place. Many women entered the workforce, putting in nine- to twelve-hour days, upending previous rhythms of domesticity.[28] Women did not have to be paid the same wage as men, for which industries welcomed them wholeheartedly.

Whenever society changes radically or customs die out, the sense of loss prompts the "survivors" to seek out the glories of the bygone golden age. In 1908, Hans Barth, an avid devotee of the Italian osteria tradition, wrote *Osteria: A Spiritual Guide to Italian Osterias from Verona to Capri*, an enological grand tour of Italy—half of which is dedicated to Rome. It was his elegy to a dying tradition, a search for the last vestiges of the true osteria:

> This book is a Holy Land, sown with crosses. A Holy Land of illusions and of
> . . . Osterias. Where for is the frenzy of the tarantella, the mandolin players
> happily drifting towards the fare served up at *Piperino*, the racket of the gamers,
> the smiling faces? If Bacchus were to return to Rome, he would cry hot tears
> and run away as fast as he could. . . . Because where can you find wine in Rome
> these days? It is harder than finding a good man in Sodom.[29]

Between the lines of inebriated lyricism is the discernible yearning of the impassioned seeker. He reviews almost one hundred thirty osterias in Rome, many with colorful names that would be lost in translation. He has a keen eye for recognizing the spirit of the age as well as the changes it is undergoing. He makes note of decline, is misty about the few genuine taverns, and perceives an overall transformation of what once was. The imitation osterias aimed at serving travelers and foreigners and relieving them of their money:

> Osteria *Jacobini* with its "nectar of Genzano" transformed into a tea-room, and
> the *Basilica di Tajano* was profaned as a sort of restaurant *chez* Maxim with silk
> covered lampshades, waiters in tuxes and a pretentious little orchestra. . . . In
> ninety out of one hundred cases when they write: "Frascati wines," it is an out-
> right lie. If every *oste* who used the name Frascati in vain were to be hung, they
> would run out of trees to make the gibbets. Wherever you see "*Vin de Frascati*"
> I recommend you flee and quickly.[30]

Barth's is one of the early gastronomic itinerate guides in search of oste-rias, trattorias, and wine; the picaresque wanderer informing curious readers how to navigate the streets and piazzas of Italy to uncover its culinary trea-sures. Another operating in a similar vein was the Touring Club Italiano, founded in 1894 by a group of bicyclists, very much in keeping with the late nineteenth-century promotion of health, exercise, and the great outdoors. In 1931, they published a special issue called the *Gastronomic Guide to Italy*. One chapter is dedicated to each region; Rome is the only city with a chapter all its own. The introduction to the cucina romanesca (which they distin-guish from the ancients by referring to the former as "Roman cuisine" and the latter as "cuisine of the Romans") reiterates the same observation on the mutability of traditional foods:

> There are many dishes pertaining to Roman cuisine, and there were even more up until not too many years ago, when genuine local traditions, not only in families, but also in the trattorias, had not yet been contaminated by the overlay and the deviations that are inevitable in a large city with an intensely modern life. . . . But there is no point in crying nostalgically over viands that have fallen into disuse, especially when what is left makes up a culinary whole with its own distinct characteristics. . . . Many of these are renowned throughout the country and can be considered among the most representative dishes of good Italian cuisine—if by this term we mean the entirety of the best regional specialties. And as it happens, many dishes served outside of Rome called *alla romana* are pure fakery, completely unknown in Rome.[31]

Paolo Monelli's *The Wandering Gormandizer: Gastronomic Travels through Italy* (1935) is the descendent of Barth's unguarded approach to culinary criticism. At the Trattoria all'Alfredo, beloved by Mary Pickford and Douglas Fairbanks, he comments on the showmen that Roman restaurateurs had become:

> It happens that this or that Roman osteria acquires some exceptional customers; the place becomes famous, prices go up and the dishes become precious. . . . But the basics of Roman cuisine are always simple and frank, so the astute restaurateur gives his high brow clientele epic names for the food—"Majestic fettuccine with double butter"—for example. So, a couple orders the fettuccine; the waiter has just now set them on a nearby table. The owner appears, mustachioed with an imposing belly, and gold silverware in his fist. He approaches the plate of fettuccine. The music stops and after an advisory drumroll a hush falls over the customers. The restaurateur feels all eyes on him. He raises high a fork and spoon, and then thrusts them into the pasta, moving them deftly, mathematically, head bowed, breath held, pinkies up. The music then explodes joyously while the man divides the portions. He puts away the gold cutlery and vanishes.[32]

Fettuccine Alfredo, an American dish of great success that no Roman knows.[33]

Mussolini and the New Roman Empire

The fascist objective of self-sufficiency was a pipe dream, not only because Italy did not have enough arable land and resources to sustain the population, but also because European prosperity required interdependence; severing ties would have only been an economic and cultural detriment. The idea that colonization in northeast Africa would to bring in more raw materials and expand the breadbasket was grossly miscalculated, in both human and financial terms, and in the end merely added to the dearth at home. The people supported Mussolini when he invaded Ethiopia in 1935 as their manifest destiny, but in 1938, when he made the Pact of Steel with Hitler, enthusiasm faded, as the writing on the wall was ominous. As a result of the Pact, the Racial Laws were instituted in Italy and after nearly seventy years of freedom, marked by notable integration both socially and professionally, the Jewish Ghetto was once again reinstated. In 1940, Italy entered into the war alongside their German ally. The people were told that it would be swift and sure but, in the meantime, they would have to tighten their belts just a bit more and accept the indignity of rationing. The need for the ration card did not disappear entirely for nearly ten years.

It was possible to use the ration card in trattorias as well, although the choice was somewhat limited. For example, at the San Carlo on Via del Corso, the menu on September 4, 1943, offered "country-style bread soup or pasta with tomato sauce" for those using the ration card, whereas for those with ready cash the selections read: "vegetable soup, cream of legumes, can-noli beans in tomato sauce, eggplant parmesan, potato gratin, tomato salad with oregano, and fruit in season."[34] The difference in the two is evident, and yet the more substantial menu is still, undeniably, wartime fare.

Under the totalitarian regime, foreign words were banned. The Touring Club Italiano, for example, became the Consociazione Turistica Italiana, for a time. All foreign films were dubbed, and even entries written on menus had to be in compliance. The details outlined in the exacting "Regulations for customers and managers of public businesses," regarding food service read:

> The composition of the obligatory fixed-price meal has been categorically es-tablished herewith in this list of foods. It is strictly prohibited to serve antipasti and abundant portions. Portions must be distributed already dressed; hence, it is also forbidden to serve oil, butter, or other fats separately. It is also forbidden to serve: (a) egg-based soups—*stracciatella, pavese, brodo all'uovo,* and the like; (b) desserts and gelato. . . . Bread must be distributed in accordance with in the amount prescribed by law.[35]

La dolce vita

Post–World War II Italian cinema was perhaps the most powerful medium through which the aftermath of war and the uphill climb to make a better life were communicated. In the film *Ladri di biciclette* (Bicycle Thieves, 1948), set in Rome, there is a poignant scene that embodies the hopes and travails of Italy during that period. The young protagonist is in a trattoria eating *mozzarella in carrozza*. As he brings the golden fried cheese to his mouth, it stretches languidly. The gesture is more than a simple response to hunger: it is the desire for the serenity and security of a job, and the possibility of eating lunch in a trattoria every now and again is a part of that. Cinema in itself was a godsend for Rome, bringing in considerable amounts of money and jobs, boosted in particular by American productions, which profited from advantageous running costs and the *Roman Holiday* atmosphere. It played an invaluable role in the extraordinary postwar boom referred to as the economic miracle.

In 1950, Remington Olmstead, California-born singer, actor, and dancer, went to Italy to take voice lessons and ended up in Rome working as a film extra and playing bit roles, as did many Americans at the time. He was a John Wayne type, a former UCLA football player, and had the looks that worked well for supporting, manly roles. He met and married a Diana Varè, a young high-society woman, and settled in Rome. The couple opened a restaurant in the heart of Trastevere in 1959 called Meo Patacca, after a local hero immortalized in a seventeenth-century poem written in Roman dialect. Other poems based on Meo followed, as well as various theater pieces and a film. The historical nature of the name is significant, given the type of ambience Olmstead was aiming to create, or rather recreate. His idea was to stage a nineteenth-century osteria, replete with wine casks, rusted farming implements, flasks, garlic braids, daggers, wagon wheels, terracotta crocks, and dim lighting, where deft waiters—dressed in velvet knee breeches, black shoes with big silver buckles, neck scarves, and berets—busily served "local fare" among which was shrimp cocktail, mountain ham with figs, bean soup à la Francofitch, cannelloni à la Meo, curried chicken pilaf, one-half free-range chicken tortured on a rotisserie, and other nonsensical dishes that get lost in translation. Musicians with guitars, mandolins, and tambourines wandered among the tables playing songs ranging from "Arrivederci Roma" to grand opera to "Moon River"—adapted for the Tiber. It was an enormous success.

An illuminating personal perspective proposes that Olmstead created the model for the modern Roman eatery:

> I was longing for knowing more about this bizarre character after listening to the fascinating memories of my father, who owned and ran a restaurant in Trastevere in the 70's.
>
> He mentioned this chap "Mr Bob" or "Sor Remy," a brilliant american [sic] guy who literally invented the typical roman restaurant tradition. It is quite

odd to say that but the roman cuisine tradition has been invented by an ameri-can [sic]. I think that you US people are aware of the fact that in Europe you are famous for so many things and for sure the Art of Cuisine is not among them.[36]

Just eating a decent meal was no longer enough. Entertainment, conspicu-ous consumption, gastronomic muscle flexing, and cocktails exploded during the economic boom. The spinal cord of the cafe society was Via Veneto, rife with people-watching and diva-spotting, while the divas themselves engaged in paparazzi-dodging. This new order was the manifestation of enormous social change that was happening at a speed unmatched in Italian history. In a few short years, Italy changed from an agricultural and rural country to one of the world's industrial powers. Around Via Veneto and in the historic center in general, flashy restaurant-bar-dancing clubs opened, mixing cosmo-politan affluence and Italian style, while on the Appian Way you could order chicken alla Caligula served by women dressed in classical garb. By 1968, Rome was home to 3,317 licensed restaurants, trattorias, osterias, pizzerias, and the like.

The Pizza Effect

Italy's youth were experiencing freedoms that had never before been allowed. Society was being reshaped and young people were at the center of the trans-formation. Eating fast and cheaply was central to their socialization, which helped pizza conquer Italy. Although pizza would go on to have unparalleled success in Rome, and despite the relative proximity to Naples, it got off to a rough start, as seen in this melodramatic excerpt:

> One day, an industrious Neapolitan had an idea. Knowing that pizza was one of the most beloved foods in Naples, and knowing that the Neapolitan com-munity in Rome was vast, he thought he would open a pizzeria in Rome. . . . You could have any pizza you wanted: with tomato, with mozzarella, with an-chovies and oil, with oil, oregano, and garlic. At first they came running, and then it tapered off. Pizza taken from its Neapolitan environment seemed to clash and represented a sort of indigestion. Its star grew pale and set in Rome; an exotic plant died in this Roman solemnity.[37]

Pizza and its prototypes had long been in existence and were associated primarily with Naples. It was a regional curiosity about which many were decidedly not curious due to the context of poverty from which it arose and the reputed unhygienic conditions of Naples. Its nonpareil success during the economic miracle was later recognized as a sociological phenomenon and dubbed "The Pizza Effect." Pizza had been exported with Italian immigrants and popularized as an ethnic food largely through Lombardi's in New York. The unsavory connotations of the Neapolitan poor did not travel with it, allowing the public to partake without prejudice.[38] American infantrymen on duty at the end of the war in Naples tasted the local fare and, finding it to their liking, facilitated the popularity of it back home, thereby lifting it out of its "ethnic" niche and launching it into the mainstream. Tourists to Italy requested pizza, puzzled that it was not, as they had thought, one of the cornerstones of "Italian cuisine." Pizza quickly became a very lucrative business, requiring very little capital to turn a sizable profit. Pizza twirlers, often featured at the front of a pizza parlor, and the large, fiery wood burning stove, added to the spectacle of consuming pizza. As pizza became associated with youth, leisure, seaside holidays, and carefree evenings out, it was then poised to take Italy by storm.

In Rome, the pizza industry exploded in the 1960s and 1970s. The first historic pizzeria in Rome, which is still in business, was the Antica Pizzeria Fratelli Ricci Est! Est! Est!, which opened in 1888 under the name Bottiglieria.[39] The founder, Ambrogio Ricci, sold his homemade wine there and with the advent of electricity, he started selling Neapolitan pizza as well. Before rustic revivalism was set in motion, the electric oven offered the reassurances of progress associated with cleanliness, freeing food and drink outlets of the smoky residual odor from wood and charcoal. Paradoxically, the electric pizza oven is used today as an indicator of "inauthentic" or second-rate pizza (see below for Roman pizza-by-the-slice).

Another questionable hallmark of progress followed at the height of the boom: artificial lighting. Florescent lights eliminated the problem of the sooty residue from lantern lights. What is now considered ambient lighting was perceived as backward. Bright lights meant modernity and added an aura of respectability, resulting in a wider range of clientele and higher profits. It is here that the "osteria" transformed into the "hostaria" and "taberna," borrowings from ancient history, wielded for modern ends. Traditions had to be re-elaborated in conjunction with the changes, which meant copious use of cream and sauces that covered nearly all of the dishes. Vittorio Metz, in his homage book to Belli and Roman cooking, suggests a recipe for the prosciutto crostini mentioned in the sonnet Belli devoted to lard. It exemplifies the combination of tradition and 1970s tastes:

> Take a loaf of square sandwich bread that is a few days old and cut twelve slices that are about the size of a 10-pack of cigarettes. Melt some lard in a pan and fry a few pieces of bread at a time, but only on one side. Once browned, arrange

the pieces of bread on a tray with lard fried side up. Take a dense béchamel sauce [prepared ahead and still hot] and mix in 100g of grated gruyere, 500g of parmesan, and 100g of prosciutto cut into thin strips. Spread this stuff on the hot crostini and then you tell me how good it is.[40]

Over time osterias lost their warmth and familiarity, appearing ever more like businesses. "Bound up in the general scheme of food service, the osteria loses its soul and becomes a shell to house pizza makers or fancy chefs."[41] A few holdouts resisted in the city center, but most moved to the outskirts, combining the idea of osteria food with a rural getaway.

Out with the Old, in with the *Nouvelle*
Between the end of the 1970s and the beginning of the 1980s, a bevy of restaurants tried to outdo the old mundane fare, seeking to win the consensus of a new generation of gourmands aware of the *nouvelle cuisine* of Bocuse, Troisgros, Guèrard, and others, promoted by the French critics Gault and Millau and imported into Milan by Gualtiero Marchesi, in his namesake restaurant on Via Bonvesin de la Riva. The food is a mix of innovation and tradition aimed at a lighter, fresher menu; the dining rooms are impeccable, as are the wine lists. La Pergola featured cream of artichokes with scampi quenelles, and strawberries with green peppercorns; Il Drapo served risotto with apples as well as squid fruit salad; at the seaside in Fiumicino, Bastianelli al Molo proposes pineapple salad with prawns, and raw fish in hot sauce; the taste of international cuisine was upheld by San Souci, French cuisine with a suggestion of Italian and George's, where lobster thermidor still haunts the menu. Papà Giovanni, near Piazza Navona, specializes in elevated Roman cuisine such as pecorino and fava bean salad, and fettuccine *al caffè*; still within the realm of Roman food and its revisitations is Agata e Romeo, which offered scalloped foie gras, rucola, black truffle, and balsamic vinegar, and an exemplary *coda alla vaccinara* (oxtail stew). The restaurant had a small plaque with their name to the left of the entrance and above the door a huge sign: *Hostaria*. But they have recently gone out of business.

Clinging to Traditions
Family-style restaurants appeal to a more or less middle-class clientele, families looking for moderate quality at a moderate price, a place to go periodically for Sunday lunch or to celebrate some occasion with the extended family. Customers are welcomed with the cordial familiarity of *benvenuto dottore, bentornata signora* . . . and served what they have come for: unsurprising dishes of ravioli, tagliatelle with tomato sauce, sliced roast beef au jus,

Figure 7.2.   Osteria da Fortunata, just off Campo de' Fiori, gives passersby an ongoing daily demonstration of traditional pasta making in the front window. Photo by Karima Moyer-Nocchi, c. 2018

potatoes, and a green salad. Once innovative dishes have passed the test of time elsewhere, they might be eased into the menu. Dishes such as tagliolini with salmon; gnocchi with tomato sauce, basil, and mozzarella; sliced steak with balsamic vinegar; tuna tartar—all toned down to suit the palate that does not want to be challenged.

Further along the continuum are the dyed-in-the-wool traditionalists serving classics of the *cucina romanesca* as if they were part of the Roman ruins. The menus are like scriptures preaching *cacio e pepe*, *matriciana*, *abbacchio*, *coda*, *carciofi*, *coppiette*, and the other well-known *romanesco* dishes. Notable among those in this genre are: Felice, Sora Lella, Paris, Pastarellaro, Scopettaro, Der Pallaro, Antico Bottaro, Augusto, Augustarello, Checchino, La Carbonara, Betto e Mary, Giggi Fazi, il Matriciano, Er Cordaro, Turiddu, Al Fidelinaro, Bucatino, Romolo, Vecchia Roma, Dar Moschino, Moro, Pallotta, Romolo a Porta Settimiana, Mastrostefano, Beltramme detto Cesaretto, Otello alla Concordia, Il Re degli Amici, Giggetto al Portico d'Ottavia, Settimio al Pellegrino, Corsetti, Sora Margarita, and Osteria da Fortunata. Of particular note is Piperno, once called Padre Abramo, custodian of the *giudie* traditions—and reviewed by Hans Barth: "Its real name is Piperno. You can only get to Monte Cenci on foot, but a carriage can let you off nearby. In the evening it is quite crowded with all sorts of people—locals, gentlemen, artists, travelers, etc."[42]

These osterias, while laudable for their heroic efforts, are striving to maintain the memory of a past whose last living vestiges disappeared completely in the late 1970s. Their central position in the ongoing life of the city was eclipsed by new trends and tastes; revival and resuscitation may keep the memory alive, but their role is now that of gatekeeper, a far cry from the bawdy, grisly, rough, suspect joints they once were. These temples are particularly sought out by tourists in search of the holy grail of authenticity, hungry to sample "traditional" Roman fare.

The Foreign Food Experience in Rome

One of the innovations that coincided with the disappearance of the osteria was interest in foreign restaurants. The first Chinese restaurant, Shangai, opened in Italy in 1949 on Via Borgognona, frequented by diplomats and a few curious locals. In 1969, two French restaurants opened, Charly's Sauciere and L'Eau Vive, the latter run by the religious order Working Missionaries of the Virgin of the Family Donum Dei. In 1974, Hamasei, the Roman offshoot of a restaurant in Tokyo, opened. The hippie culture of the 1970s welcomed the arrival of Indian restaurants, the best of which was the now defunct Surya Mahal.

A wave of red-lanterned restaurants spread across Rome in the 1980s; in most cases, mediocre eateries whose main attraction is novelty and low prices. The Chinese community has since grown significantly, giving rise to a veritable Roman Chinatown near Piazza Vittorio. The number of Chinese restaurants has increased considerably, but the quality has remained much the same. The menus are standardized, nearly identical from one to the next, but with insider knowledge it is possible to find different fare at the restaurants catering to Chinese customers. The second generation has been more enterprising, aware that patrons are more worldly and discerning, which has had an effect on the quality. Some, however, have interpreted this as the impetus to venture into other Asian cuisines, particularly Japanese, with dubious results. Although the business acuity to recognize the marketability of sushi to a public ever more focused on eating healthy is commendable, these restaurants also tend to follow a predictable industrialized standard. Chinese residents have also moved into the Italian food sector, opening cafes and pizzerias, whose hybrid menus are not well met by the Romans. The pizzeria Cinapoli on Via Trionfale is an example, where sushi and spring rolls meet with cheap, block mozzarella used on frozen pizza. Thai, Korean, Vietnamese, and Malay restaurants complete the Asian spectrum, many operated by Chinese entrepreneurs, but Rome is not a city as of yet that can boast many notable exceptions.

There was a time when there were more African restaurants, particularly Somali and Ethiopian, expressions of the communities that took up residence as a result of misguided Italian colonization. There are still some fine African restaurants along with a few rare ones from Maghreb that have not yielded to the kebab cult and make an attempt to offer North African cuisine.

Middle Eastern food, from Iran to the countries along the Mediterranean, represented mainly by Syria and Lebanon, has a history on the seven hills, but their distinguished culinary traditions seem to be unduly influenced by patrons whose generic perception of "Arabic" has homogenized the various cuisines from the Atlantic coast of Morocco to the Persian highlands and beyond. This cultural phenomenon arises from political contingencies and the mass distribution of skewered blocks of meat—almost all of them made in Germany—that end up spinning on vertical grills like unhappy dervishes. The Romans were quick to baptize these outlets *kebbabari* ("kabobers"). They are overwhelmingly successful; the umpteenth story of globalization wherein success is by no means a measure of quality.

Central and South American restaurants are constrained by stereotypes of tango, samba, salsa, and merengue as well as a barrage of maracas, rum, saudade, tequila, corazon, and "The Girl from Ipanema." Their first concern seems to be offering customers the level of entertainment and ambiance they expect, while the quality of food is a secondary consideration. Spanish restaurants fall prey to selling customers the same preconceived notions with freely flowing sangria and clattering castanets. There is hardly a sign of the rest of Europe, with the possible exception of Greek restaurants, which enjoy a modicum of success. Other restaurants in the entertainment business expressed in cookie-cutter formulas reprinted throughout the world are Hard Rock Cafe, Crazy Bull, T-Bone Station, and others of that ilk. The first of these businessmen/entertainers to open a restaurant to liven up the evenings in Rome was Jeff Blynn, who in the early 1990s opened a place in the heart of Parioli, an upmarket neighborhood hungry for gourmet hamburgers and Caesar salad. They set the stage for brunch, mingling, DJs, and theme eating.

The changes that characterize the third millennium also influence the culinary offerings of the restaurant sector at all levels, be it the fusion cuisine of the Michelin star chef, kabob ingredients on pizza, Mediterranean ceviche in *nippobrasiliana* sauce, fish carbonara, or dried Asian noodles in mainstream supermarkets. The melting pot that Rome has become is as desirable as it is necessary. Even strong gastronomic traditions, as is the Roman tradition, evolve as a result of coalescence and amalgamation brought about by various conditions in time and space. But this is not a new phenomenon in Rome; it has been the history of Roman cuisine for over two thousand years.

La cucina romana—the Next Generation

After the baroque comes the neoclassical. In the aftermath of the moving feast of the 1980s and the globalized confusion of the 1990s, Roman restaurateurs took a respectful look at the past and reinterpreted the recipes of generations of mothers and grandmothers, breathing new life into them without making them into museum pieces. They dared to branch out from foundational concepts, for example, valorizing new craft beers alongside the traditional wine. They also turned their attention to modern concerns about locally sourced foods and sustainability issues. Undoubtedly, fashion, trends, and opportunism are in the mix as well, but the current of thought that took hold shaped the menus of many food outlets and it has resonated with the public as well. Some of the protagonists exploring the possibilities in the new Roman cuisine are Adriano Baldassarre, Gabriele Bonci, Marco Bottega, Massimo Cacciani, Stefano Callegari, Giancarlo Casa, Antonello Colonna, Arcangelo Dandini, Davide Del Duca, the Di Felice brothers, Riccardo Di Giacinto, the Di Vittorio sisters, Antonello Magliari, Roberto Mancino, Giovanni Milana, Gianfranco Pascucci, Massimo Pulicati, the

Roscioli brothers, Salvatore Tassa, Danilo Valente, Eliana Vigneti Catalani, Leonardo Vignolo, and others, who at different levels and in different ways have focused their efforts on creating a contemporary Roman cuisine, and it is their ideas that are influencing the dyed-in-the-wool traditionalists.

Munching, Snacking, Sipping

In addition to that plethora of osterias, restaurants, and trattorias are various forms of street food, takeout, and food eaten standing up or perched for a few minutes on a stool: pizza, fried snacks, panini, ice cream, snow cones, roasted chestnuts, and various specialties purchased from pastry shops, *gelaterie*, *rosticcerie* (cooked food shops), groceries, bakeries, delicatessens, fry-shops, stands, and cafes.

Il bar

The function of a cafe—or *bar* as it is called in Italian—is first and foremost as a coffee distributor. The standard breakfast (in Rome, as it is throughout Italy), is *caffè e cornetto* or *cappuccino e cornetto*, the latter being the Italian *briosce*. They are shaped like croissants but made with a different dough altogether, and sold "empty" or filled with pastry cream or jam. Variations on the coffee theme are subtle:

> *Caffè*—espresso in a small cup
> *Al vetro*—espresso in a shot glass
> *Ristretto*—a dense espresso
> *Lungo*—a more watery espresso
> *Schiumato*—with a bit of milk foam
> *Decaffeinato*—decaffeinated
> *Cappuccino* or *cappuccio*—an espresso with milk processed with forced hot steam to create a foamy consistency, can be ordered normal, light, or dark
> *Latte macchiato*—hot milk with a touch of coffee
> *Caffellatte*—hot milk with coffee
> *Corretto*—with a splash of alcohol, usually sambuca or grappa

This simple start to the day is being challenged by the multinational coffee shop Starbucks. Depending on one's point of view, after years of waiting, or years of resisting, Starbucks will be (at this writing) opening two shops as a test run, one in Piazza di Spagna and the other at the Termini train station, two rather risk-free locations. If they are successful, it will usher in another one hundred fifty to two hundred branches throughout Italy in the coming years.

Bars, contrary to most other eating establishments, are open from early morning to evening. As the day wears on, many bars serve light, on-the-go lunches, and then at dusk, transform into meeting places for an *aperitivo*—a drink and *sfizi*, salty snacks and simple canapés—consumed either standing up or at a table. The current craze for the aperitivo is mostly a "millennial" phenomenon, but, as a social custom, has its roots in the nineteenth century.

But before *bar* became the common term, there were cafes. In an Italian bar, one stands to drink and eat, literally at the bar, so named because it is a *barrier* between the serving staff and the public. At a cafe, one sits, ponders, watches. Much of the conversation that brought about societal change, artistic inspiration, and democratic awareness took place at the tables of the Procope in Paris, the Florian in Venice, the Central in Vienna, the Brasileira in Lisbon, and other coffee shops throughout Europe.

In Rome in 1854, there were 217 cafes, 153 of them with an official sign. Among those listed were Affricano, degli Agonizzati, degli Artisti, dei Bicchierini, di Europa, del Giuoco Liscio, Inglese, dei Negozianti, degli Orfanelli, della Pedacchia, del Pidocchio, della Suburra, dei Svizzeri, della Vedovella, dei Virtuosi, della Zucchella—but oddly and inexplicably, the oldest and perhaps most famous was not on the list: Caffè Greco, in Via dei Condotti, mentioned previously by Gillespie.

> It has existed two hundred years on the same spot and with the same name. When you enter, you find the smoke so dense that you can scarcely see across the room, but through it dimly appear the long beards, fierce moustaches, slouched hats, slashed velvet jackets, frogged coats, and wild, but intellectual, countenances, which characterize most of the young artists of Rome. All are smoking, or taking their after-dinner coffee, or talking in a confusion of languages, compared to which Babel was a deaf-and-dumb asylum. Those who wish for the waiter, call out "Botteca!"—meaning "Shop"—or produce a sharp sound between a hiss and a whistle; to which he replies, "Eccome!"—a here I am—or "Momentino"—in a little moment—, or "Subito"—suddenly–, which last practically means "Some time in the course of the evening."[43]

The white and orange cups state, "Founded in 1760," but the actual date is uncertain. It would appear that it takes its name from Nicola della Maddalena, a Greek who, according to the church registers of San Lorenzo in Lucina, had a shop in Via Condotti in 1765.[44] In structure, it is a few rooms set up railroad car–style, one after the other, each one with a name: Rossa, Roma, Gubinelli, Venezia, Szoldaticz, and Omnibus, illuminated by skylights. Myriad VIPs passed through, traces of which were left by way of writings, paintings, photos, and memorabilia. Pictures with men in top hats, neoclassical busts, Daguerrotypes, a youthful Orson Welles, in the Omnibus room between Ennio Flaiano and Lea Padovani along with a dozen other writers and artists of the day; or Buffalo Bill, complete with boots and hat. The cafe was a portal; something imperceptible had taken hold of the public. In the words of an Englishwoman traveling in Rome:

> The Caffè Greco is situated in the Via di Condotti, which runs from the Corso into the Piazza di Spagna, and in the very midst of the English quarter. Externally, it is of unpretending aspect; it will not bear comparison with the magnificent cafes of Paris, or even those of Milan or Turin, nor even with others in the same city. A plain, quiet-looking house, with two broad windows, a glazed door, with a narrow side-entrance adjoining, a marble tablet, with the words "Caffè Greco" over the ground floor. Could this be the Caffe Greco, about which I had heard so much? this the chosen rendezvous of the genius of all countries? this that famous symposium of all nations? But by far the most interesting café in the world is the Caffè Greco at Rome.[45]

The fascination of places like these is that they preserve the aura of an era, crystalized in time so that they become veritable museums. At the end of the nineteenth century, other cafes became the artistic pulse of the city, notably Notegen on Via del Babuino and Aragno on the Corso. The hotspot would migrate and branch out internally; in the 1950s it was Via Veneto, but when the world came to visit the streets of *La Dolce Vita*, it had already moved to *Canova* and *Rosati* in Piazza del Popolo at which point it had definitively undergone the transformation, already well underway in Via Veneto, from cafe to bar.

Street Food

The most ubiquitous Roman snack is a slice of pizza, Sliced pizza is certainly not unique to Rome, but there are variations on the theme that they feel are distinctly their own. The simplest is what Romans call "white" pizza, *pizza bianca*. It is a flat bread, something between a focaccia and a pizza base, and has an airy crumb and chewy texture. It is usually eaten as is or sliced open and filled either with Roman mortadella, a flattened salami called the *spianata*, whose distinct taste derives from the wine marinated garlic used to flavor it, or Rome's own IGP-certified bolognese-style mortadella, also called *salame cotto*. This is the standard worker's pizza and traditionally comes wrapped in rough yellowish-brown paper. The *pizza bianca*, made from a soft dough of flour, water, salt, malt, yeast, and oil, originated as a means of gauging the temperature of wood-burning ovens used for bread making. This "tester" bread is at present being reviewed for IGP certification. The other simple pizza is "red" pizza, *pizza rossa*, the version with tomato sauce. Sometimes it is graced with anchovy, garlic, and parsley or cayenne, at which point it strays from its Roman origins toward the Neapolitan *marinara*. Likewise, the addition of cheese to the red pizza leads into the realm of the classic Neapolitan margherita, a simple tomato-based pizza with cheese, sparsely decorated with basil leaves. Roman pizza is more of a bread bakery item than a pizzeria product—especially the red and white varieties. "Country style" pizza is with vegetables, either stuffed inside or piled on top, like the wintertime warmer "broccoli and sausage." The most luxurious and decadent is the end of summer white pizza, with prosciutto and figs.

Even though pizza by the slice may win out on consumption, the king of Roman street foods is the *supplì*. While the origins are almost impossible to trace, this filling deep-fried ball of rice and tomato with a mozzarella center has sustained people through two world wars, reconstruction, and the economic miracle, as well as surviving the age of creamy sauces and the Mediterranean Diet.[46] However, around the beginning of 2000, it seemed as if the supplì was petering out, with the possible exception of Sisinni and a few others. Fortunately, it experienced a comeback, as it too was revisited and revalorized by pizza shops, delis, cafes, and osterias, using new flavors and fillings.

Supplì first appear on the menu of Trattoria detta del Lepre in 1846, written *soplis di riso*. The word itself is curious and may be a distorted transliteration of the French *surprise*—referring to the filling inside. Forty years later, history offers another clue in a watercolor by Roman artist Ettore Roesler Franz. It depicts a woman and a young girl in the foreground carrying empty wine flasks and looking off right where two other women are waiting at the threshold of a shop. Over the archway, FRIGGITORIA (fry-shop) is written on a large sign and in the corner of the entrance is a smaller handwritten sign saying, "*supplì al buon gusto*" (tasty supplì). Therefore, over the space of forty years, the term had come into being.

Roman folklorist Giggi Zanazzo notes in 1908 that one of the disappearing voices from the city streets was that of the ambulant supplì vendor, who wandered the streets in the early evening, carrying his wares in a contraption that kept the food warm, crying out "Steaming hot! Rice supplì."[47]

The most common supplì filling up to the twentieth century was chicken innards, fried in lard with some herbs and then mixed with a couple spoonfuls of tomato sauce. The first known written recipe is recorded in *Talisman of Happiness* as *Supplì alla Romana*,[48] where Ada Boni suggests dressing the innards up (in accordance with one's budget) with reconstituted dried mushrooms, bits of prosciutto, and mince beef from leftover stew. The rice should

Figure 7.3. *Supplì* ready to be fried up for the onslaught of customers at this popular pizza-by-the slice place just outside the national library. Photo by Karima Moyer-Nocchi, c. 2018

be prepared either with sauce from a stew or plain tomato sauce. Off heat, add butter, Parmesan, and beaten eggs. After cooling it on a platter, spread a spoonful of it in your hand. Spoon on some of the filling and two or three cubes of mozzarella or provola. They are then shaped like croquettes and coated in breadcrumbs. Fry in oil or lard until golden. The melted cheese would stretch when they were broken open, like the earpiece attached to wooden wall phones, and as such, the Romans referred to them as "*supplì al telefono.*"[49]

One romantic throwback to bygone days consists of attempts to replicate the mountain men who in times past came to town in the late autumn and winter months selling roasted chestnuts. Just as once remembered or imagined, the *caldarroste* stands consist of a warm, crackling fire set under a grate, over which the slow-roasting chestnuts with their barely blackened shells, just opening, emanate nostalgic smells of toasted, nutty goodness that promise a bit of comfort in the cold.

These delicious offerings must, however, be taken with a grain of salt, conceptually at least. Not only is their nostalgic aura questionable, but they contrast with the chestnut sellers who actually offer these wares in the streets of Rome in less contrived and grittier contexts.

Street sellers today are generally poor immigrants, not from the towns outside Rome but from beyond Europe itself. Easy prey to profiteers, they may often be paid under the table to work behind the fire pits and the mobile vending stands parked outside the Coliseum or in Piazza Navona. The romantic version of the chestnut seller serves to underline, rather than overcome, the changes.

The two legendary patriarchs of Rome, Aeneas and Romulus, tell a different story about how immigration, migration, and tradition intersect at the essence of Rome. The former was an immigrant himself, while the latter welcomed anyone and everyone to his new settlement: asylum seekers, wanderers, criminals, the destitute, fortune hunters, whoever wanted to have a hand in making Rome. So, in a sense, it still is.

When Cicero declaimed about the virtues of his republic and the rights of its citizens, he invoked the image of a Roman anywhere claiming the identity and destiny of Rome: "*Civis romanus sum.*" Now as in ancient times, the identity of Rome and its food are witness not to an inward-looking purity, but to a dynamic multiculturalism, formed by history but open to the future.

Figure 7.4.   Bangladeshi chestnut vendor in Piazza Navona. Photo by Karima Moyer-Nocchi, c. 2018

Notes

Ostium

1. Peregrine Horden and Nicholas Purcell, *The Corrupting Sea: A Study of Mediterranean History* (Oxford: Blackwell, 2000), 45.

Chapter One

1. c. 10,000 BCE.

2. Nicholas Purcell, "Rome and the Management of Water: Environment, Culture and Power," accessed July 13, 2016, https://www.academia.edu/3136285/Rome_and_the_management_of_water_environment_culture_and_power_1996.

3. 115,000–11,700 years ago.

4. In 1870, when the Papal State was annexed into the Kingdom of Italy, it measured 212,572 hectares (821 square miles), whereas the estimate calculated in 1939 during the fascist reign was 236,166 hectares (911 square miles). Enrico Filene, *L'agro romano e i suoi problemi* (Rome: Istituto di Studi Romani, 1939), 3. As of 2015, the total combined area has been renamed The Metropolitan City of Rome Capital and comprises 2,100 square miles.

5. The Roman and the English mile are nearly identical.

6. A. Afoldi, *Early Rome and the Latins* (Ann Arbor: University of Michigan Press, 1963), 298.

7. Old Latium.

8. Grant Heiken, Renato Funiciello, and Donatella De Rita, *The Seven Hills of Rome* (Princeton, NJ: Princeton University Press, 2005), 34.

9. As part of Mussolini's patriotic project to retrieve two sunken ships from the bottom of Lake Nemi, he had the lake drained and a museum built for the reconstructed boats. In 1944, American air fire hit the museum and the ships burnt to cinders.

10. Heiken, Funiciello, and De Rita, *Seven*, 30.

11. Ernesto di Renzo, *Mangiare l'autentico* (Rome: Universitalia, 2012), 143.

12. most autochthonous, others the result of prehistoric anthropogenic distribution.

13. Di Renzo, *Mangiare*, 142.

14. Giuseppina Florio, "La cucina degli antichi romani: Appunti per una tradizione," in *Le cucine della memoria Roma e Lazio*, ed. Angela Adriana Cavarra (Roma: Edizioni de Luca, 1995), 23.

15. Afoldi, *Early*, 292.

16. Pliny, *NH* 30.41.

17. Francesca Conde and Enrico De Vita, *Agro Romano antico* (Rome: Gangemi, 2011), 23.

18. Fernand Braudel, *The Mediterranean and the Mediterranean World in the Age of Philip II, Vol. 1* (Berkeley: University of California Press, 1995), 62.

19. Peregrine Horden and Nicholas Purcell, *The Corrupting Sea: A Study of Mediterranean History* (Oxford: Blackwell, 2000), 192.

20. T. J. Cornell, *The Beginnings of Rome* (London: Rutledge 1995), 32.

21. Cornell, *Beginnings*, 32.

22. Late Copper–Early Bronze Age. An admixture of Near Eastern peoples and Caucasians.

23. Peter Watson, *Ideas: A History of Thought and Invention from Fire to Freud* (New York: HarperPerennial, 2005), 55.

24. Watson, *Ideas*, 56.

25. Pope Gregory III would later (732 CE) illegalize the consumption of horse meat. Marialucia Galli, "Ippofagia su internet, l'ultima follia," accessed January 9, 2017, http://www.cavallo2000.it/detail/ippofagia_su_internet_lultima_follia-id_407.htm.

26. Horden and Purcell, *Corrupting*, 199.

27. Chris Wickham, "Pastoralism and Underdevelopment in the Early Middle Ages," in *L'uomo di fronte al mondo animale nell'alto medioevo* (Spoleto: Fondazione CISAM, 1985), 401.

28. Sergio Urilli and Fabio Brini, "Oltre la transumanza: Allevamento ovino e attività casearie alle porte di Roma," in *Roma e la sua campagna*, edited by Franco Salvatori and Ernesto di Renzo (Genoa: Tipografia Brigata, 2007), 195.

29. Wickham, *Pastoralism*, 403.

30. Afoldi, *Early*, 9.

31. Afoldi, *Early*, 5.

32. Afoldi, *Early*, 21.

33. Graeme Barker, *The Agricultural Revolution in Prehistory* (Oxford: Oxford University Press, 2006), 382.

34. Virgil, *The Aeneid*, 119–26, trans. Robert Fagles (New York: Penguin, 2006), 216–17.

35. Virgil, *The Aeneid*, 133–141, 217.

36. Named after a white sow, or boar, with a litter of thirty piglets that was found there.

37. Titus Livius, *The History of Rome by Titus Livius. Translated from the Original with Notes and Illustrations by George Baker, A.M. First American, from the Last London Edition, in Six Volumes* (New York: Peter A. Mesier et al., 1823), 1:8, accessed January 13, 2016, http://oll.libertyfund.org/titles/1754.

38. Livy, *History*, 1:9.

39. The Greek equivalent was Hypnos, whose henchwoman was Aergia, goddess of sloth and Rhea's half-sister.

40. Robert Hughs, *Rome: A Cultural, Visual, and Personal History* (New York: Knopf, 2011), ebook loc 372.

41. Beard, Mary, "Meet the Romans," accessed January 12, 2018, https://www.youtube.com/watch?v=rggk_H3jEgw, 2016.

42. Livy, *History*, 1:12.

43. Cornell, *Beginnings*, 60.

44. See chapter 2.

45. Rachel Laudan, *Cuisine and Empire: Cooking in World History* (Berkeley: University of California Press, 2013), loc 310.

46. Horden and Purcell, *Corrupting*, 206.

47. "Alimentazione in Etruria," Ministero per i Beni e le Attività Culturali, accessed January 9, 2017, http://www.beniculturali.it/mibac/multimedia/MiBAC/minisiti/alimentazione/sezioni/etastorica/etruria/index.html.

48. Cornell, *Beginnings*, 81.

49. Horden and Purcell, *Corrupting*, 205.

Chapter Two

1. Robert E. Dickinson, *City and Region: A Geographical Interpretation, Volume 2* (London: Routledge, 2002), 571.

2. Charles William Louis Launspach, *State and Family in Early Rome* (London: G. Bell and Sons, 1908), 16.

3. A. Afoldi, *Early Rome and the Latins* (Ann Arbor: University of Michigan Press, 1963), 312.

4. Launspach, *State*, 58.

5. Also thought to be Ops or *Opis*.

6. Cesare de Cupis, *Le Vicende dell'agricoltura e della pastorizia nell'agro romano, L'annona di Roma* (Roma: Tip. nazionale di G. Bertero, 1911), 2.

7. de Cupis, *Vicende*, 4.

8. Pliny, *NH* 18.5.

9. Paul Erdkamp, "Agriculture, Employment, and the Cost of Rural Labour in the Roman World," *Classical Quarterly* 49, no. 2 (1999): 558, accessed: August 28, 2016, http://asbproxy.unisi.it:2233/stable/639879.

10. Horace, *Odae* 3.6. "*mascula proles rusticorum militium, docta versare glebas Sabellis ligonibus.*"

11. Pliny, *NH* 25.9.

12. Vladimir G. Simkhovitch, "Rome's Fall Reconsidered," *Political Science Quarterly* 31, no. 2 (1916): 210, accessed July 24, 2016, doi:10.2307/2141560.

13. Columella, *De re rustica* I, preface.

14. Columella, *De re rustica*, I, preface.

15. Columella, *De re rustica*, I, preface.

16. Zeev Wiseman, *Desert Olive Oil Cultivation* (Amsterdam: Elsevier, Academic Press, 2009), 56, 58.

17. Mireille Corbier, "The Ambiguous Status of Meat in Ancient Rome," *Food and Foodways*, 3, no. 3 (1989), accessed February 15, 2017, 227 doi: 10.1080/07409710.1989.9961951.

18. Corbier, "Ambiguous." 227.

19. Galen cited in Keith Hogwood, "Bandits, Elites and Rural Order," in *Patronage in Ancient Society*, ed. Andrew Wallace-Hadrill (London: Routledge, 1990), 172.

20. Pliny, *NH*, 18.7; *Italia*, or Roman Italy, was officially created by Emperor Augustus.

21. Alexander Demandt compiled a list of 210 reasons for the Fall of the Roman Empire. This is merely one.

22. Simkhovitch,"Rome's Fall Reconsidered" 241.

23. Suetonius, *Lives of the Caesars*, Vitellius 13.

24. One of the scholarly sources that proliferated this misinformation is Lewis Mumford's *The City in History* (1961).

25. Corbier, "Ambiguous," 249.

26. Corbier, "Ambiguous," 249.

27. Strabo 15.1.22, 695 C; Columella, 3.8.; Pliny, *NH* 7.3.3.

28. Pliny specifically refers to this as being made with "zea" (XVIII, 30), which the translators Bostock/Thomas assume is rye, but Herodotus (II, 36) says, "they [Egyptians] prepare their bread with ὄλυρα which some call Zeìa (in Evans/Peacock, p. 7) related to the Greek ζείδωρος" (zeidoros) meaning "life giving." Zea (zeìa), like the Latin *far*, is emmer *Triticum turgidum subsp. dicoccum*, *Alica* was a white potage, so rendered by the addition of chalk (calcium carbonate) (Pliny, *NH* 18.30).

29. Ovid, *Fasti* 6.169–86.

30. Nicholas Purcell, "The Way We Used to Eat: Diet, Community, and History at Rome," *The American Journal of Philology* 124, no. 3 (2003): 330, Accessed July 13, 2016, http://asbproxy.unisi.it:2233/stable/1562134.

31. Pliny, *NH* 9.53.

32. Pliny, *NH* 19.19.

33. Cato, *De Agricultura* 156.

34. "The Salad," accessed June 20, 2017, http://virgil.org/appendix/moretum.htm.

35. Peter Garnsey, *Cities, Peasants and Food in Classical Antiquity* (Cambridge: Cambridge University Press, 1998), 246.

36. Peter Garnsey, "Famine in the Ancient Mediterranean," *History Today* 36, no. 5 (May 1, 1986): 26, accessed July 13, 2016, http://search.proquest.com/docview/12 99020639?accountid=13857.

37. Suetonius, *Augustus*.

38. Michele Renee Salzman, "From a Classical to a Christian City, Civic Euergetism and Charity in Late Antique Rome," *Studies in Late Antiquity* 1 no. 1 (Spring 2017): 65–85, accessed June 4, 2017, doi: 10.1525/sla.2017.1.1.65.

39. Salzman, "Classical."

40. Garnsey, Peter. "Famine," 27.

41. Peter Garnsey, *Cities*, 236.

42. Sunken merchant ships are still discovered every so often, and it is believed that many more lie on the seafloor.

43. Letizia Staccioli, "Pane e panettieri nell'antica Roma," accessed June 7, 2017, http://www.cerealialudi.org/alimentazione/pane-e-panettieri-nellantica-roma/.

44. H. E. Jacob, *Six Thousand Years of Bread: Its Holy and Unholy History* (New York: Skyhorse, 2007), 78.

45. *Triticum aestivum/compactum*.

46. "I pani di Pompeii tornano a tavola," accessed June 7, 2017, http://espresso .repubblica.it/food/dettaglio/i-pani-di-pompei-tornano-a-tavola/2217401.html.

47. Juvenal, *Satires* 5.70.

48. Naum Jasny, "The Daily Bread of the Ancient Greeks and Romans," *Osiris* 9 (1950): 243, accessed August 18, 2016, http://www.jstor.org/stable/301851.

49. "I pani."

50. Pliny, *NH* 18.27.

51. Salzman, "Classical."

52. Comune di Campodimele, accessed April 28, 2017, http://www.comune .campodimele.lt.it.

53. Pliny, *NH* 22.142.

54. Dioscorides, *Materia Medica* 3–94.

55. Glucose-6-phosphate-dehydrogenase deficiency.

56. Fritz M. Heichelheim, *Storia economica del mondo antico: IV La repubblica romana* (Rome-Bari: Laterizi & Figli 1979), 876. These lists vary and change as archeological research progresses.

57. Fabio Paraseocoli, *Al Dente: A History of Italian Food* (London: Reaktion Books, 2014), e-book loc 703.

58. Heichelheim, *Storia*, 876.

59. Horden and Purcell, *Corrupting*, 259.

60. Horden and Purcell, *Corrupting*, 273.

61. Runnels and van Andel, cited in Horden and Purcell, *Corrupting*, 273.

62. Horden and Purcell, *Corrupting*, 262.

63. Varro, *De Rustica*, 3.2.11.

64. Pliny, *NH* 19.52. "Ex horto plebei macellum, quanto innocentiore victu!"

65. Martial, *Apoph.* 14.223.

66. First recorded use of Lucullan, 1861.

67. Emily Gowers, *The Loaded Table: Representations of Food in Roman Literature* (Oxford: Oxford University Press, 1993), 21.

68. John H. D'Arms, "The Culinary Reality of Roman Upper-Class Convivia: Integrating Texts and Images." *Comparative Studies in Society and History* 46, no. 3 (2004): 432, accessed February 10, 2017. http://asbproxy.unisi.it:2233/stable/3879469.

69. John H. D'Arms, "Culinary," 449.

70. Pseudolus, 810 ff.

71. Vincent J. Rosivach, "The 'Lex Fannia Sumptuaria' of 161 BC." *Classical Journal* 102, no. 1 (2006): 7, accessed July 28, 2016, http://asbproxy.unisi.it:2233/stable/30038672.

72. Martial cited in Nicholas F. Hudson, "Changing Places: The Archaeology of the Roman 'Conviviu'" *American Journal of Archaeology* 114, no. 4 (2010), accessed July 22, 2016, http://asbproxy.unisi.it:2233/stable/25763806.

73. Hudson, "Changing," 684.

74. Hudson, "Changing," 692.

75. Petronius, *Satyricon* 40.

76. Plutarch, *Septum Sapientium Convivial* (The Dinner of the Seven Wise Men).

77. Juvenal, *Satires* 11.175.

78. Marcel Detienne, and J. P. Vernant *The Cuisine of Sacrifice among the Greeks* (Chicago: University of Chicago Press, 1989), 11.

79. Seneca, *Moral Letters* 87.17, 88.18, 95.23; Petronius, *Satyricon* 2, Robert Curtis, "Professional Cooking, Kitchens, and Service Work," in *A Cultural History of Food in Antiquity*, ed. Paul Erdkamp (London: Bloomsbury, 2016), 123.

80. The question of whether it was Aurelian or Severus Alexander who introduced bread in place of wheat in the dole is a matter of scholarly dispute.

81. Paul Erdkamp,"The Food Supply of the Capital," in *The Cambridge Companion to Ancient Rome* (Cambridge: Cambridge University Press, 2013), 267.

82. *Edictum de preriis rerum venalium*, Bibliotheca Augustana, accessed June 14, 2017, http://www.hs-augsburg.de/~harsch/Chronologia/Lspost04/Diocletianus/dio_ep04.html.

83. Corbier, "Ambiguous," 237.

84. Corbier, "Ambiguous," 231–32.

85. A. H. M. Jones, "The Roman Colonate." *Past & Present*, no. 13 (1958): 1–13, accessed July 26, 2017. http://asbproxy.unisi.it:2233/stable/649865.

86. Jones, "Colonate," 6.

87. Jones, "Colonate," 3.

88. With the division of the empire, Egypt was assigned to Byzantium, and the rest of the African holdings, Gaul, and Macedonia supplied Rome.

89. H. Moss, *The Birth of the Middle Ages, 395–814* (London: Oxford University Press, 1935), 27.

90. Lewis Mumford, *The City in History*, excerpt chapter 8, accessed June 9, 2016, http://www.panarchy.org/mumford/rome.html.

91. Nicholas Purcell, "The Populace of Rome in Late Antiquity: Problems of Classification and Historical Description," in *The Transformations of Vrbs Roma in Late Antiquity*, ed. W. V. Harris (Portsmouth, RI: Journal of Roman Archeology, 1999), 155.

92. Nicholas Purcell, "The Populace," 139.

93. Procopius, *Secret History*, 23.

94. Procopius, *History of the Wars* 7.17.7–12.

95. Procopius, *History of the Wars*, 7.17.12–19.

96. Procopius, *History of the Wars*, 7.17.12–19.

97. *The Book of the Popes (Liber pontificalis)* vol I, trans. Louise Ropes Loomis, 158.

98. Procopius, *History of the Wars*, 7.20.26–31.

99. Paolo Delogu, "Rome in the Ninth Century: The Economic System," in *Post-Roman Town, Trade and Settlement in Europe and Byzantium, Volume 1:The Heirs of the Roman West*, ed. Joachim Henning (Berlin: De Gruyter, 2007).

100. Cris Wickham, *Framing the Middle Ages: Europe and the Mediterranean 400–800* (Oxford: Oxford University Press, 2005), 292.

101. Gregory of Nazianzus, In laudem Basilii, 34–35, citation in: Erdkamp, "Agriculture, Underemployment," 563.

102. Coinage had increasingly less actual gold and silver and had thereby become worthless and suspect.

103. cf. Mark Koyama, accessed August 18, 2016, https://medium.com/@Mark-Koyama/why-did-the-roman-economy-decline-225deada66ea#.yh8syqn8s; Peter Brown, *The Rise of Western Christendom: Triumph and Diversity, A.D. 200–1000* (Malden, MA: Wiley-Blackwell, 2013), xxiv; Peter Watson, *Ideas: A History of Thought and Invention from Fire to Freud* (New York: HarperPerennial, 2005), 236.

104. de Cupis, *Le vicende*, 26–27.

105. Brown, *The Rise*, xxvii.

106. Delogu, "Rome," 105.

107. Detienne and Vernant, *Cuisine*, 17.

108. *Pistacia terebinthus*. A Mediterranean tree related to the pistachio tree.

109. Patrick Morrisroe, "Chrism," in *The Catholic Encyclopedia*, vol. 3 (New York: Robert Appleton Co. 1908,) accessed June 10, 2016, http://www.newadvent.org/cathen/03696b.htm.

110. Detienne and Vernant, *Cuisine*, 17.

111. Corbier, "Ambiguous," 248.

112. Andrew McGowan, "Food, Ritual, and Power," in *Late Ancient Christianity: A People's History of Christianity*, vol. 2, ed. Virginia Burrus (Minneapolis: Fortress, 2005), 149.

113. McGowan, "Food," 150.

Chapter Three

1. Cato, *On Agriculture*, 78.

2. Cato, *On Agriculture*, 79.

3. Columella, *De re rustica*, 57.12.

4. Mark Grant, *Galen on Food and Diet* (London: Routledge, 2000), 11.

5. Grant, *Galen*, 64.

6. Grant, *Galen*, 80.

7. Ovid, *Metamorphoses*, 8:611–78 "Lelex tells of Philemon and Baucis."

8. Apicius, *De re coquinaria*, 4.2.14.

9. Barbara Flower and Elisabeth Rosenbaum, *The Roman Cookery Book* (London: George G. Harrap & Co., 1958), 19.

10. Apicius, *De re coquinaria*, 5.2.12.

11. Plautus, *Pseudolus* I, 810.

12. The collective unwritten laws of moral and social behavior in accordance with Roman ancestral customs.

13. Variously called *liquamen*, *hallec*, *muria*, etc.

14. This method, which originated in Bithynia, Anatolia, is only one of many. *Geponica*, 20, 46.

15. Anne Willan, *The Cookbook Library* (Berkeley: University of California Press, 2012), 14.

16. Pope Gregory, *Moralia* 31.45.89.

17. Martin Luther, cited in Ken Albala, *Food in Early Modern Europe* (Westport, CT: Greenwood Press, 2003), 200.

18. From 1378–1417, there were three claimants to the papal throne. Rome would eventually win out over Avignon and Pisa.

19. *Libre de Sent Soví* (1324) is one of the main sources of Catalan cuisine that would have been in circulation at the time, and one of the foundational texts of Spanish cuisine. It is also speculated that Martino himself spent some time in Neapolitan court circles. *De Arte Coquinaria* may be a later version of an anonymous recipe collection titled *The Neapolitan Recipe Collection*, perhaps also written by Martino. Regardless, had it not been for Platina's revision and revitalization of Martino's text, it is unlikely that *De Arte Coquinaria* would have found a readership outside of his immediate circle.

20. What is called *blancmange* today is nearly identical to *panna cotta*, but quite different from the dish described here.

21. Subtitle of Luigi Ballerini's edition of *De Arte Coquinaria*.

22. One of the proposed starting dates is the 1453 fall of Constantinople.

23. Luigi Ballerini, introduction to *The Art of Cooking* by Martino of Como (Berkeley: University of California, 2005), 59.

24. Luigi Ballerini, introduction, 28–29.

25. Sugar was previously considered a spice and like salt had been sprinkled on ubiquitously as a flavor enhancer.

26. Earlier prototype recipes for a macaroni and cheese dish were in circulation that predate written Italian recipes. One example comes from the English cookery book *Forme of Cury* (1390): Makerouns. Take and make a thynne foyle of dowh, and kerue it on pieces, and cast hym on boiling water & seeþ it wele. Take chese and grate it, and butter imelte, cast bynethen and abouven as losyns; and serue forth.

Translation: Macaroni. Take a piece of thin pastry dough and cut it in pieces, place in boiling water and cook. Take grated cheese, melted butter, and arrange in layers like lasagna; serve.

27. Mary Ella Milham, introduction to *Platina's On Right Pleasure and Good Health: A Critical Abridgement and Translation of "De honest voluptate et valetudine"* (Asheville, NC: Pegasus Press, 1999), xviii.

28. Mary Ella Milham, introduction to *Platina: On Right Pleasure and Good Health*, ed. (Tempe, AZ: Medieval & Renaissance Texts & Studies, 1998): 47.

29. Milham, introduction to *Platina's*, iv.

30. Milham, introduction to *Platina's*, v.

31. Attributions to other sources given occasionally within the text, but unevenly and inconsistently—acknowledging insignificant bits and ignoring larger borrowings—as further scholarship has uncovered.

32. Milham, introduction to *Platina*, 51.

33. Milham, introduction to *Platina's*, xviii.

34. Although he had been actively working alongside the official librarian, he became the first librarian of the new Vatican Library when it opened on June 15, 1475.

35. Peacock colors.

36. Meg Licht, "Elysium: A Prelude to Renaissance Theater." *Renaissance Quarterly* 49, no. 1 (1996): 1–29, accessed August 14, 2017, doi:10.2307/2863263.

37. Milham, introduction to *Platina*, 55.

38. Romoli, *Dottrina*, 2.21.

39. Terence Scully, introduction to *The Opera of Bartolomeo Scappi (1570), L'arte et prudenza d'un maestro cuoco* (Toronto: University of Toronto Press, 2008), 18.

40. Scully, *Opera*, 61.

41. Claudio Bemporat, *Storia della gastronomia Italiana* (Milan: Ugo Mursia, 1990), 105. Over time, the order in which foods were served would be refined and standardized.

42. One of three recipes containing tomato.

43. Occhialini, *Memorie*, x.

44. Occhialini, *Memorie*, xv.

45. Leonardi, *Modern*, 1.17.

46. Leonardi, *Modern*, 1.7.

47. Leonardi, *Modern*, 1.9.

48. Vitaliano Bossi and Ercole Salvi, *L'imperatore dei cuochi* (Rome: Edoardo Perino, 1894), #71, 24.

49. Bossi and Salvi, *L'imperatore*, #746, 184.

50. Bossi and Salvi, *L'imperatore*, #208, 315, #67, 278.

51. Bossi and Salvi, 370.
52. Domenico Orano, *Come vive il popolo a Roma* (Pescara: Ettore Croce, 1912), 191.
53. Orano, *Come*, 201.
54. Orano, *Come*, 282.
55. Orano, *Come*, 432–33.
56. Orano, *Come*, 652.
57. Orano, *Come*, 649.
58. Orano, *Come*, 448–449.
59. Ada Boni, *Talismano della Felicità*, fourth edition (Rome: Carlo Colombo, 1934), 11–12.
60. Ada Boni, *La cucina Romana* (Rome: Newton Compton, 1983), 9.
61. Mostly by Bartolomeo Pinelli, (1781–1835). Born and died in Trastevere.
62. See chapter 6.
63. See chapter 4.
64. Another Roman specialty also called "*coppiette*" is strips of spiced dried meat.
65. Boni, *Cucina*, 137–38.

Chapter Four

1. Chris Wickham, "Pastoralism and Underdevelopment in the Early Middle Ages" (paper presented at the *Centro di Studi Sull'Alto Medioevo*, 7–13 April, 1983), in *L'uomo di fronte al mondo animale nell'alto medioevo*, 401–51 (Spoleto: Fondazione CISAM, 1985), 410.
2. The liturgical vestment the pope conferred on bishops consisting of a wide circular band worn around the neck, with tabs that extended slightly down the chest and back.
3. Ezio Maurizi, "La Via Salaria" in Il cibo dei pellegrini, ed. Gianni Franceschi (Rome: Studio Ricciardi & Associati, 1999), 15.
4. Alexandra Witze, "Science: The Miraculous Microbes of Bolsena," New Science, June 4, 1994, accessed October 1 2017, https://www.newscientist.com/article/mg14219282-300-science-the-miraculous-microbes-of-bolsena/.
5. Lorenzo Abbamondi, "A tavola coi papi," in Le cucine della memoria Roma e Lazio, ed. Angela Adriana Cavarra, second edition (Rome: Edizioni de Luca, 1995), 500.
6. June di Schino, "La giornata del Romeo" in Il cibo dei pellegrini, ed. Gianni Franceschi (Rome: Studio Ricciardi & Associati, 1999), 70.
7. Maria Attilia Fabbri Dall'Oglio, "Pellegrini di lusso," in Il cibo dei pellegrini, ed. Gianni Franceschi (Rome: Studio Ricciardi & Associati, 1999), 53–54.
8. Fabbri Dall'Oglio, "Pellegrini," 54.
9. The name for those whose profession is making salumi, or cured pork products.
10. Willy Pochino, Le curiosità di Roma (Rome: Newton Compton, 1985), 352.

11. Richard Lassels, *The Voyage of Italy; or, A Compleat Journey through Italy* (Paris:1660), 5.

12. Lassels, *The Voyage of Italy*, 17.

13. William Beckford, *Dreams, Waking Thoughts, and Incidents*, accessed October. 3, 2017. http://www.gutenberg.org/files/7258/7258-h/7258-h.htm.

14. Gilbert Burnet, *Burnet's Travels* (London: Ward and Chandler, 1738), 157.

15. Tobias Smollett, *Travels through France and Italy* (London: Oxford University Press, 1919), 323.

16. Amelia Rauser, "Hair, Authenticity, and the Self-Made Macaroni," *Eighteenth-Century Studies* 38, no. 1 (2004): 101, accessed January 15, 2016, https://www.academia.edu/1967485/Hair_authenticity_and_the_self-made_Macaroni,.

17. Rauser, "Hair," 106.

18. Elizabeth Raffald, *The Experienced English House-Keeper for the Use and Ease of Ladies, House-Keepers, Cooks, &c.* (Manchester: J. Harrop, 1769), 261.

19. Mathew Sturgis, *When in Rome, 2000 Years of Sightseeing* (London: Frances Lincoln, 2011), 172.

20. *Murray's Hand-Book of Rome & Its Environs* (London: John Murray, 1864), xii.

21. Luigi Delatre, *Ricordi di Roma* (Florence: Gazzetta d'Italia, 1870), 16–17.

22. Delatre, *Ricordi*, 8–9.

23. A political slogan popular between 1861 and 1870.

24. Isabella Clough Marinaro and Bjørn Thomassen, eds., *Global Rome: Changing Faces of the Eternal City* (Bloomington: Indiana University Press, 2014), 10.

25. Mina Novello, "Pranzi reali," in *Pranzo al Quirinale*, ed. Albina Malebra and Isabella Massabò Ricci (Candelo: Arti Grafiche Biellesi, 2004), 102.

26. Ciampi, "L'alimentazione," 46.

27. Riccardo Filiberto Medici, *L'agro Romano che scompare* (Rome: Quaderni della Maremma, 1953), 33.

28. Filiberto Medici, *L'agro*, 20.

29. William Wetmore Story, *Roba di Roma*, 2 vols, eighth edition (Boston: Houghton, Mifflin and Company, 1887), 358–59.

30. Wetmore Story, *Roba*, 361.

31. Wetmore Story, *Roba*, 364.

32. Boni, *Talismano*, 12.

33. See also Maestro Martino, "Roman-Style Macaroni," *The Art of Cooking*; Bartolomeo Scappi, "To prepare a thick macaroni soup in the Roman Style," *Opera*; "Makarouns," The Forme of Cury, http://www.gutenberg.org/ebooks/8102.

34. "Hollywood on the Tiber," *Time* June 26, 1950, 92–94.

35. "The 2008 Global Cities Index," accessed January 31, 2018, https://web.archive.org/web/20100107184223/http://www.foreignpolicy.com/story/cms.php?story_id=4509.

36. Clough Marinaro and Thomassen eds. *Global*, 1–2.

37. "Immigrazione, Roma si conferma Capitale:+ 115% di stranieri in 15 anni," Il Tempo, June 22, 2015, accessed January 31, 2018, http://www.iltempo.it/roma-cap-itale/2015/06/22/news/immigrazione-roma-si-conferma-capitale-+-115-di-stranieri-in-15-anni-980276/.

38. At the same time, Rome has the highest percentage of civil marriages in the country at over 50 percent.

39. Seventy percent of the immigrants who come to Rome live in the capital city. Most are Romanian, seconded by Filipinos.

40. Cristina Bassi, "L'esercito delle badanti in Italia: Due su tre non sono in regola." Il Giornale, June 24, 2015, accessed October 8, 2017, http://www.ilgiornale.it/news/lesercito-delle-badanti-italia-due-su-tre-non-sono-regola-1144790.html.

41. Giuseppe Cucinotta, "E adesso badanti e colf sono romane," Corriere de la Serra—Roma, November 18, 2012, accessed October 8, 2017. https://roma.corri-ere.it/roma/notizie/cronaca/12_novembre_18/badanti-romane-indagine-federcasal-inghe-2112758860479.shtml.

42. Simone Cinotto, introduction in Quaderni Storici, Rivista quadrimestrale, April 1, 2016, 5.

43. Ciampi, "L'alimentazione," 50–51.

44. Previously the JNRC served badly formed croissants, destined to be discarded, but after consulting with a dietician they changed to a more nutritionally substantial breakfast.

45. From an interview with one the JNRC directors.

Chapter Five

1. Livy, History of Rome 6.25.

2. Plural of forum.

3. Claire De Ryyt, Macellum: Marché alimentaire des Romains (Louvain-la-Neuve: Institut supérieur d'archéologie et d'histoire de l'art, 1983), 227–30.

4. Claire Holleran, Shopping in Ancient Rome: The Retail Trade in the Late Republic and Principate (Oxford: Oxford University Press, 2012), 94.

5. Holleran, Shopping, 238.

6. Jerome Carcopino, La vita quotidiana a Roma all'apogeo dell'Impero (Bari: Laterza, 1978), 204.

7. Holleran, Shopping, 240–41.

8. Juvenal, Satires, 11.64–76. Translation A. S. Kline.

9. Holleran, Shopping, 152.

10. 39 hectares.

11. In modern Italian testa means "head," which comes from the idea of the cranium as a vessel-like container.

12. Holleran, Shopping, 183.

13. Joan M. Frayn, *Markets and Fairs in Roman Italy* (Oxford: Clarendon Press, 1993), 5.

14. Holleran, *Shopping*, 135.

15. Holleran, *Shopping*, 230.

16. Seneca, *Epistulae Morales ad Lucilium*, 56.2; quoted in Holleran, *Shopping*, 211

17. Hippolyte Taine, *Italy, Rome and Naples*, trans. J. Durand, 4th edition (New York: Henry Holt and Company, 1875), 12.

18. *De romans piscibus libellus*, 1524.

19. For more on the *Cucina ebraica* see chapter 6.

20. After the unification of Italy, the market moved from the Portico to Piazza San Teodoro.

21. Joseph Collins, *My Italian Year* (London: Forgotten Books, 2015), 168.

22. List compiled by the *Dipartimento Attività Economiche e Produttive, Formazione e Lavoro del Comune di Roma*, updated August 8, 2013.

23. Hippolyte Taine, *Voyage en Italie, vol II, Florence et Venise* (Paris: Librarie Hachette et Co., 1866), 3–4.

24. The norcino worked salt curing pork and were known for their skill in animal castration.

25. The piazza of the Pantheon.

26. Henry Noel Humphreys, *Rome and Its Surrounding Scenery* (London: David Bogue, 1845), 160

27. Humphreys, *Rome*, 163–64.

28. Story of the origin of the water buffalo: "When the first created man saw the animals that God had made, it is said that he presumptuously, over-rating his powers, asked that he too might be given the creative power to fashion others like them. God granted his request and man tried his prentice hand. But the result was the buffalo, and man seeing that it was not good, asked in disgust that the creative power might be taken back again from him for ever. The buffalo, however, remained as the only living handiwork of man." F. B. Bradley-Birt, *Chota Nagpore: A Little-known Province of the Empire*, second edition (London, 1910), 115.

29. Paul the Deacon, *History of the Langobards*, book 4, trans. William Dudley Foulke (Philadelphia: Univerity of Pennsylvania Press, 1907). chap. 10.

30. Ugo Pesci, *Come siamo entrati a Roma* (Milan: Fratelli Treves, 1895), 98.

31. Andrea Belli, *Delle case abitate in Roma da parecchi uomini illustri*, second edition (Rome: Morini e Morini, 1850), 64.

32. Literally, "Swisses" (Swiss patties).

33. Literally, "another pair of handcuffs."

34. Francesco Duscio, *La Romanesca: Cucina popolare e tradizione romana* (Roma: Fuoco edizioni, 2014).

35. Personal contribution elaborated expressly for *The Eternal Table* from Katie Parla, coauthor of *Tasting Rome*.

36. Carlo Emilio Gadda, *Quer pasticciaccio brutto de via Merulana* (Milan: Garzanti, 2007).

Chapter Six

1. Livio Jannattoni, *Il ghiottone* (Milano: Bramante, 1965), 216.

2. See chapter 4.

3. *Registrum coquine* (1431).

4. Bruno Laurioux, "Le registre de cuisine" de Jean de Bockenheim, cuisinier du pape Martin V," accessed January 23, 2018, http://www.persee.fr/doc/mefr_0223-5110_1988_num_100_2_2987#mefr_0223-5110_1988_num_100_2_T1_0725_0000, 738.

5. The letter was discovered in the Ferrara library and published in 1876.

6. Sante Lancerio, "Della qualità dei vini," in *L'arte della cucina in Italia*, ed. Emilio Faccioli (Turin: Einaudi, 1987), 339.

7. Alessandro Petronio, *Del viver delli romani et di conservar la sanità* (1592), 58–59.

8. Andrea Bacci, *Del Tevere* (Venetia: 1576), 4.

9. Successive popes and doctors continued to praise the curative powers of the water through the ages until construction in the area during the fascist era contaminated it. In 1966, it was declared nonpotable.

10. John B. Buescher, "In the Habit: A History of Catholicism and Tobacco," *Catholic World Report*, November 9, 2017, accessed January 26, 2018, http://www.catholicworldreport.com/2017/11/09/in-the-habit-a-history-of-catholicism-and-tobacco/.

11. See also chapter 4 regarding *mercanti di campagna*.

12. Ricardo Filiberto Medici, *L'agro romano che scompare* (Rome: Quaderni della Maremma, 1953), 35–42.

13. In butcher shops and osteria/trattorias the terms are used loosely and also includes the male calves.

14. Edict of the Reverend Apostolic Chamber, December 4, 1787.

15. Game was part of the goods that *pollaroli* were permitted to sell. In 1625, the license to hunt was suspended between March 1 and August 31, during which time fowl vendors, inns, and pie makers were not allowed to sell or prepare foods with game.

16. February 20, 1675.

17. Wine, along with meat, was forbidden in the early centuries of the Church.

18. Gaetano Moroni, *Dizionario di erudizione storico-ecclesiastica da s. Pietro sino ai nostri giorni specialmente intorno ai principali santi* (Venice: Emiliana, 1846), 62.

19. Laura Posa Andeoli, "'Effermeridi' Alimentari settecentesche," in *Le cucine della memoria—Roma e Lazio* (Rome: De Luca, 1995), 68.

20. The stoics of ancient Greece also taught that the path to higher spiritual ground lie in ignoring hunger and other material desires.

21. Published first in Milan and then in Rome.

22. Rita Fioravanti, "La crisi del settore agro-alimentare a Roma e nel Lazio dall'inizio del settecento all'occupazione Napoleonica," in *Le cucine della memoria: Roma e Lazio* (Rome: De Luca, 1993), 93.

23. Example: Nicola Maria Nicolai, *Memorie, leggi ed osservazioni sulle campagne e sull'Annona di Roma*, 1803.

24. Giggi Zanazzo, *Usi, costumi e pregiudizi del popolo di Roma* (Turin: Società Tipografico-Editrice Nazionale, 1908), 241.

25. Antonietta Amicarelli Scalisi, "Cucina e alimentazione di Roma e del Lazio negli editti e bandi della biblioteca Casantense, in *Le cucine della memoria: Roma e Lazio* (Rome: De Luca, 1993), 273.

26. Lorenzo Abbamondi, "A tavola coi papi," in *Le cucine della memoria: Roma e Lazio* (Rome: De Luca, 1993), 517.

27. The Jewish community in Rome is the oldest in Europe, having arrived in the second century BCE, with many more following after 63 BCE when Pompey conquered Judea.

28. Traditional fare or classic dishes in Italian are referred to as *tipico*. Everywhere in Italy this is translated as "typical," which in English has other meanings and connotations that generally run from neutral to negative, whereas, in reference to food, in Italian *tipico* has a positive, homey meaning.

29. Hasia Diner, "Jewish Peddlers During the Great Jewish Migration," *Quaderni Storici* 151 (April 2016): 29.

30. In 1555, under Paul IV (1555–1559), the Jewish Ghetto was created. Over the centuries, tolerance waxed and waned under the various popes, but the confinement would not be abolished until 1870—only to be reinstated once again under Mussolini in 1938.

31. See Maestro Martino, chapter 3.

32. Giuliano Malizia, *La cucina romana e ebraico-romanesca* (Rome: Newton Compton, 2001), 108.

33. Bossi and Salvi, *L'imperatore*, #479, 382.

34. Bianca Maria Zaccheo, "Tradizioni della cucina ebraico-romana del Portico d'Ottavia," in *Le cucine della memoria—Roma e Lazio* (Rome: De Luca, 1993), 544–45.

35. Fabio Parasecoli, *Al Dente: A History of Food in Italy* (London: Reaktion Books, 2014), loc 2199.

36. Karima Moyer-Nocchi, *Chewing the Fat: An Oral History of Italian Foodways from Fascism to Dolce Vita* (Perrysburg, OH: Medea, 2015), 22.

37. Steve Siporin, "From Kashrut to Cucina Ebraica: The Recasting of Italian Jewish Foodways," *Journal of American Folklore* 107, no. 424 (Spring, 1994): 272.

38. Paraphrased from Katie Parla and Kristina Gill, *Tasting Rome* (New York: Clarkson Potter, 2016), 113.

39. Vincenzo Misserville, "Romano lo volemo (er cocommero)," *Strenna dei Romanisti* 21 (April 1960): 264.

40. God of healing. His legacy today is the snake entwined staff, the symbol of medicine.

41. Misserville, "Romano," 266.

42. See chapter 2.

43. Roman dialect. *Mattatoio* in Italian.

44. Anna Alloro, "'Sette cose fa la zuppa . . .' ovvero L'arte di mangiar bene con poco, e vivere felice," in *Le cucine della memoria—Roma e Lazio* (Rome: De Luca, 1993), 347–48.

45. Livio Jannettoni, *Osterie e feste romane* (Rome: Newton Compton, 1977), 62.

46. Jannattoni, *Il Ghiottone*, 215.

47. Secondino Freda, *Roma a Tavola* (Milan: Longanesi, 1973), 185–86.

48. Association suggested by Luigi Ballerini, "Food for the Bawdy: Johann of Bockenheim's Registrum Coquine," *Gastronomica* 1, no. 3 (Summer 2001): 37.

49. Alberto Capatti, lecture, University of Rome, Tor Vergata, 2016.

50. Secondino Freda, "Roma a tavola," *Strenna dei Romanisti* 44 (April 21, 1983): 174.

51. Freda, "Roma," 175–76.

52. Freda, "Roma," 176–77.

53. Ippolito Cavalcanti, *Cucina teorico-pratica*, second edition (Naples: G. Palma, 1839), 364.

54. Both of these approaches are under the entry *carbonara, pasta alla* in Marco Guarnaschelli Gotti, *Grande enciclopedia illustrata della gastronomia* (Milan: Selezione dal Reader's Digest, 1990).

55. For example, *alla carrettiera, alla boscaiola, alla vaccinara, alla macellara,* and so on.

56. Alberto Capatti, *Storia della cucina italiana* (Milan: Guido Tomassi, 2014), 86–87.

57. *La cucina di famiglia: Raccolta di ricette pratiche e consigli per ben cucinare.*

58. The first milk shop in Rome.

59. Adolfo Giaquinto, *Bojerie romanesche e cispatane* (1890).

60. Luigi Volpicelli, "Cucina Romana dell'Artusi," *Strenna dei Romanisti* 28 (April 21,1967): 459–60.

61. Artusi is from Forlimpopoli, Romagna, but lived and worked in Florence.

62. Volpicelli, "Cucina," 460.

63. Luigi Carnaccina cited in, Freda, *Roma*, 190.

64. "Snails large and small. You can pick them out with pins if they are tiny."

65. Paola Angori, "Cibi e tradizioni romane nei periodici Casanatensi" in *Cucine della memoria Roma e Lazio* (Rome: DeLuca, 1993), 161–62.

66. *La festa di San Giuseppe fra frittelle, sonetti e lunari,* accessed January 24, 2018, http://romacult.blogspot.it/search/label/festa%20di%20san%20Giuseppe.

67. Giuseppe Ceccarelli (Ceccarius), "Tradizioni romane: La devozione delle frittelle," *La Tribuna: l'idea nazionale* 49, no. 67 (March 19 1931): 6.

68. Moyer-Nocchi, *Chewing*, 178.

69. Miriam Mafai, *Pane nero* (Rome: Ediesse, 2008), 184.

70. Mafai, *Pane*, 194.

Chapter Seven

1. "I censimenti precedenti: La storia dal 1861 a oggi," Istat, accessed February 1, 2018, https://www.istat.it/it/censimenti-permanenti/censimenti-precedenti.

2. Andrew Wallace-Hadrill, *Herculaneum: Past and Future* (London: Frances Lincoln, 2011), 80.

3. Federica Grossi, "Bar, Fast Food e tavole calde" *LANX* 9 (2011): 8.

4. Steven J. R. Ellis, "Eating and Drinking Out," in *A Cultural History of Food in Antiquity*, vol. 1, ed. Paul Erdkamp (New York: Bloomsbury, 2012), 111.

5. Ellis, "Eating," 111.

6. Book of Leviticus 25, 10–14.

7. Benvenuto Cellini, *Vita* (Turin: Einaudi,1973), 74.

8. Cellini, *Vita*, 80.

9. The word used is *barone*, but it is meant ironically.

10. Andrew Graham Dixon, *Caravaggio: Vita sacra e profana* (Milan: Mondadori, 2011), 271–72.

11. Giovanni Volfango Goethe, *Ricordi di viaggio in Italia* (Milan: F. Manini, Milano, 1875), 167–68.

12. See chapter 6.

13. Sante Lancerio, "Della qualità dei vini," in *L'arte della cucina in Italia*, ed. Emilio Faccioli (Turin: Einaudi, 1987), 330. In the 1876 publication the contributor declared 1539 as the original date.

14. Gianni-Emilio Simonetti, "I vini d'Italia giudicati da Papa Paolo III (Farnese) e dal suo bottigliere Sante Lancerio," *La Gola* no. 1 (October 1982): 16.

15. Lancerio, "Della qualità, 333.

16. Ada Corongiu, "Cucina e alimentazione romana nelle opere a stampa dei secoli XV e XVI," in *Le cucine della memoria:—Roma e Lazio* (Rome: De Luca, 1993), 32.

17. *De naturali vinorum historia, de vinis Italiae et de conviviis antiquorum*, 1596.

18. Ariel Toaff, *Il prestigiatore di Dio: Avventure e miracoli di un prestigiatore ebreo nelle corti del Rinascimento* (Milano, Rizzoli, 2010), 127.

19. *Raccolta delle leggi e disposizioni di pubblica amministrazione nello Stato Pontificio*, Stabilimento Governativo, volume V (Rome, 1834/1870), 625.

20. By hanging a sign, one was registered to pay taxes and held accountable for that line of work.

21. Alessandro Rufini, *Notizie Storiche intorno alla origine dei nomi di alcune osterie, caffè, alberghi e locande esistenti nella città di Roma* (Rome: Tipografia Legale, 1855).

22. W. M. Gillespie, *Rome: As Seen by a New-Yorker in 1843–4* (New York: Wiley and Putnam, 1845) 126-132.

23. Livio Jannattoni, *Il ghiottone* (Milano: Bramante, 1965), 241.

24. Vittorio Metz, *La cucina di G. Giachino Belli* (Tivoli: De Rossi, 1972), 21.

25. This most likely refers to cazzimperio, a dish of raw vegetables eaten at the end of the meal to refresh the mouth.

26. Augusto Jandolo and Ettore Veo, eds., *Osterie Romane* (Milan: Ceschina, 1929), 209.

27. Jandolo and Veo, *Osterie*, 210.

28. Domenico Orano, *Come vive il popolo a Roma: Saggio demografico sul quartiere Testaccio* (Pescara: Ettore Croce, 1912), 617–25.

29. Hans Barth, *Osteria: Guida spirituale delle osterie italiane da Verona a Capri,* (Padova: Franco Muzzio, 1998), 17.

30. Barth, *Osteria*, 153.

31. Touring Club Italiano, *Guida gastronomica d'Italia* (Milan: Colombi, 1931), 314–15.

32. Paolo Monelli, *Il ghiottone errante: Viaggio gastronomico attraverso l'Italia* (Milano: Touring, 2005), 115–6.

33. In the United States, February 7 is National Fettuccine Alfredo Day.

34. Gianni Franceschi, "Il rancio unico al ristorante," in *A Roma negli anni difficili: A tavola con l'Accademia* (Rome: Ricciardi & Associati, 1995), 30.

35. Franceschi, "Il rancio," 31.

36. Matt Blake, "Who was . . . Remington Olmstead?" *The Wild Eye*, June 17, 2009, accessed February 9, 2018, http://www.thewildeye.co.uk/blog/performers-direc tors/who-was-remington-olmstead/.

37. Matilde Serao, *Il ventre di Napoli* (Milano: Fratelli Treves, 1884), 21.

38. This is not to deny the prejudice against Italians in general or wariness for their foodways.

39. Bottle-shop or liquor store.

40. Metz, *La cucina*, 22.

41. Alberto Capatti, *L'osteria nuova* (Bra: Arcigola Slow Food, 2000), 183.

42. Barth, *Osteria*, 174.

43. Gillespie, *Rome*, 133.

44. Emma Amadei, "Il caffè Greco ieri e oggi," *Strenna dei Romanisti* 35 (1974): 21.

45. L. C. Henley, "A Scene at Rome, 'Il caffè greco,'" *London Society*, October, 1866, 362–67.

46. They may have been inspired by the Sicilian arancini, which long predate supplì, as Sicily's history of rice cultivation dates back to Arab dominance.

47. Giggi Zanazzo, *Usi, costumi e pregiudizi del popolo di Roma* (Turin: Società tipografico-editrice nazionale, 1908), 429.

48. Published from 1925 to 1933 by Edition della rivista Preziosa; also by Colombo from 1929; picked up after World War II by Dumas publishing.

49. Ada Boni, *Talisman della felicità*, fourth edition (Rome: Carlo Colombo, 1934), 220–21.

Bibliography of Referenced Works

Abbamondi, Lorenzo. "A tavola coi papi." In *Le cucine della memoria Roma e Lazio*, edited by Angela Adriana Cavarra, 495–526. Second edition. Rome: Edizioni de Luca, 1995.

Afoldi. A. *Early Rome and the Latins*. Ann Arbor: University of Michigan Press, 1963.

Albala, Ken. *Food in Early Modern Europe*. Westport, CT: Greenwood Press, 2003.

Alloro, Anna. "'Sette cose fa la zuppa . . .' ovvero L'arte di mangiar bene con poco, e vivere felice." In *Le cucine della memoria: Roma e Lazio*, edited by Angela Adriana Cavarra, 329–413. Rome: De Luca 1993.

Amadei, Emma. "Il caffè Greco ieri e oggi." *Strenna dei Romanisti* 35 (1974): 21–27.

Amicarelli Scalisi, Antonietta. "Cucina e alimentazione di Roma e del Lazio negli editti e bandi della biblioteca Casantense." In *Le cucine della memoria: Roma e Lazio*, edited by Angela Adriana Cavarra, 263–308. Rome: De Luca, 1993.

Angori, Paola. "Cibi e tradizioni romane nei periodici Casanatensi." In *cucine della memoria: Roma e Lazio*, edited by Angela Adriana Cavarra, 157–63. Rome: De-Luca, 1993.

Bacci, Andrea. *Del Tevere*. Venetia, 1576.

Ballerini, Luigi. "Food for the Bawdy: Johann of Bockenheim's Registrum Coquine," *Gastronomica* 1, no. 3 (Summer 2001): 32–39.

Barker, Graeme. *The Agricultural Revolution in Prehistory*. Oxford: Oxford University Press, 2006.

Barth, Hans. *Osteria: Guida spirituale delle osterie italiane da Verona a Capri*. Padova: Franco Muzzio, 1998.

Belli, Andrea. *Delle case abitate in Roma da parecchi uomini illustri*. Second edition. Rome: Marini e Morini, 1850.

Benporat, Claudio. *Storia della gastronomia Italiana*. Milan: Ugo Mursia, 1990.

Boni, Ada. *La cucina romana*. Rome: Newton Compton, 1983.

———. *Talismano della felicità*. Fourth edition. Rome: Carlo Colombo, 1934.

Bossi, Vitaliano, and Ercole Salvi. *L'Imperatore dei cuochi*. Rome: Edoardo Perino, 1894.

Bradley-Birt, F. B. Chota Nagpore: A Little-known Province of the Empire, second edition (London, 1910).

Braudel, Fernand. *The Mediterranean and the Mediterranean World in the Age of Philip II, Vol. 1*. Berkeley: University of California Press, 1995.

Brown, Peter. *The Rise of Western Christendom: Triumph and Diversity, A.D. 200–1000*. Tenth anniversary revised edition. Malden, MA: Wiley-Blackwell, 2013.

Burnet, Gilbert. *Burnet's Travels*. London: Ward and Chandler, 1738.

Capatti, Alberto. *Storia della cucina italiana*. Milan: Guido Tomassi, 2014.

Carcopino, Jerome. *Daily Life in Ancient Rome: The People and the City at the Height of the Empire*. London: Routledge, 1941.

Cavalcanti, Ippolito. *Cucina teorico-pratica*. Second edition. Naples: G. Palma,1939.

Ciampi, Gabriella. "L'alimentazione popolare a Roma e nell'Agro romano." In *Storia d'Italia, annali 13, L'alimentazione*, edited by Alberto Capatti, Alberto De Bernardi, and Angelo Varni, 41–64. Turin: Einaudi, 1998.

Cinotto, Simone. "Introduction." *Quaderni Storici* (April 1, 2016): 3–22.

Clough Marinaro, Isabella, and Bjørn Thomassen. *Global Rome: Changing Faces of the Eternal City*. Bloomington: Indiana University Press, 2014.

Collins, Joseph. *My Italian Year, Observations and Reflections in Italy during the Last Year of the War*. London: Forgotten Books, 2015.

Conde, Francesca, and Enrico De Vita. *Agro romano antico*. Rome: Gangemi, 2011.

Cornell, T. J. *The Beginnings of Rome*. London: Rutledge, 1995.

Corongiu, Ada. "Cucina e alimentazione romana nelle opere a stampa dei secoli XV e XVI." In *Le cucine della memoria: Roma e Lazio*, edited by Angela Adriana Cavarra, 27–34. Rome: De Luca, 1993.

Curtis, Robert. "Professional Cooking, Kitchens, and Service Work." In *A Cultural History of Food in Antiquity*, edited by Paul Erdkamp, 133–32. London: Bloomsbury 2016.

De Cupis, Cesare. *Le Vicende dell'agricoltura e della pastorizia nell'agro romano, L'annona di Roma*. Roma: Tip. nazionale di G. Bertero, 1911.

De Ruyt, Claire. *Macellum: Marché alimentaire des Romains*. Louvain-la-Neuve: Institut supérieur d'archéologie et d'histoire de l'art, 1983.

Delatre, Luigi. *Ricordi di Roma*. Florence: Gazzetta d'Italia, 1870.

Delogu, Paolo. "Rome in the Ninth Century: The Economic System." In *Post-Roman Towns, Trade and Settlement in Europe and Byzantium, Vol 1: The Heirs of the Roman West*, edited by Joachim Henning. Berlin: De Gruyter, 2007.

Detienne, Marcel, and J. P. Vernant. *The Cuisine of Sacrifice among the Greeks*. Chicago: University of Chicago Press, 1989.

Di Renzo, Ernesto. *Mangiare autentico*. Rome: UniversItalia, 2012.

Di Schino, June. "La giornata del Romeo." In *Il cibo dei pellegrini*, edited by Gianni Franceschi, 70–72. Rome: Studio Ricciardi & Associati, 1999.

Dickinson, Robert E. *City and Region: A Geographical Interpretation.* Volume 2. London: Routledge, 2002.

Diner, Hasia. "Road Food: Jewish Peddlers during the Great Jewish Migration." *Quaderni Storici* 151 (April 2016): 23–49.

Dixon, Andrew Graham. *Caravaggio: Vita sacra e profana.* Milan: Mondadori, 2011.

Duscio, Francesco. La Romanesca: Cucina popolare e tradizione romana. Rome: Fuoco edizioni, 2014.

Ellis, Steven J. R. "Eating and Drinking Out." In *A Cultural History of Food in Antiquity,* edited by Paul Erdkamp, 95–112. New York: Bloomsbury, 2012.

Erdkamp, Paul. "The Food Supply of the Capital." In *The Cambridge Companion to Ancient Rome,* 262–27. Cambridge: Cambridge University Press, 2013.

Fabbri Dell'Oglio, and Maria Attilia. "Pellegrini di lusso." In *Il cibo dei pellegrini,* edited by Gianni Franceschi, 58–60. Rome: Studio Ricciardi & Associati, 1999.

Filene, Enrico. *L'agro romano e i suoi problemi: Quaderni della Roma di Mussolini, Il piano regolatore di Roma Imperiale IX.* Rome: Istituto di Studi Romani, 1939.

Filiberto Medici, Riccardo. *L'agro romano che scompare.* Rome: Quaderni della Maremma, 1953.

Fioravanti , Rita. "La crisi del settore agro-alimentare a Roma e nel Lazio dall'inizio del settecento all'occupazione Napoleonica." In *Le cucine della memoria: Roma e Lazio,* edited by Angela Adriana Cavarra,77–97. Rome: De Luca, 1993.

Florio, Giuseppina. "La cucina degli antichi romani: Appunti per una tradizione." In *Le cucine della memoria Roma e Lazio,* edited by Angela Adriana Cavarra, 13–26. Second edition. Rome: Edizioni de Luca, 1995.

Flower, Barbara, and Elisabeth Rosenbaum. *The Roman Cookery Book: A Critical Translation of "The Art of Cooking" by Apicius for Use in the Study and the Kitchen.* London: George G. Harrap & Co.,1958.

Franceschi, Gianni. "Il rancio unico al ristorante." In *Roma negli anni difficili: A Tavola con l'Accademia,* 29–31. Rome: Studio Ricciardi & Associati, 1995.

Frayn, Joan M. *Markets and Fairs in Roman Italy.* Oxford: Clarendon Press, 1993.

Freda, Secondino. "Roma a tavola." *Strenna dei Romanisti* 44 (April 21, 1983): 173–80.

———. *Roma a Tavola.* Milan: Longanesi, 1973.

Gadda, Carlo Emilio. *Quer pasticciaccio brutto de via Merulana.* Milan: Garzanti, 2007.

Garnsey, Peter. *Cities, Peasants and Food in Classical Antiquity.* Cambridge: Cambridge University Press, 1998.

Giaquinto, Adolfo. *Bojerie romanesche e cispatane.* Rome, 1890.

Gillespie, William Mitchell. *Rome: As Seen by a New-Yorker in 1843–4.* New York: Wiley and Putnam, 1845.

Gowers, Emily. *The Loaded Table: Representations of Food in Roman Literature.* Oxford: Oxford University Press, 1993.

Grant, Mark. *Galen on Food and Diet.* London: Routledge, 2000.

Grossi, Federica. "Bar, fast food e tavole calde," *LANX* 9 (2011): 1–46.

Touring Club Italiano. *Guida Gastronomica d'Italia.* Milan: Colombi, 1931.

Heichelheim, Fritz M. *Storia economica del mondo antico: IV La repubblica romana*. Rome-Bari: Laterizi & Figli, 1979.

Heiken, Grant, Renato Funiciello, and Donatella De Rita. *The Seven Hills of Rome*. Princeton, NJ: Princeton University Press, 2005.

Henley, L. C. "A Scene at Rome, ' Il caffè greco.'" *London Society* (October 1866): 362–67.

Hogwood, Keith. "Bandits, Elites and Rural Order." In *Patronage in Ancient Society*, edited by Andrew Wallace-Hadrill, 171. London: Routledge, 1990.

Holleran, Claire. *Shopping in Ancient Rome: The Retail Trade in the Late Republic and Principate*. Oxford: Oxford University Press, 2012.

"Hollywood on the Tiber," *Time* (June 26, 1950): 92–94.

Horden, Peregrine, and Nicholas Purcell. *The Corrupting Sea: A Study of Mediterranean History*. Oxford: Blackwell, 2000.

Hughes, Robert. *Rome: A Cultural, Visual, and Personal History*. New York: Knopf, 2011.

Humpreys, Henry Noel. *Rome and Its Surrounding Scenery*. London: David Bogue, 1845.

Jacob, H. E. *Six Thousand Years of Bread: Its Holy and Unholy History*. New York: Skyhorse, 2007.

Jannattoni, Livio. *Il giottone romano*. Milan: Bramante, 1965.

———. *Osterie e feste romane*. Rome: Newton Compton, 1977.

Lancerio, Sante. "Della qualità dei vini." In *L'arte della cucina in Italia*, edited by Emilio Faccioli. Turin: Einaudi, 1987.

Lassels, Richard. *The Voyage of Italy; or, A Compleat Journey through Italy*. London: John Starkey, 1670.

Laudan, Rachel. *Cuisine and Empire: Cooking in World History*. Berkeley: University of California Press, 2013.

Launspach, Charles William Louis. *State and Family in Early Rome*. London: G. Bell and Sons, 1908.

Malizia, Giuliano. *La cucina romana e ebraico-romanesca*. Rome: Newton Compton, 2001.

Martino of Como. *The Art of Cooking*. Edited by Luigi Ballerini. Translated by Jeremy Parzen. Berkeley: University of California, 2005.

Maurizi, Ezio. "La Via Salaria." In *Il cibo dei pellegrini*, edited by Gianni Franceschi, 14–15. Rome: Studio Ricciardi & Associati, 1999.

McGowan, Andrew B. "Food, Ritual, and Power." In *Late Ancient Christianity: A People's History of Christianity, Vol. 2*, edited by Virginia Burrus, 145–64. Minneapolis: Fortress, 2005.

Metz, Vittorio. *La cucina di G. Giachino Belli*. Tivoli: De Rossi, 1972.

Misserville, Vincenzo. "Romano lo volemo (er cocommero)." *Strenna dei Romanisti* 21 (April 1960): 264–65.

Moroni, Gaetano. *Dizionario di erudizione storico-ecclesiastica da s. Pietro sino ai nostri giorni specialmente intorno ai principali santi*. Venice: Emiliana. 1846.

Moss, H. *The Birth of the Middle Ages, 395–814*. London: Oxford University Press, 1935.

Moyer-Nocchi, Karima. *Chewing the Fat: An Oral History of Italian Foodways from Fascism to Dolce Vita*. Perrysburg, OH: Medea, 2015.

Murray's Handbook of Rome and Its Environs. London: John Murray, 1864.

Novello, Mina. "Pranzi Reali." In *Pranzo al Quirinale, Cerimoniale e scenografia dal regno alla Repubblica*, edited by Albina Malebra and Isabella Massabò Ricci. Candelo: Centro Studi Piemontesi, Docbi, 2004.

Occhiolini, Giovanni Battista, *Memoria sopra il meraviglioso frutto americano chiamato volgarmente patata ossia pomo di terra. Con la descrizione della maniera di piantarlo, coltivarlo, del di lui vantaggio, del modo di ridurlo a farina, ed a pane, di cavarne amido, cipria, di farne salde, bosima, &c*. Rome: Giunchi, 1784.

Orano, Domenico. *Come vive il popolo a Roma: Saggio demografico sul quartiere Testaccio*. Pescara: Ettore Croce, 1912.

Jandolo, Augusto, and Ettore Veo, eds. *Osterie Romane*. Milan: Ceschina, 1929.

Parla, Katie, and Kristina Gill. *Tasting Rome: Fresh Flavors and Forgotten Recipes from an Ancient City*. New York: Clarkson Potter, 2016.

Paul the Deacon. *History of the Langobards*, book 4. Translated by William Dudley Foulke. Philadelphia: Univerity of Pennsylvania Press, 1907.

Pesci, Ugo. *Come siamo entrati a Roma*. Milan: Fratelli Treves, 1895.

Petronio, Alessandro. *Del viver delli romani et di conservar la sanità*.1592.

Platina. *Platina: On Right Pleasure and Good Health*. Translated by Mary Ella Milham. Tempe, AZ: Medieval & Renaissance Texts & Studies, 1998.

Platina. *Platina's On Right Pleasure and Good Health: A Critical Abridgement and Translation of "De honest voluptate et valetudine,"* by Mary Ella Milham. Asheville, NC: Pegasus Press, 1999.

Pocino, Willy. *Le curiosità di Roma: Storie, aneddoti e segreti legati a luoghi, tradizioni e monumenti esitenti o scomparse di una città irripetibile*. Rome: Newton Compton, 1985.

Posa Andeoli, Laura. "'Effermeridi' Alimentari settecentesche." In *Le cucine della memoria: Roma e Lazio*, edited by Angela Adriana Cavarra, 67–72. Second edition. Rome: De Luca, 1995.

Procopius, *History of the Wars*, Books 6 and 7. Translated by H. B. Dewing. Cambridge, MA: Harvard University Press, 1962.

Purcell, Nicholas. "The Populace of Rome in Late Antiquity: Problems of Classification and Historical Description." In *The Transformations of Vrbs Roma in Late Antiquity*, edited by W. V. Harris, 135–61. Portsmouth, RI: Journal of Roman Archeology, 1999.

Raffald, Elizabeth. *The Experienced English House-Keeper for the Use and Ease of Ladies, House-Keepers, Cooks, &c. Wrote Purely from Practice . . . Consisting of near 800 original receipts, most of which never appeared in print*. Manchester: J. Harrop, 1769.

Rufini, Alessandro. *Notizie storiche intorno alla origine dei nomi di alcune osterie, caffè, alberghi e locande esistenti nella città di Roma*. Rome:Tipografia Legale, 1855.

Scappi, Bartolomeo. *The Opera of Bartolomeo Scappi (1570): L'arte et prudenza d'un maestro cuoco*. Translated with commentary by Terence Scully. Toronto: University of Toronto Press, 2008.

Serao, Matilde. *Il ventre di Napoli*. Milan: Fratelli Treves, 1884.

Simonetti, Gianni-Emilio. "I vini d'Italia giudicati da Papa Paolo III (Farnese) e dal suo bottigliere Sante Lancerio." *La Gola* no. 1 (October 1982): 16–18.

Siporin Steve, "From Kashrut to Cucina Ebraica: The Recasting of Italian Jewish Foodways." *Journal of American Folklore* 107, no. 424 (Spring 1994): 268–81.

Smollett, Tobias. *Travels through France and Italy*. London: Oxford University Press, 1919.

Sturgis, Mathew. *When in Rome, 2000 Years of Sightseeing*. London: Frances Lincoln Limited, 2011.

Taine, Hippolyte, *Voyage en Italie, vol. 2: Florence et Venise*. Paris: Librarie Hachette et Co., Paris, 1866.

———. *Italy, Rome and Naples*. Translated by J. Durand. Fourth edition. New York: Henry Holt and Company, 1875.

Urilli, Sergio, and Fabio Brini. "Oltre la transumanza: Allevamento ovino e attività casearie alle porte di Roma." In *Roma e la sua campagna*, edited by Franco Salvatori and Ernesto di Renzo, 194–209. Genoa: Tipografia Brigata, 2007.

Virgil. *The Aeneid*. Translated by Robert Fagles. New York: Penguin, 2006.

Volpicelli, Luigi. "Cucina romana dell'artusi." *Strenna dei Romanisti* 28 (1967): 456–63.

Wallace-Hadrill, Andrew. *Herculaneum: Past and Future*. London: Frances Lincoln, 2011.

Watson, Peter. *Ideas: A History of Thought and Invention from Fire to Freud*. New York: HarperPerennial, 2005.

Wetmore Story, William, *Roba di Roma*. Eighth edition. Boston: Houghton, Mifflin and Company, 1887.

Wickham, Chris. "Pastoralism and Underdevelopment in the Early Middle Ages." Paper presented at the *Centro di Studi Sull'Alto Medioevo*, April 7–13, 1983. In *L'uomo di fronte al mondo animale nell'alto medioevo*, 401–51. Spoleto: Fondazione CISAM, 1985.

———. *Framing the Middle Ages: Europe and the Mediterranean, 400–800*. Oxford: Oxford University Press, 2005.

Willan, Anne. *The Cookbook Library*. Berkeley: University of California Press, 2012.

Zaccheo, Bianca Maria. "Tradizioni della cucina ebraico-romana del Portico d'Ottavia." In *Le cucine della memoria: Roma e Lazio*, edited by Angela Adriana Cavarra, 541–52. Rome: De Luca, 1993.

Zanozzo, Giggi. *Usi, costumi e pregiudizi del popolo di Roma*. Turin: Società tipografico-editrice nazionale, 1908.

Electronic Sources

Amburn, Brad. "The 2008 Global Cities Index." *Foreign Policy*, October 6, 2009. Accessed January 31, 2018. https://web.archive.org/web/20100107184223/http://www.foreignpolicy.com/story/cms.php?story_id=4509.

Bassi, Cristina. "L'esercito delle badanti in Italia: Due su tre non sono in regola." *Il giornale*, June 24, 2015. Accessed October 8, 2017. http://www.ilgiornale.it/news/lesercito-delle-badanti-italia-due-su-tre-non-sono-regola-1144790.html.

Beard, Mary, *Meet the Romans*. Accessed January 12, 2016. https://www.youtube.com/watch?v=rggk_H3jEgw.

Beckford, William. *Dreams, Waking Thoughts, and Incidents; In a Series of Letters from Various Parts of Europe*. Accessed October 3, 2017. http://www.gutenberg.org/files/7258/7258-h/7258-h.htm.

Blake, Matt. "Who Was . . . Remington Olmstead?" *The Wild Eye*, June 17, 2009. Accessed February 9, 2018. http://www.thewildeye.co.uk/blog/performers-directors/who-was-remington-olmstead/

Buescher, John B. "In the Habit: A History of Catholicism and Tabacco." *Catholic World Report*, November 9, 2017. Accessed January 26. 2018. http://www.catholicworldreport.com/2017/11/09/in-the-habit-a-history-of-catholicism-and-tobacco/.

Comune di Campodimele. Accessed April 28, 2017. http://www.comune.campodimele.lt.it

Corbier, Mireille, "The Ambiguous Status of Meat in Ancient Rome," *Food and Foodways*, 3, no. 3 (1989): 223–64. Accessed February 15, 2017. doi: 10.1080/07409710.1989.9961951.

Cucinotta, Giuseppe. "E adesso badanti e colf sono romane." Accessed October 8, 2017. http://roma.corriere.it/roma/notizie/cronaca/12_novembre_18/badanti-romane-indagine-federcasalinghe-2112758860479.shtml.

D'Arms, John H. "The Culinary Reality of Roman Upper-Class Convivia: Integrating Texts and Images." *Comparative Studies in Society and History* 46, no. 3 (2004): 428–50. Accessed February 10, 2017. http://asbproxy.unisi.it:2233/stable/3879469.

E. C. "I pani di Pompeii tornano a tavola." *L'espresso*, December 4, 2013. Accessed June 7, 2017. http://espresso.repubblica.it/food/dettaglio/i-pani-di-pompei-tornano-a-tavola/2217401.html.

Erdkamp, Paul. "Agriculture, Underemployment, and the Cost of Rural Labour in the Roman World." *Classical Quarterly* 49, no. 2 (1999): 556–72. Accessed August 28. 2016. http://asbproxy.unisi.it:2233/stable/639879.

Galli, Marialucia. "Ippofagia su internet, l'ultima follia." Accessed January 9, 2017. http://www.cavallo2000.it/detail/ippofagia_su_internet_lultima_follia-id_407.htm.

Garnsey, Peter. "Famine in the Ancient Mediterranean." *History Today* 36, no. 5 (May 1, 1986): 24–31. Accessed July 30, 2016. http://search.proquest.com/docview/1299020639?accountid=13857.

Hudson, Nicholas F. "Changing Places: The Archaeology of the Roman 'Convivium.'" *American Journal of Archaeology* 114, no. 4 (2010): 663–95. Accessed July 22, 2016. http://asbproxy.unisi.it:2233/stable/25763806.

"I censimenti precedenti: La storia dal 1861 a oggi." Istat. Accessed February 1, 2018. https://www.istat.it/it/censimenti-permanenti/censimenti-precedenti.

"Immigrazione, Roma si conferma capitale:+ 115% di stranieri in 15 anni." *Il Tempo*, June 22, 2015. Accessed Jan 31,2018. http://www.iltempo.it/roma-capitale/2015/06/22/news/immigrazione-roma-si-conferma-capitale-+-115-di-stranieri-in-15-anni-980276/.

Jasny, Naum. "The Daily Bread of the Ancient Greeks and Romans." *Osiris* 9 (1950): 227–53. Accessed August 18, 2016. http://www.jstor.org/stable/301851.

Jones, A. H. M. "The Roman Colonate." *Past & Present*, no. 13 (1958): 1–13. Accessed July 26, 2017. http://asbproxy.unisi.it:2233/stable/649865.

Laurioux, Bruno "Le registre de cuisine" de Jean de Bockenheim, cuisinier du pape Martin V." *Mélanges de l'Ecole française de Rome: Moyen-Age, Temps modernes* 100, no. 2 (1988):709–60. Accessed January 23, 2018. http://www.persee.fr/doc/mefr_0223-5110_1988_num_100_2_2987#mefr_0223-5110_1988_num_100_2_T1_0725_0000.

Licht, Meg. "Elysium: A Prelude to Renaissance Theater." *Renaissance Quarterly* 49, no. 1 (1996): Accessed August 14, 2017. 1-29. doi:10.2307/2863263.

"La festa di San Giuseppe fra frittelle, sonetti e lunari." *Romacult*. Accessed January 24, 2018. http://romacult.blogspot.it/search/label/festa%20di%20san%20Giuseppe.

Leclercq, Henri. "Holy Water." In *The Catholic Encyclopedia*. Vol. 7. New York: Robert Appleton Co. 1910. Accessed April 3, 2016. http://www.newadvent.org/cathen/07432a.htm.

Livius, Titus (Livy), *The History of Rome by Titus Livius. Translated from the Original with Notes and Illustrations by George Baker, A.M. First American, from the Last London Edition, in Six Volumes.* New York: Peter A. Mesier et al., 1823, Vol. 1. Accessed January 13, 2016. http://oll.libertyfund.org/titles/1754.

Ministro per I Beni e le Attività Culturali, "Alimentazione in Etruria." Accessed January 9, 2017. http://www.beniculturali.it/mibac/multimedia/MiBAC/minisiti/alimentazione/sezioni/etastorica/etruria/index.html.

Morrisroe, Patrick. "Chrism." In *The Catholic Encyclopedia*. Vol. 3. New York: Robert Appleton Co. 1908. Accessed April 3, 2016. http://www.newadvent.org/cathen/03696b.htm.

Parasecoli, Fabio. *Al Dente: A History of Food in Italy.* E-book. London: Reaktion Books, 2014.

Pizzuti, Francesca. "I carciofi di Caravaggio." Accessed February 4, 2018. http://www.aromaweb.it/articoli/curiosita/i-carciofi-di-caravaggio/#comment-17043.

Purcell, Nicholas. "The Way We Used to Eat: Diet, Community, and History at Rome." *American Journal of Philology* 124, no. 3 (2003): 329–58. Accessed: July 13, 2016. http://asbproxy.unisi.it:2233/stable/1562134.

———. "Rome and the Management of Water: Environment, Culture and Power." Accessed July 13, 2016. https://www.academia.edu/3136285/Rome_and_the_man agement_of_water_environment_culture_and_power_1996.

Rauser, Amelia. "Hair, Authenticity, and the Self-Made Macaroni." *Eighteenth Century Studies* 38, no. 1 (2004): 101–17. Accessed January 15, 2016. https://www .academia.edu/1967485/Hair_authenticity_and_the_self-made_Macaroni.

Rosivach, Vincent J. "The 'Lex Fannia Sumptuaria' of 161 BC." *Classical Journal* 102, no. 1 (2006): 1–15. Accessed: July 28, 2016. http://asbproxy.unisi.it:2233/ stable/30038672.

Salzman, Michele Renee. "From a Classical to a Christian City, Civic Euergetism and Charity in Late Antique Rome," *Studies in Late Antiquity* 1, no. 1 (Spring 2017): 65–85. Accessed June 4, 2017. doi: 10.1525/sla.2017.1.1.65.

Simkhovitch, Vladimir G. "Rome's Fall Reconsidered." *Political Science Quarterly* 31, no. 2 (1916): 201–43. Accessed: July 24, 2016. doi:10.2307/2141560.

Staccioli, Letizia. "Pane e panettieri nell'antica Roma," *Cerealia.* accessed June 7, 2017, http://www.cerealialudi.org/alimentazione/pane-e-panettieri-nellantica-roma/.

Virgil. "The Salad." Virgil.org. Accessed June 20, 2017. http://virgil.org/appendix/ moretum.htm.

Witze, Alexandra. "The Miraculous Microbes of Bolsena." *New Scientist*, June 4, 1994. Accessed October 1 2017. https://www.newscientist.com/article/mg14219282 -300-science-the-miraculous-microbes-of-bolsena/.

Index

About the Author

Karima Moyer-Nocchi was born in the United States and immigrated to Italy in 1990. She is a lecturer at the University of Siena in the Modern Languages Department and teaches food studies at the University of Rome, Tor Vergata. Her first book, *Chewing the Fat—An Oral History of Italian Foodways from Fascism to Dolce Vita* (2015) received international critical acclaim. She currently resides in Umbria.

CPSIA information can be obtained
at www.ICGtesting.com
Printed in the USA
LVHW091535280619
622665LV00008B/116/P

9 781442 269743